TABLE OF CONTENTS

Top 20 Test Taking Tips

1. Carefully follow all the test registration procedures
2. Know the test directions, duration, topics, question types, how many questions
3. Setup a flexible study schedule at least 3-4 weeks before test day
4. Study during the time of day you are most alert, relaxed, and stress free
5. Maximize your learning style; visual learner use visual study aids, auditory learner use auditory study aids
6. Focus on your weakest knowledge base
7. Find a study partner to review with and help clarify questions
8. Practice, practice, practice
9. Get a good night's sleep; don't try to cram the night before the test
10. Eat a well balanced meal
11. Know the exact physical location of the testing site; drive the route to the site prior to test day
12. Bring a set of ear plugs; the testing center could be noisy
13. Wear comfortable, loose fitting, layered clothing to the testing center; prepare for it to be either cold or hot during the test
14. Bring at least 2 current forms of ID to the testing center
15. Arrive to the test early; be prepared to wait and be patient
16. Eliminate the obviously wrong answer choices, then guess the first remaining choice
17. Pace yourself; don't rush, but keep working and move on if you get stuck
18. Maintain a positive attitude even if the test is going poorly
19. Keep your first answer unless you are positive it is wrong
20. Check your work, don't make a careless mistake

Understanding Students with Cognitive Impairments

Piaget's stages of cognitive development

Sensorimotor stage

Piaget defined four stages of cognitive development. He called the first stage sensorimotor to characterize infants' cognitive processes: they perceive sensory information from their surrounding environments and respond to these by engaging in motor activities, e.g., rooting, suckling, looking, listening, reaching, and grasping. Piaget divided the sensorimotor stage into six substages: Reflexes, from 0–1 month; Primary Circular Reactions from 1–4 months wherein infants finds accidental actions like thumb-sucking pleasurable and then intentionally repeats them; Secondary Circular Reactions from 4–8 months when infants intentionally repeat actions to evoke environmental effects; Coordination of Reactions from 8–12 months, featuring obviously intentional actions, comprehension of cause and effect, and combining schemas (concepts); Tertiary Circular Reactions from 12–18 months, when children experiment with trial-and-error; and Early Representational Thought from 18–24 months, when children begin representing things or events with symbols. A significant sensorimotor development is Object Permanence, i.e., realizing things still exist when out of sight.

Preoperational stage

Piaget called his second stage of cognitive development, between the ages of 2–7 years, Preoperational, because children have not yet developed the ability to perform mental operations, i.e., mentally manipulating information, and do not understand concrete logic. Piaget called children in this stage egocentric, i.e., they cannot assume another's perspective. For example, Preoperational children can select a picture matching a three-dimensional scene they just saw, but cannot select a picture matching what someone else would see from a different physical location/position. They do not understand what Piaget termed conservation, the concept that quantities remain constant regardless of shape or appearance. For example, children judge the same amount of liquid differently by its appearance in differently shaped containers (short wide versus tall narrow), even when seeing it poured from one to the other. Piaget identified additional characteristics of Preoperational thinking as animism (attributing human qualities to inanimate objects) and magical thinking (attributing external events to one's internal thoughts).

Concrete Operations stage

Around ages 7–11 years, children are in what Piaget termed the Concrete Operations stage. A salient feature of this stage is that children develop the ability to think logically and conduct mental operations with regard to concrete objects. However, they still have trouble comprehending hypothetical and abstract concepts. A significant ability developing during this stage is the understanding of reversibility, i.e., that actions can be reversed. Whereas the younger Preoperational child watching someone pour liquid from a short, wide container to a tall, narrow one believes the taller container has more liquid, the Concrete Operations child sees the amount is the same despite different container shapes. Reversibility aids this insight. Children in Concrete Operations also understand sequences between mental categories, e.g., their pet is a poodle, a poodle is a dog, and a dog is an animal. The introduction of formal school subjects, especially math, is no coincidence with the age range of this stage because children in Concrete Operations are first able to do simple arithmetic computations.

Formal Operations

Piaget termed his final stage of cognitive development, from around age 12 into adulthood, as Formal Operations. This reflects the individual's ability to understand and manipulate completely abstract concepts without needing to refer to concrete objects. This stage also features the development of logic, the addition of deductive reasoning to the inductive reasoning children develop in the previous stage of Concrete Operations, and systematic planning. Children/teens/adults can now consider hypothetical situations; apply general principles to predict specific events (deductive reasoning) as well as make generalizations from multiple specific details (inductive reasoning, which typically develops during Concrete Operations); and plan organized, systematic approaches to problem-solving. They are more fully able to consider another's viewpoint and feelings, and can understand abstract concepts like liberty, justice, democracy, truth, and beauty.

Delays in cognitive development

Whether caused by neurological deficits or damage, deprivation or other environmental factors, or a combination, some children do not develop cognitive skills typically. They may develop them much later than others or not at all. They may also demonstrate differences in the quantity and quality of their cognitive skills. Children with cognitive developmental delays, for example, can have significant difficulty with learning colors, shapes, and similar basic concepts. They often have trouble learning more advanced concepts, such as counting numbers, reading printed language, and writing language. In addition, children with delayed and/or deficient cognitive development can demonstrate a failure to generalize things they learn to other situations or contexts. Moreover, when children have problems with adjusting to new situations and changes in their environments, this can be a sign of delayed or deficient cognitive development.

Atypical social and emotional development

When children experience developmental delays that are manifested in the social and emotional domain, one characteristic is being too trusting of others, which allows others to take advantage of them. This is often associated with intellectual disability or intellectual disabilities. Another characteristic of some children with atypical social and emotional development is not reading or understanding others' nonverbal cues indicating emotional states or social conventions, and/or linguistic cues during interpersonal interactions, preventing them from responding appropriately. This is commonly associated with autism spectrum disorders. Autistic children also may show excellent verbal skills in monologues, but be unable to initiate and maintain conversations and have difficulty with turn-taking. Some children fail to develop the ability to consider others' viewpoints at typical ages, remaining egocentric; this interferes with social interaction. This is common to various conditions, including intellectual disability, autism, and behavior disorders. Children with ADHD tend to have difficulties with impulse control, emotional self-regulation, and sustaining attention, interfering with social interactions as much as with academic performance.

Atypical development of gross motor skills

Motor development follows a hierarchical pattern. In other words, for example, if a child cannot stand, s/he cannot walk, and if s/he cannot walk, s/he cannot run. When a baby is between 3 and 12 months old, some signs of atypical gross motor skills development include that the child does not open his/her hands during the normal age range; that the child has trouble holding his/her head up; the child cannot sit up without support, and/or the child has difficulty sitting up even with support; and the child does not begin to pull up on furniture or stand up during this age range. Between 12 and 36 months, signs of delayed/atypical development include problems with walking and/or running; with ascending or descending stairs; with rolling, catching, and throwing a ball; and with jumping and hopping. Children with atypical motor development may demonstrate higher or lower muscle tone than normal and problems with motor planning, motor coordination, balance, and proprioception.

Fine motor skills

Young children need fine motor skills to play with toys, eat meals, turn lights on/off, and hold crayons, paintbrushes, spoons, etc. During evaluations, many children perform poorly on certain tasks, from delays not in cognitive development but in fine motor development. Oral/motor skills, like the control of jaw, lip, mouth, and tongue movements for eating and speaking, are included in fine motor skills. While occupational therapists work with other fine motor skills, speech-language pathologists and occupational therapists may both work to remediate oral/motor skill deficits. If a baby has trouble orally grasping the nipple or bottle to nurse, this can indicate delayed fine motor development. Babies whose hands are in fists more often than open may have fine motor delays. A baby having problems manually bringing toys to his/her mouth and/or mouthing them can have atypical fine motor development. Difficulty holding small objects with a pincer grasp or with a thumb and a forefinger is another sign of delayed fine motor development.

Early language development

The development of language skills is critical to the development of cognitive, emotional, and social skills. These are all interrelated, so problems in any one area usually cause problems/delays in others. Receptive language is the ability to understand spoken and written language. Receptive language develops before expressive language: children must understand what they hear before they learn to speak, and to read and comprehend written language before they learn to write. Hence a child's receptive vocabulary typically exceeds his/her expressive vocabulary: s/he can understand more words than s/he can use. Nonverbal receptive language includes understanding others' facial expressions. Verbal receptive language includes understanding what others say; understanding qualitative concepts like big/little and tall/short and quantitative concepts like a lot, a little, all, none, etc.; understanding and following simple directions; listening to stories; understanding and following complex/multiple directions to do a series of things; and understanding others' questions. Written receptive language includes identifying upper- and lowercase letters and numbers, and also reading and comprehending simple and complex sentences and paragraphs.

Receptive, expressive, and pragmatic language and delayed or atypical development

Receptive language is comprehending language we hear and read. Expressive language is our production of spoken and written language. Pragmatic language is our using receptive and expressive language to facilitate social interactions. Expressive and pragmatic language depend upon receptive language, which precedes them. If a baby is not imitating others' vocal sounds or behaviors or responding to hearing his/her name called and/or seems not to be listening to others' speech by the age of 12 months, this can indicate delayed/deficient receptive language development. By three years, if a child does not follow instructions and/or does not learn to speak normally, this can indicate receptive language delay. When children frequently ask others to repeat and/or have trouble answering questions by five years old, they may have receptive language delays. By seven years, signs of receptive language deficits include having trouble understanding stories told/read aloud; avoiding participating in social activities; and having trouble processing or making sense of verbal information. Having trouble reading sentences by nine years old is another sign.

Expressive language development

Expressive language is that language we produce in order to communicate with others, whether through spoken or written words, vocal sounds, facial expressions, physical gestures, and/or body language. Babies and children develop expressive language gradually and in a cumulative sequence. Nonverbal expressive language consists of all of that expressive communication that does not involve the use of words. For example, when a baby cries, that is a form of nonverbal expressive language. Smiling also communicates pleasure, recognition, and/or affection toward others. Laughing expresses amusement or delight. Frowning expresses displeasure, sadness, or anger. When infants and toddlers learn to wave "bye-bye," they are using nonverbal expressive language. When babies and young children point at things, they nonverbally communicate a variety of messages—like "I want that"; "Look at that"; "What is that?"; "I see that." When young children throw objects, whether to express anger, protest something, or get an adult to retrieve it as a game, this is also nonverbal expressive language.

Vocal and spoken verbal expressive language in babies and young children: Verbal expressive language can be spoken or written. In infants, early forms of verbalization also include vocalizations. For example, babies "coo" by repeating prolonged vowel sounds; "grunt" or make guttural sounds expressing satisfaction/contentedness; and soon begin to babble by repeating consonant-vowel combinations like "babababa," "dadadada," etc. Babies also imitate adults' vocal sounds and facial expressions. Their first words are often parent names like "Mama" and "Dada," which coincide closely with babbling sounds. As their speech develops, they echo/repeat others' utterances. In the holophrastic stage, toddlers use single words to express phrase concepts, like "up" to mean "Pick me up" or "Look at the bird up there." They combine pointing with nouns to identify people, animals, and things, like "baby," "doggie," or "car." They soon learn to use the socially conventional utterances "thank you" and "please." Toddlers then learn to combine two words to express phrase concepts, like "Daddy go" or "Mommy shoe," which can also convey a variety of meanings.

Development of spoken verbal expressive language skills: Once they can speak using more than one-word expressions, young children begin to ask questions and answer others' questions. They progress to correctly using words expressing qualitative concepts, including opposites like big and little, tall and short, etc.; and quantitative concepts, including opposite and relative quantities like all, none, a lot, or a little. As their expressive language skills develop, they reflect children's receptive understanding of the concepts underlying the words. The toddler's basic "She walk" phrase gives way to the more advanced present progressive verb tense "She is walking" in preschoolers. Children begin to use pronouns like "I" and "you," rather than using no pronouns or only "me" or "Mommy." They then develop possessive pronouns like "mine" and "my" [+ object]. They start including prepositions like on, in, over, and under. They use past tenses, both regular and irregular ("gave") and future constructions like "will/is going to" [+verb]. They progress from two-word to three- and four-word phrases, and then full sentences with subject, auxiliary verb, verb, and object.

Activities that reflect written expressive language skills development: Children learn to speak before they learn to write, though there is also some overlap in their developing spoken and written expressive language skills. These both also depend on the development of the receptive language skills of listening and reading comprehension. Young children first learn to trace letters, then they copy them, and then they write them. They follow the same progression with tracing, copying, and writing numbers. They copy examples of simple words, like "Mom," and then do the same with more complex words like "truck." Once they have copied words and can remember letters, they progress to writing the letters in sequence to spell written words (d-a-d-d-y). Thereafter, they learn to write consecutive words that form sentences, such as "I love my kitty." Eventually, school-age children can write connected sentences that form paragraphs, like "I love my kitty. One day my friends will come over. I will show my kitty to my friends."

Signs in babies and young children are of atypical development or delays: Babies normally babble at a few to several months. An infant's not babbling by eight months is a sign of delayed/atypical spoken language development. A child not uttering any words by 18 months is not developing expressive language normally. Children over two years using only single words show atypical development. After four years, speaking mainly in "baby talk" is atypical. Echolalia (continually repeating what others say) is normal in younger children, but beyond three years is atypical. Talking to oneself aloud is typical of toddlers, but children continuing this practice extensively past three years show delayed development. Children older than three years who do not take conversational turns but talk "in circles" are not developing typically. Children over four years who have trouble expressing their needs and wants show atypical development. Answering open-ended questions ("What did you do at Jimmy's?") with single words indicates a delay in a six-year-old. Overgeneralizing, i.e., naming many objects with one word like calling all vehicles cars, is another sign of delayed expressive language development.

Babies who make no, or very little, eye contact with others by 12 months of age are not developing typically. Another sign indicating a need for evaluation is not pointing at things by this age. Children who demonstrate few or no skills at taking turns by a year old can have expressive language delays. Little or no demonstration of joint attention, i.e., attending to the same thing as his/her parent, is another sign of developmental delay. So is a lack of joint action, i.e., engaging in the same activity as the parent. Children who consistently hit others or have temper tantrums when they cannot communicate a message to others show signs of delayed expressive language. Crying, yelling, and similar shows of frustration when trying to communicate also indicate developmental delays. In addition, young children with such delays may rarely if ever initiate conversations with others, and may not want to engage in activities with others.

Physical and motor development of children with Down syndrome

Children with Down syndrome show overall slower development in physiology and motor skills. They grow more slowly in physical size and also ultimately attain smaller full statures than typically developing children. They tend to have lower/weaker muscle tone, or hypotonia. They commonly start walking significantly later than other children. Even once they learn to walk, they may not develop physical coordination, balance, and proprioception as soon or ever as well as other children. The oral-motor skills components of motor development are also slower to develop in those with Down syndrome, compounded by having large, thick, often protruding tongues, which can interfere with eating skills and clear speech. Additional physiological stigmata of Down syndrome include small hands and feet; short, stubby fingers; short, thick necks; small heads, flattened in back; small noses; and Asian-appearing eyes with epicanthal folds. Down syndrome children are more likely to have celiac disease (gluten intolerance), gastroesophageal reflux, hypothyroidism, hearing and vision problems, and to develop senile dementias earlier than normally.

Development of students with autism spectrum disorders

<u>Language</u>
An estimated one-half of those on the autism spectrum never develop verbal language skills. The other half range from echolalia as their only speech production to perfectly functional, high-level speech, and everything in between. Some autistic students display advanced vocabularies and fluent speech in long monologues about topics interesting them, often including the highly specialized and/or technical, but are unable to initiate or maintain two-way conversations with others. These individuals have difficulty with turn-taking and the give-and-take of verbal interactions. Some high-functioning autistic persons can conduct normal conversations with others, but their speech patterns may sound a bit singsong, odd, or quirky. Many autistic students have difficulty understanding emotional overtones in others' speech, such as sarcasm or humor. Additionally, they often cannot understand nonverbal cues like facial expressions, gestures, and body language indicating emotions or social customs, though many can learn this through explicit training.

<u>Social and emotional</u>
Emotional and social differences can be observed in autistic people from early childhood, when many of them avoid eye contact with others and resist physical contact with parents, like flinging themselves backward from being hugged/held or going rigid in their bodies when held. Many also engage in repetitive, stereotypic self-stimulating behaviors like rocking. Students with autism experience the same internal emotions as others, but may not express these normally. Moreover, they often have great difficulty noticing or understanding the emotions of others and their expression of them. As a result, their behavior in social situations can appear rather strange, especially from high-functioning autistic individuals with above-average intelligence. For example, as autism expert John Gerdtz once related, "It's really strange when you're talking with someone who has a PhD in mathematics, and he suddenly turns and walks away right in the middle of the conversation." Autistic individuals frequently fail to follow social conventions because they do not understand them.

<u>Behavioral differences</u>
One area of behavioral difference among the autistic is language: some people with autism spectrum disorders (ASDs) have few or no verbal skills; others have limited speech and

language; others have more functional, but odd-sounding speech and language; and still others have highly functioning verbal skills. Some are able to speak extensively on favorite topics but cannot start or continue social conversations. Another area is social and emotional: those with ASDs have difficulty observing, interpreting, and using socially accepted behaviors indicating emotions. A common autistic deficit is tolerating interruptions, changes, or transitions in activities. Autistic people frequently display narrowly limited interests and activities, and rigid thinking and behavior. The lower functioning often engage in repetitive behaviors; the higher functioning can focus intensely on a single activity for long periods, but not shift or divide their attention. Some autistic individuals react to sudden changes, or sensory input they find painful due to hypersensitivity, with panic reactions including screaming, self-injurious behavior, and/or withdrawal into rocking, counting, or other repetitive self-soothing actions.

Deaf students

Differences in learning
Hearing children are surrounded by speech sounds from birth, and they absorb a great deal of their knowledge and understanding of language and speech through this immersion. However, deaf children do not benefit from sensory input in the auditory mode. Those whose parents use sign language and/or speech reading learn to comprehend and produce language through the visual modality instead. This is a major difference, because the main basis for communication among the majority of the population is auditory; and written language, with its relationship to spoken language, has the same auditory basis. Instead of auditory cues like tone of voice, grammatical inflections (like verb tense or plural endings), or intonations like the rising end of a question, deaf students rely exclusively on visual cues like facial expressions, gestures, and body language; and in ASL (American Sign Language), built-in signs conveying grammatical information.

Similarities to hearing students
Although a major difference in deaf students is that they learn language through visual rather than auditory modalities, they also have many similarities to hearing students. They have the same need to communicate and interact socially with others. Unfortunately, the majority of hearing people do not know sign language; and while many deaf people can visually read speech, many others who sign exclusively and adhere to deaf culture function best within the signing deaf community and are at significant disadvantages in hearing milieus. While deaf students often do not understand humor based on word play or sound, they do appreciate humor, and the deaf culture has its own inside jokes. Deaf students have equal interests in competing in sports and academics as hearing students do. They feel the same emotions as others. While they hug each other more and spend longer times on good-byes, their social interactions still fulfill the same needs for belonging, connection, and communication.

Blind students

Differences from sighted students
Blind students with normal hearing do not miss out on the auditory medium wherein children learn to understand and use speech and language as deaf students do. However, while they can learn spoken language normally, they cannot learn to read and write visually as other children can. They must learn Braille and have access to Braille publications to read and/or listen to books on tape. Today they have the added advantage of computer text-to-

speech software. Another significant difference is that blind students cannot learn their way around schools and other large, complex buildings simply through the experience of navigating them a few times. Sighted individuals often take this for granted. Blind students usually need help from Orientation and Mobility specialists to learn how to get around in indoor and outdoor settings. Without the benefit of the multitude of visual information others have, it can be very confusing not to know just which way to go, but even where one is and in what position relative to one's surroundings (orientation).

Similarities to sighted individuals

Although the totally blind cannot read printed text, blind students still often want to read and enjoy it. Some read available Braille texts by touch. Others listen to books on tape and/or use text-to-speech computer software, greatly expanding their options of available texts. Though blind students may not understand visual humor like sight gags, they still appreciate humor. Students not blind from birth have additional frames of reference for understanding visual expressions and comparisons. For example, Helen Keller, who became deaf-blind at 19 months, reportedly was told she had blue eyes and asked, "Are they like wee skies?" Without hearing or sight, Keller had to learn tactile finger-spelling to communicate, yet her accomplishments made her famous. A woman who became blind around nine years old found hilarious a coworker's description of another employee bundled up in a fur coat and hat with only her nose protruding. Blind people have the same social, communication, and emotional needs; they just need supplementary auditory information/verbal descriptions of what they cannot see.

Differences and similarities of physically disabled students

Physically normal students, and sometimes even educators, may not realize that even navigating through a school building—a seemingly simple everyday activity they take for granted—is not the same for the physically disabled. For example, buildings with traditional construction frequently include doorways too narrow for wheelchairs, solid obstacles impossible or difficult to move around, or stairs and grades not safely traversed using crutches. Federal legislation protecting the rights of the disabled has now mandated that all new constructions be accessible to them; however, this does not address old/existing buildings that often cannot be retrofitted. Also, physically disabled students have the same needs and desires to compete, win, and play as others, which should not be discounted. For example, wheelchair basketball and races are popular alternatives. In some schools, students in wheelchairs are also included in regular sports teams and games.

Family's role

Families play a critical role by frequently serving as their disabled child's first case manager. In this capacity, they are the most consistent and know the most about their child's abilities and needs. Families help coordinate the services disabled children need. They help them explore career possibilities and interests. They supply housing, transportation, adaptive equipment, and other necessities. When young people with disabilities progress from high school to college or employment and community living, their families support the transitions they must make. Families can help their children achieve greater understanding of themselves and their disabilities. However, many families do not realize how crucial such self-knowledge is, and many assume the schools teach this when they seldom do. Also, when educators and families avoid directly discussing disabilities and focus instead on abilities and strengths, children can grow up not realizing their disability's impact and the accommodations to facilitate their success. Students who avoid identification as disabled for fear of labeling and stigma are frequently unprepared for self-advocacy.

Understanding, communication, and disclosure of disability

Young people with disabilities will benefit by learning to understand themselves more fully; to understand their disabilities more completely; and to explain their disabilities more effectively to others. They will often need help from experts to make decisions whether to disclose their disability to others and to become more prepared for such disclosure. Even more importantly, young people with disabilities need to gain a better comprehension of how their opportunities in social, educational, and employment contexts can often be enhanced by disclosing their disabilities in certain situations. Where appropriate, disclosure of disability can give them access to services and accommodations they would not be entitled to if they were not disabled. Experts have prepared informational publications to support them in this issue. For example, the National Collaborative on Workforce and Disability for Youth (NCWD-Y) has published *The 411 on Disability Disclosure: A Workbook for Youth with Disabilities* to help youth and parents make informed decisions about disclosure and its various impacts.

Financial and service challenges on family systems

The challenges and demands on family systems are compounded when a member has a disability, and such challenges are typically long-term. Regardless of the type of family, the age of the disabled member, and the type of disability, many of the family demands are the same. For example, obtaining appropriate health services, social services, and educational services of sufficient quality often entail significant economic burdens, as do modifying the home to accommodate a disability and procuring adaptive equipment, medications, and special diets. Although families may qualify for public funding, e.g., from Medicaid, Social Security SSI, or private health insurance, additional challenges are not only to discover which programs and services their child is eligible for, but moreover to interact with various bureaucracies to confirm such eligibility—frequently on a repeated basis. Another major problem is service coordination among providers, like doctors, teachers, counselors, physical and occupational therapists, social workers, and dieticians. Frequently providers are not informed of one another's actions and may give contradictory information.

Impact on families

Emotional and caregiving
Caring for a disabled child or family member, particularly one with more severe disabilities, is a daily stressor that can exhaust caregivers and all family members emotionally and physically. Emotional stress includes anxiety, anger, guilt, and insecurity—about the disability's cause, other family members' needs, whether caregivers are doing enough, the future, etc. Families grieve the disabled member's functional losses, initially and recurrently. A member's disability frequently causes major changes in family life. Members, especially females, may discard or alter jobs and/or career plans for caregiving duties. Some members feel too involved in care while others feel left out, and within-family relationships change. Different loyalties and/or alliances develop within the family. Past research has found that while disability tended to increase marital tension, it did not necessarily increase divorce rates.

Family resources, social roles, lifestyle, leisure time, and community interactions

When a family member has a disability, it can deplete the family's resources in terms of money, time, and energy far out of proportion to other demands. This often detracts from meeting other needs of the family and its other members. The family members find they must change their lifestyle, for example, spending less money, time, and energy on leisure activities and staying at home more. Families may abandon their plans and dreams for the future because they no longer have enough of these resources to pursue them. Community members may exclude the disabled member and family; avoid them; and/or denigrate them with looks or comments. Though federal legislation mandates inclusion, many communities do not have the resources, facilities, and programs to enable full inclusion. Many families state they feel burdened not by the disabled member, but by rejection, judgment, stigmatization of the member and family, and other negative behaviors and attitudes—from not only strangers, but also service providers, friends, and relatives.

Variation in the impact of disabilities on families

Research shows the functioning and health of family members can be compromised by disability's additional demands. This includes elevated risks of behavioral and psychological symptoms in other family members. But despite this greater risk, studies also find that the majority of children and adults in families with a disabled member do not demonstrate such behavioral or psychological problems. This is attributed to the family members' adaptive abilities: they find and apply various coping skills to address the additional stresses caused in their life by the disability. Even though having a disabled member can cause families to experience grief, fatigue, depletion of resources, and other stressors, many families have also reported experiencing greater family closeness, acceptance of other people, new friendships, deepened spiritual faith, greater self-efficacy and sense of competence, more respect for life, and becoming stronger as a family. Thus, both negative and positive consequences are associated with having a family member with a disability.

Differential psychosocial effects

Families are affected differentially by the degree of a member's disability: its type, i.e., whether it is a motor, sensory, or cognitive disability; how visible the disability is; how much pain or other symptoms are involved; the disabled member's life expectancy or prognosis; how much treatment and/or care is required; and whether the disability is progressive, constant, or relapsing in nature. Some experts believe these characteristics have more influence on a chronic condition's psychosocial impact than the diagnosis itself. Constant disabilities, e.g., spinal cord injuries, necessitate major initial family restructuring, plus long-term endurance and persistence. While the family can plan for a known future, they can still become exhausted, especially if community resources are lacking. Progressive disabilities, e.g., dementia or degenerative arthritis, cause grief over continuous losses, uncertainty about living arrangements and degrees of dependency, and increasing demands in caretaking. Relapsing disabilities, e.g., cancer or epilepsy, require less continual care but more ability to shift suddenly from normal to crisis mode and rapidly activate resources.

Differential impacts of cognitive or intellectual disabilities

Research studies have shown that families appear to have more difficulty coping with cognitive or intellectual disabilities. Mental impairments can limit the disabled member's ability to assume responsible roles or to live independently, and/or increase the demands on families to be more vigilant to protect the disabled member. In cases of severe or profound intellectual disability, families may experience additional stress caused by boundary ambiguity—i.e., the disparity between the disabled member's physical and psychological presence makes his or her membership in the family unclear to the other members, as the disabled member is present as a part of the family in some ways, but in other ways is absent or only partially present. The ambiguity of this situation causes families more stress, as it can be more difficult for them to plan the roles of the other family members when they do not know what they can expect.

Effects of medical advances

When the life expectancy of a disabled member is unclear, the family finds it harder to plan its members' future roles in life; to know future care costs; or, when the member needs help with daily living activities, to decide on optimal living arrangements. For example, individuals with Down syndrome often have congenital heart defects and died younger in the past, but with improved medical care, they now live longer. And between 1970 and 1991, the survival of American children with cystic fibrosis increased by 700 percent, from a median life expectancy of eight years to twenty-six years. This opens up new questions about marriage, procreation, and other difficult family choices. Ethical problems are also presented when medical advances can extend the lives of those with serious medical conditions. Considerations include weighing benefits versus costs, when and/or why to intervene and how aggressively. Family members may disagree about these. Moreover, courts and/or hospitals may prohibit chosen family actions. Such cases provoke much controversy (witness the 1998–2005 case of Terri Schiavo).

Considerations for families regarding functional status

A person's functional status is the extent to which s/he can perform activities of daily living (ADLs) like self-feeding, toileting, or walking. The severity of impairment in these activities caused by a disability can be assessed. The human help, support, and equipment an individual will require is inversely related to his/her functional status, and families are typically the main providers of such assistance. Providing it can constitute a burden for them, compromising their physical and mental health. For instance, research has found that parents and particularly mothers whose disabled children have lower functional status have more symptoms of depression. Another factor to consider is that when disabled children and their parents both grow older, and/or when grandparents are caregivers, their ability to provide the same amounts and durations of care can become more limited due to the physical stresses of caregiving, which may be unmanageable for many elderly persons.

Significance of age of disability onset and the age of parents at onset or diagnosis

In contrast to disabilities manifested in late adulthood, which are more predictable and less disruptive psychologically to families, disabilities occurring earlier in life are perceived as less normal, affect development more, and require making more adjustments for longer times. Congenital disabilities shape the identity and life of a child, so the child and family are not required to adjust to a sudden loss of function. An example is the difference between a child born with spina bifida versus a normal adolescent who sustains an injury and suddenly becomes paraplegic. Parental age at onset is also a factor in family response to disability. Adolescent parents still have salient developmental needs themselves; plus, they usually have fewer resources and less maturity for coping with the additional demands of their child's disability. Older parents have greater risks of bearing children with Down syndrome and other disabilities, lesser endurance for caregiving, and more fears about who will care for their child after their deaths.

Interrelationship of disability and child development

Because childhood development is sequential, the mastery of skills at each level or stage depends upon the successful completion of the previous stage. Therefore, the earlier in a child's life the onset of a disabling condition is, the more it interrupts the child's developmental progress. Accomplishing developmental tasks is complicated in many ways for children with disabilities. This influences what family roles the child can adopt and consequently affects the family. If an infant's disability prevents the infant from responding to parental efforts at nurturing, this impedes the development of bonding, secure attachment, and trust, undermining parenting competence. Toddlers must actively explore their social environments to develop self-control and autonomy. But sensory, motor, or cognitive disabilities can hamper such exploration. Parents may be overprotective for fear of additional damage or injury, and/or, due to guilt or sympathy, overindulgent. Others' negative feedback about the child's disability can reinforce these parental behaviors, additionally limiting the child's development of self-control and autonomy.

Challenges with attending school

As Freud, Erikson, Piaget, and others have observed, when children begin school, their social and emotional focus shifts from the parent-child relationship to developing social relationships outside of the home with peers, children of other ages, and adults other than parents. The focus of child development consequently shifts from mainly personal skills and parental attachment to social competencies and interpersonal skills. In spite of government mandates of special education and inclusion, schools still vary significantly in their effectiveness with these. Insufficient funding for special education programs; inadequate training of school staff for accommodating instruction to special needs; and frequently, negative attitudes regarding disabilities in school personnel and other children, constitute some of the obstacles faced by children with disabilities and their parents. Because of the variance among schools in this respect, some families realize great resources in school programs, while others realize great additional challenges in trying to advocate for their disabled children's educational rights with schools and other service providers.

Challenges of adolescent development

As especially elucidated by Erikson, adolescents have the developmental tasks of developing their individual identities, separating from their childhood relationships with parents, and becoming more independent. Having a disability makes these tasks more challenging for a teenager. While normally developing adolescents often engage in risk-taking, e.g., experimenting with alcohol and tobacco, as part of this process, teens with disabilities may refuse prescribed medications, diets, or other disability-related treatments as their form of the risk-taking part of the developmental process. The natural adolescent development of sexuality also involves additional complications for disabled teens, as they often experience anxieties and fears about their desirability, performance, and future potential for marriage and reproduction. The complications they encounter can include being exploited sexually by others for the cognitively disabled, risk of contracting sexually transmitted diseases, and possible higher risks of pregnancy for girls with disabilities.

Amphetamines for ADHD

Many adults do not understand why a child who is already hyperactive would be prescribed a stimulant drug, thinking this would only make them even more so. However, stimulants like amphetamines often have the effect of helping children with ADHD to focus their attention better for longer time periods. This compares to the effects of caffeine and controlled amphetamine doses in helping normal but tired adults concentrate better. Serious amphetamine side effects include rapid, uneven, or pounding heartbeat; burning or pain with urination; increased talkativeness; other unaccustomed behaviors; extremes of depression or elation; muscular twitches/motor tics; physical tremors; hallucinations; and dangerous elevations in blood pressure, with symptoms like buzzing in the ears, severe headaches, shortness of breath, cardiac arrhythmias, chest pain, confusion, anxiety, seizures, and others. Less serious side effects include blurred vision, dizziness, weakness, moderate headaches, irritability, restlessness, agitation, insomnia, dry mouth, bad taste in the mouth, constipation, diarrhea, stomachache, nausea, vomiting, fever, loss of appetite, weight loss, hair loss, loss of libido, and others.

Depakote

Depakote is an anticonvulsive prescribed to control seizures. It can sometimes cause pancreatitis or liver damage. If so, symptoms include jaundice, low-grade fever, pale/clay-colored stools, dark-colored urine, loss of appetite, upper stomach pain, nausea, and vomiting. Emergency medical attention should be pursued if the child has these symptoms. Additional serious side effects include agitation, anxiety, depression, hostility, mental or physical hyperactivity, restlessness, suicidal or self-injurious ideations, confusion, fainting, weakness, bruising easily, urine in the blood, body aches, swollen glands, other flu-like symptoms, decreased urination, excessive sleepiness, incoordination, nystagmus, double vision, painful skin, burning eyes, rashes with blisters and peeling, and other symptoms. Allergic reactions to Depakote cause symptoms of breathing difficulty, hives, and/or swelling of the throat, tongue, lips, or face. Less serious side effects include mild sleepiness, mild weakness, upset stomach, constipation, diarrhea, tremors, changes in vision, hair loss, an unpleasant/unusual taste in the mouth, and others. Educators should always know students are taking seizure medications. They should not first assume behavior or mental disorders or sleep deprivation.

Pulmozyme

A doctor may prescribe Pulmozyme to a patient who has cystic fibrosis. This condition causes thick mucus secretions in the lungs, interfering with normal breathing. Excessive DNA in the pulmonary secretions causes these symptoms. Pulmozyme is a synthesized protein that breaks down this extra DNA. It makes the lung secretions thinner and thus less likely to obstruct breathing, and also decreases the patient's risk of respiratory tract infections. Pulmozyme is given in solution via inhalation from a nebulizer. Allergic reactions to Pulmozyme cause symptoms like breathing difficulty, swelling of the face, lips, or tongue, hives, swelling/closing of the throat, chest pain, and/or fever. Emergency medical attention or immediate physician contact are indicated for these, which are the primary serious side effects. Less serious Pulmozyme side effects include changes in the voice; a sore throat; laryngitis; rashes; conjunctivitis, or red, irritated, or inflamed eyes; nasal congestion and/or discharge; and other symptoms, for which a doctor should be consulted.

Medications for childhood anxiety disorders

According to psychiatrists, children with anxiety are often prescribed the wrong medications when practitioners fail to understand the children's experiences and lack knowledge of evidence-based anxiety treatments. Anxious children have attentional difficulties, not from attention deficits but worries. They are often misdiagnosed as having ADHD and prescribed stimulants. These improve concentration, but not mood; they can even increase anxiety and the insomnia it causes. Alpha-two agonists, e.g., clonidine or guanfacine, lower arousal levels and can calm children, but do not treat their anxiety. Some practitioners even prescribe antipsychotics, also inappropriate for anxiety disorders. Serotonin-specific reuptake inhibitor (SSRI) antidepressants are most effective in research studies and patient treatments by experienced psychiatric physicians. These can improve children's anxiety relatively fast, e.g., beginning in a week or two, and are most effective in conjunction with cognitive-behavior therapy. Benzodiazepines (Valium, Librium, Dalmane, Halcion, Xanax, Ativan, etc.), used as anti-seizure treatments, sleep aids, and muscle relaxants as well as anxiolytics, also provide short-term help for extreme anxiety, but not long-term help like SSRIs.

Medications for childhood schizophrenia

While the symptoms of childhood schizophrenia can differ from adult symptoms, the same antipsychotic medications are prescribed to children as adults (though in different dosages), in conjunction with psychotherapy. A few of these drugs include Haldol, Thorazine, Stelazine, Mellaril, Risperdal, Loxitane, Moban, and lithium, which is also often prescribed for bipolar disorder. Antipsychotics in the phenothiazine class, such as Thorazine, Stelazine, and Mellaril, have significant risks of side effects like tardive dyskinesia, which refers to repetitive, involuntary movements that can be irreversible even upon discontinuing treatment; dystonias, like involuntary tongue thrusts, muscular rigidity, etc.; and extrapyramidal syndrome, involving muscle spasms, which are usually reversible on discontinuing treatment but may need other treatments to resolve when they are serious or interfere with breathing. Another side effect is pseudoparkinsonism, which mimics the symptoms of Parkinson disease including "pill-rolling" finger tremors, "mask-like" flat facial appearance, a shuffling gait, and muscular rigidity. A very serious side effect is neuroleptic malignant syndrome. Thorazine and other phenothiazines can also themselves cause psychiatric side effects.

Gabapentin

Although gabapentin is prescribed to adults for the nerve pain of shingles and for Restless Legs Syndrome, it is prescribed to children primarily for seizure disorders. For epilepsy, it is prescribed alone or with other medications to children at least 12 years old as well as adults, and with other medications to children aged 3–12 years for partial seizures. Caution is advised with patients having liver disease, kidney disease, or heart disease. Gabapentin can cause suicidal or self-injurious ideations in some patients. It can also cause depression, anxiety, changes in mood or behavior, agitation, hostility, restlessness, or physical or mental hyperactivity. Serious gabapentin side effects include increased instead of decreased seizures; fever, body aches, swollen glands, flu-like symptoms; bleeding or bruising easily; skin rashes; severe tingling, numbness, or pain; muscular weakness; chest pain, heart arrhythmia, shortness of breath; rapid weight gain, edema/swelling; less/no urination;

confusion; nausea, vomiting; worsened/new coughing; difficulty breathing; nystagmus; and upper stomach pain, loss of appetite, dark urine, and jaundice (signs of liver damage).

Gabapentin is prescribed to children to control seizures. It is also prescribed to adults for Restless Legs Syndrome and for nerve pain secondary to shingles. It may be prescribed to some children for whom other anti-seizure medications have not been effective. Some less serious side effects of gabapentin include sleepiness, dizziness, weakness, fatigue; constipation, diarrhea, nausea; blurred vision; headaches; swelling of the breasts; dryness of the mouth; and loss of coordination or balance. In children particularly, gabapentin is more likely to cause problems with memory, changes in behavior, difficulty concentrating, and restless, aggressive, or hostile behavior. If parents or caregivers observe any of these side effects in children who are taking gabapentin, they should always contact the prescribing physician. Educators should always ensure they are informed when students are taking seizure medications, especially younger children less likely to know/understand or volunteer this information. They should not automatically assume a child has an attention deficit or behavior disorder instead. They should also realize this is probably the reason if a student seems sleepy.

Medical needs for spina bifida

Spina bifida is a neural tube defect: the neural tube that will become the baby's brain, spinal cord, and enclosing tissues does not close completely. Of its several types, spina bifida occulta frequently needs no treatment. Spina bifida meningocele requires surgery to replace the meninges back into the spinal column and close the vertebral opening. Spina bifida myelomeningocele needs surgery within 24 to 48 hours of birth to lessen infection risk and protect the spinal cord from further trauma. Surgeons sometimes install a shunt in the infant's brain during surgery to control hydrocephalus, a buildup of fluid in the brain. Fetal surgery, before week 26 of gestation, reduces children's needs for brain shunts, crutches/walkers/braces, etc., but is risky for mothers and highly elevates premature birth risk. Despite early surgery, children with myelomeningocele often have lower-body paralysis and bladder and bowel problems. Treatment includes exercises preparing for later assisted walking. Myelomeningocele complications include tethered spinal cord from postoperative scar tissue, inhibiting growth. Surgery can restore some function and mitigate the extent of disability

Medical needs for muscular dystrophy

Muscular dystrophy, a genetic condition, makes muscle fibers unusually vulnerable to damage, causing progressive weakness. Symptoms include breathing/swallowing difficulties and limb contractures. Some forms affect the heart and other organs. Among at least seven forms of MD, the Duchenne type comprises roughly half of all cases and is most common in boys. Children learning to walk may fall often; have trouble getting up, running, and jumping; waddle when walking; and have enlarged calf muscles. They also often have learning disabilities. With no cure, treatment focuses on decreasing/preventing spinal and joint deformities and enabling mobility as long as possible. Prednisone and other corticosteroids can slow progression of some forms of MD and enhance muscular strength, but also weaken bones, elevating fracture risks, with long-term use. Surgeries can loosen contracted joints, correct spinal scoliosis to ease breathing, and install pacemakers for MD-related heart conditions. Range-of-motion exercises improve flexibility. Braces support weak muscles, stretch muscles and tendons, and preserve flexibility, slowing contracture progression. Some patients need C-PAP sleep apnea devices or ventilators.

Medical needs for cystic fibrosis

Children who inherit cystic fibrosis have a genetic defect that makes normally thin, slippery secretory juices become thick and sticky. These fluids, which normally lubricate the tissues, when thickened obstruct passageways, ducts, and tubes, particularly in the lungs and pancreas. CF has no cure, and treatment involves complex management. However, improved detection and intervention have decreased complications and ameliorated symptoms, allowing children to live longer. Treatment focuses on loosening and eliminating mucus from the lungs; preventing and controlling lung infections; preventing and treating intestinal obstructions; and supplying sufficient nutrition. This includes antibiotics; mucus-thinning medications; bronchodilators to keep airways open; pancreatic enzymes to improve nutrient absorption; chest clapping by hand or mechanical device, inflatable vibrating vests, and breathing masks/tubes; breathing exercises and strategies; nutritional counseling; energy-conserving techniques; counseling, and/or support groups. Additional procedures include oxygen therapy to prevent pulmonary hypertension, endoscopy and lavage to suction mucus, surgical nasal polyp removal, feeding tubes for supplemental nutrition, surgical removal of bowel obstructions, and lung transplants.

Treatments addressing medical needs of cerebral palsy

Damage or deficient development in the brain before birth usually causes cerebral palsy, which affects muscle tone, posture, and movement. It can include spasticity causing muscular rigidity and incoordination, athetosis causing involuntary movements and exaggerated reflexes, or both. Its effects can range from an unsteady gait or slight limp to complete loss of walking and speech, and every degree in between these. Botox can help isolated spasticity, and muscle relaxants can help generalized spasticity. CP patients benefit from physical therapy to improve motor development, mobility, strength, balance, and flexibility. Splints or braces can stretch stiff muscles, prevent contractures, and help some children walk. Occupational therapists provide adaptive equipment and alternate strategies to help children participate independently in daily routines and activities. Speech-language therapists help children speak clearly, use sign language or communication boards/devices, and improve eating/swallowing muscle use. Orthopedic surgery for severe deformities or contractures can reposition bones or joints; lengthen contracted tendons and muscles to reduce pain and increase mobility; and sometimes sever extremely spastic muscles.

Typical human cognitive development through life

According to Jean Piaget, who developed a widely regarded theory of cognitive development, people progress through clearly defined stages of mental abilities via a combination of biological maturation and experience gained from interacting with the environment. Infants learn through environmental input to their senses, through experimenting with their motor abilities, and receiving feedback about their actions from the environment. Young children's thinking is intuitive, animistic, and magical, but not logical. Their thinking is egocentric and thus unable to consider others' perspectives. Older children develop abilities to think logically and to perform and reverse mental operations, but only with concrete objects as referents. Preteens and adolescents develop abstract thought. They can understand and create logical structures, as well as perform and reverse mental operations without using concrete objects. Adults continue to refine and expand their abilities to understand abstract concepts; conduct complex mental operations; handle multiple levels of thinking; and exercise higher-order cognitive skills in critical thinking, including decision-making, prioritizing, organizing, evaluating, judging, analyzing, and synthesizing.

Receptive language development

Newborns show awareness of environmental sounds, startling or crying at unexpected sounds, quieting at new sounds, awakening at loud noises, and attending to others' speech. By three months they turn to face persons speaking, smile at recognized voices, stop crying upon hearing familiar voices, respond to comforting tones in familiar and unfamiliar voices, and halt activities to attend closely to unfamiliar voices. Around four to six months, babies respond to "no" and changes in speakers' vocal tones, as well as birdsong, machines, toys, music, and rhythm. They also look for sources of new sounds. From 7 to 12 months, they turn and look at the faces of people calling their names, listen when spoken to, and recognize nouns naming familiar things (such as Mommy, ball, car, phone, doggie, key). They respond to simple questions ("More juice?") and requests ("Give it to Mommy"). They play "patty-cake" and other simple games. Children at one to two years are able to point to several body parts and pictures others name. They follow simple commands and questions and listen to songs, rhymes, and simple stories, wanting to hear the same ones repeatedly.

Whereas children one to two years old can follow single commands ("Get your socks"), at two to three years they progress to two-stage commands ("Get your socks, and put them in the hamper"). They understand opposite concepts like hot/cold, stop/go, or nice/yucky. They notice doorbells or phones ringing and may show excitement, point, try to answer, or get their parents to answer these. Three to four-year-olds respond to being called from another room and comprehend simple questions using "who," "what," and "where." While all newborns and younger children should receive hearing screenings, less obvious hearing problems often become apparent at three to four years. Four- to five-year-olds enjoy hearing stories and can answer simple questions about these. By this age, children are capable of understanding almost all the spoken language that they hear. Beyond the age of five years, children expand their vocabularies and learn to read. As they get older, they continue these processes, developing greater comprehension of words naming abstract concepts, compound and complex sentences, and other more sophisticated linguistic structures.

Normal expressive language development

Newborn infants express feelings of pain, discomfort, and pleasure through vocalizations. By three months, babies make cooing and "goo-ing" sounds expressing contentment. They make some sounds repetitively. They smile upon seeing parents. Their crying differentiates to express various needs, such as a "hungry" cry versus a "pain" cry. Babies start babbling and other vocal play around four to six months. Their babbling often mirrors the intonational patterns of verbal speech. They communicate needs and wants to parents using gestures and sounds, including expressing urgency. From 7 to 12 months, infant babbling expands to include long and short vowel and additional consonant sounds. Babies now use speech sounds and other sounds to get and keep parents' attention, rather than simply crying. Their first words emerge (words like Mama, bye-bye, night-night), albeit often with unclear articulation. Children one to two years old ask two-word questions ("What's that?"

"Where kitty?" "More cookies?") and make "Stage 1" type sentences like "Daddy go" or "More play." They articulate more initial word consonants, speaking more clearly.

Two-year-olds show dramatic increases in their spoken vocabulary. They can name most familiar objects. They make one- to three-word utterances that their families usually understand. Toddlers request or point out things using nouns to name them ("elephant"), adjectives to describe them ("big"), or interjections to comment on them ("Wow!"). Three- to four-year-old children are able to speak in sentences combining four words or more. They now talk about experiences, events, people, and places outside of home. By this age, their speech is usually fluent and understandable to people outside of their families. By five years old, children typically have clear, fluent speech and voices adults can listen to comfortably. They can speak in long sentences using details, coordinating conjunctions, and dependent clauses. They sometimes tell long, imaginative, involved stories using standard grammar and staying on-topic. Though they may still distort more difficult consonant sounds, they show otherwise correct pronunciation. Children five years and older easily communicate with peers and familiar adults. They may start conversations with strangers, and invent and tell "tall tales."

Social development

Erikson's theory focuses on stages in lifetime human psychosocial development. Each stage involves a central conflict to resolve; success and failure produce different outcomes. Infants develop basic trust or mistrust in the world, environment, and society depending on whether their needs are fully met, inconsistently met, or not met. Toddlers develop a sense of either autonomy (independence) with high self-esteem, or shame and self-doubt with low self-esteem, through success or failure in toilet-training; learning to walk, talk, and feed themselves; developing fine motor skills; and learning right from wrong. They develop control over bodily functions and learn to assert their wills. Three- to five-year-olds develop a sense of initiative or guilt through imitating adult behaviors in play activities. Six- to twelve-year-olds develop a sense of industry or inferiority as they attend school and make friends, acquiring many new skills and much new information. Relationships extend from the immediate family to the school and the community.

Erikson proposed that infants develop basic trust vs. mistrust; toddlers, autonomy vs. shame and self-doubt; young children, initiative vs. guilt; and elementary school-age children, industry vs. inferiority, through interactions with parents and society. Adolescents develop a sense of identity vs. role confusion, discovering and defining who they are individually, their personal philosophies and roles in society, and navigating social interactions and moral matters. Peer groups gain more importance. Young adults' task is resolving the nuclear conflict of intimacy vs. isolation. Having established their identities as adolescents, they now successfully establish intimate relationships with others, or fail and become isolated. The psychosocial task of middle adulthood is to resolve the conflict of generativity vs. stagnation. They find meaning through passing cultural values to offspring, creating legacies for future generations, and contributing to society; or, if failing to be or feel productive, end up in stagnant, self-absorbed ruts. Older adults develop integrity vs. despair, finding wisdom, meaning, and satisfaction at lives well-spent; or sadness, fear of death, and/or dogmatism at perceived life failures.

Similarities and differences in the growth and development of individuals with and without various disabilities

Not all disabilities cause differences in all aspects of individual growth and development. For example, blind children are generally not found to demonstrate delays in their development of receptive language comprehension and spoken language. Obviously, they cannot learn to read and write through visual modalities, but they can learn to read and write or type Braille via touch, and read via hearing using text-to-speech software. Deaf children, on the other hand, are known to demonstrate delayed development of reading and writing skills. Deafness or blindness alone does not cause delays or deficits in normal physical maturation. Down syndrome can cause cognitive impairment ranging from mild to profound, and delayed physical development. Other genetic syndromes, and various kinds of neurological damage before, during, or after birth that cause cognitive impairment, are often also accompanied by delayed or arrested physiological development. Neurological damage causing cognitive impairment may also cause cerebral palsy, affecting motor control, and seizure disorders. In general, many individuals with significant cognitive impairment usually also have impaired fine motor skills.

Alzheimer's disease and similar dementias related to aging

Aging adults without dementias commonly experience some cognitive decline, particularly in speed, flexibility, and short-term memory, but these are minor. In Alzheimer's disease and similar dementias, however, adults typically demonstrate significant losses in short-term, then long-term memory; disorientation to place and time; confusion; and impaired judgment. They may exhibit awareness and frustration with memory loss early on, but soon will not recognize they have the disease and deny it. As the disease progresses, they often forget to turn off stoves, close or lock doors, and other normally habitual activities. They develop difficulty remembering how to execute familiar everyday tasks. They cannot remember relatives and friends not seen recently. Eventually, this progresses to not recognizing current spouses, siblings, or children. Verbal skills deteriorate, especially reading, writing, and spoken word-finding. Some patients experience mood swings, personality changes, even paranoia; others maintain calmer or happier affects but do not really know what is going on around them. Alzheimer's also impairs walking, speaking, and swallowing. Ultimately, conscious patients may become unresponsive, lose consciousness, suffer strokes, and die. The rate of disease progress varies considerably among individuals.

Ways that disabilities affect development and functioning

Physical, motor, and sensory disabilities obviously alter normal physical, motor, and sensory development and functioning. In some cases, these physiological functions and their development can be enhanced through early and ongoing intervention. In others, where there is no function—as with paralysis, blindness, deafness, and such—many individuals learn alternative means of accomplishing daily life activities. For example, blind people can use other sensory abilities, such as their hearing and speech, to learn receptive and expressive language. They may also use hearing for text-to-speech software for reading, and their tactile sense to learn Braille for reading and to use a cane to check for obstacles ahead when walking. Deaf individuals use vision, hand movements, facial expressions, and body positions and movements to communicate using sign language and speechreading. With non-cognitive disabilities, the chief emotional and social effects are often frustration and isolation. Cognitive disabilities are often accompanied by emotional and social immaturity. Emotional and social skills may develop at later than normal ages, or may seem fixed at earlier age levels.

Growth and development of typical and autistic individuals

Individuals with autism spectrum disorders (ASDs) without additional disabilities do not usually show differences in physical development from typical progress. Motor deficits are also not common in the development of individuals with ASDs. However, depending on the individual and degree of involvement on the autism spectrum, the most striking differences tend to be in the areas of language, social and emotional development, and behavior. Roughly half of autistic individuals have intellectual disabilities while the other half do not. Those who do are affected to varying degrees in language, motor skills, emotional and social skills, and behavior. Those without intellectual disabilities are still likely to have ASD-specific cognitive impairments. For example, roughly half of autistic individuals are nonverbal; those who are verbal range from fluent speech in the high-functioning to limited verbal abilities in others. Inability or difficulty to understand others' social and emotional cues is common in autism, as is difficulty interacting socially or making friends. Behavioral rigidity, including repetitive activities, need for strict routines, and limited range of interests, is also typical in ASDs.

Diagnosis of intellectual disabilities or intellectual disability

According to the American Association on Intellectual and Developmental Disabilities (AAIDD, formerly known as the American Association on Mental Retardation/AAMR), establishing a diagnosis of intellectual disability or intellectual disabilities requires three criteria: (1) The onset of this disability was before a child was 18 years old. (2) The individual displays significant deficits, not only in intellectual ability, but also in adaptive behavior. The former is generally measured using standardized IQ tests; the latter is measured using standardized adaptive behavior scales and checklists, and can also be informally assessed through observation and recording of the individual's behavior in various life situations and tasks, and interviewing caregivers and/or close family members familiar with the individual's daily functioning. (3) The individual's intelligence testing results in an IQ level of 70 or lower on tests (where "average" intelligence equals 100, as in most standardized tests). Intelligence should be determined using multiple testing instruments. IQ levels of 70 or below represent approximately 2% of the population receiving the lowest scores on standardized intelligence tests.

Levels of severity in intellectual disabilities based on IQ scores

The traditional practice of classifying levels of intellectual disabilities uses ranges of scores on standardized intelligence (IQ) tests. IQ scores from 70 to about 55/50 are classed as mild intellectual disabilities. Scores from 55/50 to 40/35 are classified as moderate intellectual disabilities. Scores from 40/35 to 25/20 are termed severe intellectual disabilities. Scores below 25/20, and test responses too minimal to measure with scores, are deemed profound intellectual disabilities. These scores and levels are most used in clinical settings, while in school settings it is common to hear more general terms such as "mild disabilities" or "severe disabilities." The American Association on Intellectual and Developmental Disabilities (AAIDD, formerly American Association on Mental Retardation/AAMR) proposed levels in 1992 related to amounts of support needed rather than IQ scores. These are intermittent support, which indicates episodic need for assistance; limited support, for those needing support for specific periods of time; extensive support, indicating support is regularly needed for an extended time period; and pervasive support, meaning the individual needs intensive, lifetime-long support.

Causes of cognitive impairments and contributing etiological factors

Many cases of cognitive impairment and/or intellectual disabilities have unknown etiologies. These are generally attributed to environmental deprivation early in life, such as lack of intellectual and linguistic stimulation; heredity, as when both parents had below-average intelligence; or both. Known causes of cognitive impairments in children include genetic syndromes like Down syndrome and Fragile X syndrome; brain injury before, during, or after birth, such as anoxia or hypoxia (no oxygen or insufficient oxygen to the brain); and maternal exposure to toxins. Alcohol abuse during pregnancy may cause fetal alcohol syndrome, including cognitive impairment and other symptoms. Maternal exposure to tobacco, other drugs (prescription, over-the-counter, herbal, and illegal), heavy metals like lead and mercury, radiation, air pollution, and many other environmental toxins can all damage fetal brains and have variously been associated with low birth weight, developmental delays, intellectual disabilities, attention deficit hyperactivity disorder (ADHD), and such. Mothers abusing drugs like heroin and crack cocaine deliver addicted babies who display withdrawal symptoms and severe sensory and cognitive impairments.

Down syndrome

Genetically normal humans have 23 pairs of chromosomes, for a total of 46. Due to a genetic mutation, babies born with Down syndrome have an extra full or partial copy of chromosome 21, meaning there are three instead of two, hence the name Trisomy 21. Individuals with Down syndrome range anywhere from profound intellectual disabilities to a normal IQ, though some degree of cognitive impairment is more prevalent. These individuals exhibit short physical stature; short, stubby fingers; thick tongues, often contributing to distorted or unclear speech; thick necks; Asian-appearing eyes; and thin, fine hair. They tend to have slow metabolisms, which may contribute to overweight, though many receiving good dietary and exercise management avoid this. People with Down syndrome frequently have congenital heart defects. This historically contributed to shorter life spans, but with medical advances many patients are living longer. Parents and teachers are familiar with a trait of stubbornness typical of Down syndrome. Most Down syndrome individuals have pleasant, passive, affectionate personalities; are rarely aggressive to others; and enjoy social interaction.

Additional conditions that cause cognitive impairments

A metabolic disorder, rare but medically well known today that causes cognitive impairment is phenylketonuria (PKU). Babies born with PKU, caused by both parents carrying the recessive gene for it, lack the enzyme for metabolizing the essential amino acid phenylalanine, present in certain protein foods and artificial sweeteners. Symptoms in infants include vomiting and seizures. Once PKU was discovered, newborns have been screened for it. Eliminating phenylalanine from the diet prevents brain damage in most, though a few are still affected. Untreated PKU individuals, in addition to intellectual disabilities, exhibit pale hair, eyes, and skin. An endocrine disorder, specifically thyroid deficiency due to lack of dietary iodine (rare since iodized salt was introduced), birth injuries, or infectious diseases, causes what has historically been called cretinism. In addition to intellectual disabilities, individuals have dwarflike symptoms: very short (about three feet) stature, stubby limbs, slightly bowed legs, scoliosis, large heads, and other symptoms. Cranial anomalies causing cognitive impairments include microcephaly (undersized head), macrocephaly (oversized head), and hydrocephalus, a buildup of cerebrospinal fluid in the cranium.

Intellectual functioning and adaptive functioning

Intellectual functioning is equated with intelligence. While controversy has historically surrounded the definition of intelligence, the majority of standardized intelligence tests measure an individual's performance of such skills as general knowledge, word vocabulary, problem solving, and reasoning, which have been found predictive of the person's ability to learn. Adaptive functioning differs from intellectual functioning in that it represents the practical and social skills an individual demonstrates to function in the activities of everyday life. For example, adaptive skills include communication skills; interactional social skills; self-care skills like toileting, dressing and undressing, and feeding oneself; household skills such as cleaning, laundry, and shopping; money management skills; and skills in using transportation, and so on. Individuals with cognitive impairments do not necessarily display matching levels in both areas. For example, some autistic children have very high intelligence but lack communication and/or social interaction skills. And some individuals with intellectual disabilities show clear intellectual deficits, yet they have developed excellent social skills.

Autism spectrum disorders (ASDs)

While about half of autistic individuals have dual diagnoses with intellectual disabilities, half do not. Even so, these latter individuals still exhibit specific cognitive deficits. For example, they often do not understand nonliteral uses of language like sarcasm, humor, metaphors, and other figurative expressions. They may not understand emotional content in language, only literal, linear, and logical content. They may feel normal emotions but be unable to express these in words, hugs, other physical contact, or other socially conventional ways. They typically have great difficulty noticing, recognizing, and understanding others' emotional and social cues, such as smiles indicating happiness or friendliness, facial expressions showing sadness or anger, and gestures and body language communicating social and emotional content. Hypersensitivity to sensory input is common: sounds are too loud, lights and colors too bright; scratchy clothes are intolerably painful. Unaddressed, these sensitivities can cause behavioral problems. Even high-functioning autistics tend to require rigid schedules and routines, having difficulty with changes and transitions.

Even without intellectual disabilities, individuals with ASDs range from being minimally affected to profoundly involved. Many autistic individuals with high or normal intelligence are nonverbal. Some speak only or mostly in echolalia (repeating others' words); some produce original speech but are very limited in vocabulary and have small repertoires of repetitive utterances. Others have normal vocabularies and speak fluently but with slightly odd, sing-song rhythms and intonations. Still others have completely normal speech and language. Typical behavioral characteristics include focusing in depth on one topic for long times rather than showing breadth among many topics of interest. In this sense, autistic students are opposites of ADHD students. They tend to engage in repetitive actions. They are often interested in numerical and linear activities. Those with good verbal abilities may engage in composing lists, classifying words, analyzing word components, and so on. Typically, they show more ability, understanding, and comfort in solitary activities than social interactions. In a normal, intellectual discussion, it is not unusual for a high-functioning, autistic Ph.D. suddenly to walk away mid-conversation.

Preventing cognitive impairments

Expectant mothers may avert cognitive damage to their unborn babies by not ingesting drugs, including alcohol and tobacco; avoiding (when possible) undue exposure to environmental toxins like air pollution, radiation, or lead in paint; and not eating fish known for high mercury levels. They should also have regular prenatal medical checkups; take prenatal vitamins; eat nourishing diets; engage in regular, nonstrenuous exercise; and avoid or alleviate emotional stress by maintaining or seeking social, financial, and emotional support; pursuing counseling if needed; and engaging in fulfilling activities. Parents protect children from traumatic brain injuries by handling infants properly, making children wear helmets for bicycling, and supervising their play activities. They should prevent children's exposure to lead in paint, mercury in foods, and limit exposure to environmental radiation and pollution. Providing environments with structure and mental stimulation also prevents cognitive underdevelopment. While causes of Alzheimer's dementia and associated tau protein neurofibrillary tangles and beta-amyloid protein plaques in aging adults are unknown, early diagnosis and treatment minimizes and slows cognitive impairment.

Effects of cognitive impairments

Depending on the type and severity of impairment, some individuals do not develop physically to normal adult size. Generally, those with the most severe or profound brain damage are more likely to suffer from seizure disorders and cerebral palsy. Repeated seizures may incur further brain damage. Cerebral palsy (CP) damages the brain's motor control, causing paralysis or weakness and incoordination of the muscles. CP symptoms range from mild, like a slight limp, to profound, with quadriplegia and spasticity, hypotonia, and/or athetosis. The most severe CP significantly restricts an individual's physical abilities, requiring total physical care. A sensory factor to consider in students with neurological damage or defects is that some show abnormally low sensitivity to pain: they can injure themselves and not feel pain or even be aware of the injury. At the other extreme, many individuals with autism are hypersensitive to sensory stimuli, finding intolerable what others find normal. Generally (but not always), the more severe the cognitive impairment, the more likely fine and/or gross motor skills are affected.

Although cognitively impaired students generally feel the same emotions all people do, such as happiness, sadness, depression, anger, and frustration, they may not express them the same way. For example, cognitive deficits may prevent a student from converting those feelings into words when he or she cannot grasp abstract concepts embodied in language. Also, limited vocabulary development sometimes prevents a student from articulating feelings. Another limiting aspect is lack of emotional self-control or self-regulation. Some students have delayed emotional development commensurate to their delayed cognitive development, so others may perceive them as emotionally immature: although their emotional age matches their mental age, neither matches their chronological age, which can confuse those unfamiliar with intellectual disabilities. Other students have neurological conditions that actually impair self-control (frontal lobe damage, tuberous sclerosis, etc.). Many cognitively impaired students are socially inclined and develop good social skills.

Those with mental levels of young children may be egocentric, causing difficulty seeing others' viewpoints, but many others are able to learn this with instructional support.

Cognitive impairments impact cognitive and linguistic development

One of the most valuable generalizations about the cognitive development of students with cognitive impairment is that they learn in the same way as all people do, only slower. Aside from specific considerations like individual learning styles, and conditions like specific learning disabilities or autism that can make certain modalities more or less successful for learning, most cognitively impaired students learn in the same sequences and manner that everybody does, but at a much slower rate. Thus parents and educators need great patience and persistence in teaching them. These students need information broken down into much smaller increments, much more repetition, and far more time devoted to each task. Some students have great difficulty retaining information. This is especially true with traumatic brain injuries, and anytime memory is affected. Language development generally is delayed, and ultimately limited, commensurately with the degree of cognitive impairment. Profoundly intellectually disabled individuals are generally nonverbal.

Degrees of independence in self-care

Students diagnosed with mild levels of cognitive impairment, in the IQ score range of 70 to 51, are not very different from normal-IQ peers in many respects. With appropriate instruction, they often learn to live independently or with minimal support. Those with moderate impairments, in the IQ range of 50 to 36, can learn with instruction to perform personal self-care and many activities of daily living, as well as vocational tasks to work for pay, usually in sheltered or supported work settings. Students with severe impairments in the IQ range of 35 to 21, given sufficient intensive instruction, can still learn fundamental self-care tasks; also, typically with supervision, they are able to contribute somewhat to their self-support. Students testing with IQ scores below 20 have profound intellectual impairment. They most often are dependent on others for personal care. In addition to their cognitive-developmental levels limiting which self-care tasks they are capable of learning, these students are more likely to have accompanying conditions, such as cerebral palsy and seizure disorders, which physically prevent their performing them.

Assessing Students with Cognitive Impairments and Developing Individualized Programs

Accommodations and modifications for students with cognitive disabilities

Assessment instruments often must be adjusted for students with special needs. For example, a student who cannot read and write at grade level may yet perform at grade level on a test given orally using oral responses. Parental concerns that testing accommodations are "crutches" and their child will never learn to perform without extra support are addressed by educators who liken accommodations to glasses for a student who cannot read without them or leg braces for a student's physical disability. Accommodations compensate for deficit areas and may strengthen weak areas. Testing modifications more substantially alter the quality and quantity of materials, including difficulty level, amount or number of items tested, and the nature of assessment and presentation of material. For students with more severe disabilities, modifications generate different standards. For those with complex special needs, alternative assessments are sometimes more suitable. For example, a student who is unable to compute fractions with pencil and paper could demonstrate a different but related conceptual/skill area by cutting an apple in half.

Alternative assessments at home with cognitively impaired children

Students with cognitive impairments generally have difficulties with reading, writing, and spelling. Most standardized tests being in written form poses a disadvantage. To enable their children to show what they have learned, creative parents might substitute assessments wherein students give speeches or oral presentations, produce artwork, build models, and demonstrate processes or procedures. Parents can create rubrics showing preset standards being evaluated: a chart, grid, or graph shows performance criteria vertically and descriptions of excellent/good/fair/poor performance horizontally. Parents should discuss the individual performance criteria with the child. This enables students to know exactly what will be evaluated, and what they must do for their performance to be graded as excellent. It also improves the parents' teaching skills and has often been found to serve as a motivational stimulus for students to achieve at higher levels.

Accommodations for students with cognitive impairments

Standardized tests are called "high-stakes testing" because they influence end-of-year evaluations, grade promotions, and other important education decisions. Accommodations and modifications regularly needed by a student must be included in his/her IEP. Standardized test publishers commonly indicate standard or permissible testing accommodations that will not change the test's validity, ensuring it is still measuring what it is supposed to measure. For example, some written tests may be read aloud to students who cannot read at grade level, but not reading tests, which would be invalidated as they would then test listening comprehension, not reading ability. Accommodations publishers identify as "nonstandard" may still be used when a student requires or normally receives them, but scores cannot then be compared meaningfully to group norms. Though not a completely accurate, norm-referenced picture of student performance, this still fairly depicts individual performance. Educational consultants can assist parents regarding whether specific standardized tests scheduled for their child allow accommodations, and if so, which ones. Students needing many accommodations to perform at grade level pose difficulties for group administrators and are better served by one-on-one testing.

Accommodating assessment instruments for cognitively impaired students

Accommodations to test presentation include reducing clutter to make the printed layout clearer, enlarging type fonts and worksheets, repeating spoken directions, boxing math problems to facilitate visual tracking, highlighting important vocabulary words, and using recorded instead of printed text. Accommodations to student test responses include letting students mark answers in the test book rather than on separate paper; allowing oral rather than written test responses; assigning written short-answer rather than essay responses; and permitting nonverbal responses, such as pointing to correct multiple-choice answers in lieu of writing or speech. Accommodations to test setting include providing an individual carrel, finding quieter surroundings, providing special lighting, incorporating background music, and/or testing in a separate room. Accommodations to test scheduling or timing include allowing more time for completing tests, scheduling frequent breaks, and testing at different times of day. Accommodations to pacing include presenting test content more slowly and reviewing more often.

Assessment programs that are included in the Michigan Educational Assessment System

The MEAS incorporates the Michigan Educational Assessment Program (MEAP), Michigan's Alternate Assessment Program MI-Access, and English Language Proficiency Assessment (ELPA). Michigan's Office of Educational Assessment and Accountability provides information on which assessment accommodations are standard and nonstandard, as well as which are permitted/not permitted for the National Assessment of Educational Progress (NAEP), Michigan Merit Exam (MME), and English Language Learners (ELLs). A school's or district's meeting No Child Left Behind's Adequate Yearly Progress (AYP) is influenced by whether accommodations are standard or nonstandard. Nonstandard accommodations render student scores ineligible for the MME. Examples of nonstandard accommodations include using a calculator on sections of MEAP math tests prohibiting calculators, or being read aloud passages in MEAP's reading assessment designed to test decoding ability. State government documents specify the information provided is not to be used as a "checklist" for deciding which assessments to administer to a disabled student, but rather to ascertain whether accommodations applicable to certain students are standard or nonstandard for the MEAS and permitted or not permitted for the NAEP, MME, and ELLs.

Emotional, social, and behavioral assessment of cognitively impaired students

School and other psychologists typically include emotional, social, and behavioral assessments in their psychological assessments. Cognitive impairments often contribute to emotional, behavioral, and/or social problems. Limitations in a student's abilities to understand may lead to inappropriate behaviors, and frustrated feelings contribute to acting-out or withdrawal behaviors. Developmental delays may result in emotionally and socially immature behavior. A significant factor in the cognitively impaired is often limited communication skills: students unable to verbalize and use other socially acceptable means of communicating their needs, emotions, and thoughts are more likely to communicate through their behavior, even when it is inappropriate. Psychologists assess emotional functions and behavior via formal and informal methods. They may use direct student observation; student, parent, and teacher interviews; standardized rating scales normed to same-age peer samples and completed by teachers, parents, and/or students; and projective measures, wherein they ask students to complete a sentence, tell a story about a picture, or make a drawing.

Interpreting a cognitively impaired student's standardized test scores and results

Standardized tests commonly represent results in standard scores, with a mean/average of 100 and a standard deviation (SD) from the mean of 15. Sixty-eight percent of a typical student population will score within one SD (15 points) of the mean/average that is between 85 and 115. Scores much lower, ruling out other causes, may indicate cognitive impairment. Behavioral or emotional rating scales may use T-scores, with a mean of 50 and an SD of 10. The normal range is thus between 40 and 60. A T-score of 75 in categories such as aggression or depression is considered significant. Parents and other interested parties should understand percentile scores do not equal percentages of correct test answers. Percentiles are a statistical method of ranking students among their age peers. If an average IQ score of 100 is in the 50th percentile for an age group, 50% of students that age scored greater than 100 and 50% 100. A student scoring at the 27th percentile scored higher than 27% of age peers. Also, parents should not assign too much weight to grade-level equivalents, which can be extremely misleading.

Components, content, and abilities measured in cognitive assessments

School psychologists include cognitive assessment within their psychological assessments of students. Cognitive assessment indicates a student's intellectual performance compared to age-level peers. Some tests, like the Peabody Picture Vocabulary, measure only the student's receptive knowledge of word meanings. Most IQ tests give an overall score that is obtained as a composite of scores on various scales testing verbal abilities, nonverbal abilities, memory, spatial abilities, and processing speed. Each scale typically contains subscales to measure different forms or facets of each ability area. Cognitive assessments are designed to indicate a student's relative abilities to interpret information through visual, auditory, and other modalities, and in which one(s) the student is most successful—how well the student retains information, how quickly or slowly s/he processes information in various modalities, and how well s/he solves problems.

Educational assessment

Educational assessments are usually administered by special education teachers or educational diagnosticians. Educational assessments measure a student's academic functioning relative to age peers. The main areas on which educational assessments focus are typically reading, writing, mathematics, and spoken language. Within each of these areas, subtests are included to measure component aspects. For example, in the area of reading, subtests might include reading comprehension, reading speed, and sight word recognition. Educational assessments do not test specific material taught in classroom lessons. Rather, they test the student's attainment of the general skills they are required to have in order to learn and achieve in the related academic subjects. Students cannot study in preparation for an educational assessment the way they would study specific subject matter to prepare for a test covering classroom lessons in academic subject content. The skills measured in educational assessments are broader, encompassing the skills foundations the student needs to succeed academically.

Scaled scores on standardized tests

Whereas standard scores have a mean of 100 and a standard deviation (SD) of 15, scaled scores have a mean of 10 and an SD of 3. Therefore a scaled score of 13 is above average. For example, the Wechsler Intelligence Scales for Children (WISC) test uses scaled scores on each of its subscales, and these are combined for a composite score designed as the full-scale IQ score. Stanine scores are basically reduced counterparts of standard scores. They have a mean of 5 and a range between 1 and 9. The main disadvantage of stanines is that they yield a broader, or coarser, measure. Their main advantage is that this coarser measurement permits easier comparison among scores on different standardized tests. Parents and teachers can monitor student progress over time by drawing a normal/"bell" curve, and placing the student's scores from separate administrations of a standardized test along the standard score axis. Scores decreasing over time indicate a need to make instructional and/or other (medical, emotional, etc.) changes for the student.

Grade equivalent (GE) scores

A GE score does not mean that a student performs at grade level in all parts of a skill or area tested. One GE score should never be used for placement without additional strongly supporting documentation from other sources. GE score changes from one school year to the next mean less at higher grade levels: students do not progress as steadily in mastering skills as in lower grades. GE scores do not match across subjects. GEs are metrically inadequate, may be misleading, and should not be literally interpreted. For example, a third-grader receives a score of 1.9, meaning month 9 of first grade, in math. This student got a few addition problems correct on the test, two subtraction problems correct, got no subtraction with regrouping problems correct, and got several single-digit multiplication problems correct. One cannot assume this student's math skills are identical to those of an end-of-year first-grader: the test results show some skill deficits, but also some second- and third-grade math skills, surpassing what is expected of first-graders.

Communicating cognitively impaired students' assessment results to various stakeholders

When conveying the meaning of assessment results to the cognitively impaired student, one should use terms commensurate with the student's developmental level; for instance, "You are doing great with your numbers. We are going to do some more work with your words." When communicating with general education teachers, psychological or special education jargon should be avoided, and any technical terms should be defined or paraphrased in clear, nontechnical English. Psychologists and special education professionals should be careful not to "talk down" to students or classroom teachers. They should use similarly clear language with parents, while also avoiding jargon limited to educators (unless the parents are also educators). When talking to school administrators, assessors should focus on the student's educational strengths and needs, and on the types of educational interventions and programs that would most benefit student performance. Culturally responsive professionals should best obtain interpreters for explaining assessment findings to parents who speak little/no English. They should also be sensitive to varying cultural attitudes, and describe student attributes to parents accordingly.

IEP process for students with cognitive impairments

If prereferral classroom interventions on a student's behalf have been ineffective or insufficient, a multidisciplinary evaluation team is assembled to identify a disability and determine the best placement, program, and service delivery options. This team may include a special educator, psychologist, physical therapist, occupational therapist, speech-language pathologist, vision specialist, hearing specialist, and other professionals, depending on the individual student's needs. Once they obtain the parents' written consent, the team members will conduct assessments of the student's developmental skills including speech and language/communication skills, gross and fine motor skills, and particular academic skills like reading and mathematics. Team members compile test results into a comprehensive evaluation report, classifying the student educationally and identifying skills the student needs, as well as the support necessary to acquire these. Parents review the report; some may disagree. Parents and school personnel collaboratively develop a plan for the student. They attend an IEP meeting, including a general education teacher to provide input for the IEP to help the student with standard curriculum.

Diagnosis of cognitive impairments

When assessing a child for cognitive impairment, sensory deficits such as visual and hearing impairments should first be ruled in or out as they can interfere with student performance in classes, on tests, and in interviews. Emotional and behavioral disturbances must also be assessed independently of cognitive assessments: While cognitive impairments can lead to related emotional and behavioral problems in many students, it is also true that emotional or behavioral disorders by themselves can significantly alter a student's responses to assessments as well as their everyday classroom behaviors. Because the student is a whole person and these factors interact in complex ways, differential diagnosis is very important to avoid misdiagnosing cognitive impairment where there is none, or failing to diagnose a cognitive impairment in the presence of more obvious emotional and/or behavioral symptoms. Neither a below-average IQ test score, nor school performance below age or grade level, nor an adaptive skills deficiency alone can determine cognitive impairment; the student must demonstrate all three of these to be diagnosed with cognitive impairment.

Using assessment results to determine a cognitively impaired student's eligibility for special education and related services

When a student's teacher, parents, or physician has concern that the student is experiencing difficulty in school, the teacher may initiate the referral process by notifying the school psychologist or counselor. School personnel then must collect data specific to the student's school progress and problems. They obtain this information through student conferences, parent conferences, observing the student, and analyzing the student's performance. Performance analysis is based on observations of the student's attention in class; behavior; schoolwork completion; test responses and results; class work and homework; etc. School personnel then try various student-specific classroom interventions/strategies. If these do not help, further evaluation for a specific disability is indicated. A multidisciplinary team of professionals will evaluate the student using observations, standardized test scores; daily class work, homework, quizzes, and tests to determine eligibility for special services.

Identifying a disability does not guarantee service eligibility; the disability must compromise the student's functioning in school.

IEP teams

<u>Addressing the needs of linguistically and culturally diverse students</u>
When a student is suspected to have cognitive impairment and/or demonstrates difficulties in school and preliminary classroom interventions are unsuccessful, a multidisciplinary team conducts evaluations of the student's developmental and academic skill levels. If the student is also identified as an ELL (English language learner) or ESL (English as a second language) student, s/he will also be given tests of English literacy and/or English language proficiency. These determine how much English the student knows, as well as approximate grade level equivalents in various aspects of English language. Individual ELL/ESL students are often at respectively different levels of reading, writing, listening, and speaking English, depending on their backgrounds and experiences. Many schools have educational programs for bilingual students. In schools where some students are both ELL/ESL and cognitively impaired, they may be placed together—in the same special or mainstream classes—according to similar ages, cognitive or developmental levels, grade levels of learning, and/or a combination of these.

<u>Developing, implementing, and amending IEPs</u>
When a student has been identified with cognitive impairment and found eligible for special services, the federal government requires public schools to develop an IEP to direct the student's educational programming. The student, parents, teachers, and therapists and other service providers attend IEP meetings to develop a plan that will address teaching the skills the student needs, and the support necessary for learning these skills, both identified through evaluations. The IEP should include the student's present level of performance. The team develops more general, global learning goals for the student to attain, plus more specific, detailed learning objectives within these goals. A goal example might be to read at grade level; accompanying objectives might specify the amounts of material to read, the time frames, and the number or percentage of correct responses to achieve on a reading test/measure. Service specialists should monitor whether classroom teachers and others are actually implementing the IEP. IEPs must be reviewed annually. However, goals, objectives, and criteria may be adjusted anytime as needed.

Services that might be specified in a cognitively impaired student's IEP

Students with cognitive impairments, depending on their individual needs, may have specifications in their IEPs to receive special education instruction, nursing services, other medical services, vision therapy, hearing therapy, audiological services, speech-language therapy, physical therapy, occupational therapy, or counseling. When multiple services are recommended for a student, it may become impossible to fit them all into the school schedule. In these cases, services may be delivered in consultative form. For example, if a student has fine motor deficits that impede handwriting, an occupational therapist may not deliver hands-on therapy, but offers accommodations that the classroom teacher should incorporate into whole-class handwriting lessons. Or the OT might deliver one-on-one fine motor therapy to the student in class while other students practice handwriting, so therapy does not interrupt the school day or detract from the students' classroom time. Similarly, a physical therapist may give the physical education teacher accommodations to incorporate, or deliver individualized therapy during PE classes.

Considerations important to the sequencing and evaluation of short- and long-term IEP goals

In developing IEP goals, following the proper developmental sequence is important. Objectives and instruction to achieve them should always proceed from simplest to most complex, shortest to longest, concrete to abstract, and least to most difficult. The most basic skills should always be taught first, not only following the difficulty sequence, but also providing foundations on which more advanced forms of skills are built. For example, if a student with deficits in communication, decision-making, and problem-solving has a goal to request needed help, the ultimate long-term objective might be requesting help in school in 90% of need instances. If the student currently requests help 10% of the time, a shorter-term objective could be increasing this by 20% more per school year over four years. Short-term objectives within this might be 5% increases every two months. Evaluations of progress should not be a single observational session or test, but include multiple measures to ensure accuracy, obtain an average, and measure the behavior's consistency.

How and why IFSPs, IEPs, and transition plans are used

When young children and preschoolers are identified with cognitive impairments, service professionals may collaborate with the child and parents to develop an individualized family service plan (IFSP). Because younger children are not yet attending elementary school, these plans typically involve more plan implementation by parents and service providers. Plans will not refer to school curriculum or academic subject content. They focus on helping children attain functional skills like self-care, communication, and daily living activities, to meet their age/developmental levels. IFSPs may also include measures to help children attain school readiness. They specify which services a child needs—in the home and/or community—to learn identified skills needed. IEPs are used in schools to define skills a student needs to learn, and the instruction and services needed to support those goals. Transition plans are developed in advance of life changes like promotions to higher grades or schools, graduation, employment, and community living. Cognitively impaired students' learning processes are slower, requiring more repetition, review, and reinforcement: they must begin learning transitional skills years in advance.

Prioritizing parts of the general school curriculum for students with cognitive impairments

When working with cognitively impaired students, teachers should focus on the aspects of each area of general curriculum that will give students the most functional forms or applications of skills. For example, it is less important for students with severe reading impairment to read literature with difficult language and concepts for enjoyment than it is to read road signs with street names, traffic indicators, and warnings (such as walk/don't walk); signs inside buildings indicating exits and entrances, fire or emergency exits, elevators and stairwells, male/female/unisex bathrooms, and cafeterias; "no" signs like no talking/running/smoking/cell phones/cameras; and labels on consumer products. It is less useful for a student to compute square roots than to identify coin and paper money denominations and make correct change in stores, restaurants, and workplaces. Rather than expending great time and energy with little to no success in differentiating between word forms for items like hamburger, cheeseburger, and fries, students with severe reading deficits may instead be taught to recognize pictures of these on register keys and computer touch-screens at fast-food restaurants, affording them usable job skills.

Early developmental screening of children

The U.S. Department of Education finds significant disparity between the numbers of children below three years old being served by federally supported early intervention programs and the numbers below 18 years old who have developmental, learning, or behavioral disabilities. Birth to age three is a critical period for child development; therefore, delayed identification may impinge on a child's chances of future success. Screenings for developmental delays or disabilities and monitoring a child's cognitive, emotional, and social development take only a few minutes and may be incorporated into physician well-baby visits. Parents may complete screening forms at home before visits, in the doctor's waiting room, or in the examining room with professional assistance. Physicians observe how the child interacts with other people, attends to the speech of others, and comprehends and uses language, as well as the age-appropriateness of developmental milestones. Pediatricians should pay attention to parental observations and combine these with their own findings to attain a deeper, richer, more complete picture of the child's development.

Prereferral process in public schools for students with disabilities

Prereferral in schools is done prior to referral for evaluation to determine eligibility for special education services. If a child is having academic and/or behavioral problems and/or is suspected of cognitive impairment, the school first determines whether modifications and accommodations in the regular classroom might improve the student's learning. The school prereferral team's job is to work together to identify the student's strengths and needs, implement teaching strategies suited to these attributes, and assess the effects of this implementation to promote student success in the general education classroom. Teams may include classroom teachers, counselors, administrators, school psychologists, special education teachers, and speech-language pathologists and other related service providers. Most schools include parents, who know the child best and can identify specific concerns. If interventions selected do not succeed, the team may try different interventions or refer the student for a special education eligibility evaluation. Parents may request evaluation at any time without waiting for the prereferral process to begin or end.

Supplying background information to school personnel to aid in the evaluation of a student suspected of cognitive impairment

A student's parents are typically the best sources of information about their child's developmental history, areas of strengths and needs, family history, and overall school history. The family doctor, pediatrician, or other physician can give medical history information about specific diagnoses, incidents, and procedures. However, parents are often best able to provide the child's overall nonclinical medical history with continuity over time. If the child has been seen by service providers such as early intervention specialists, speech-language pathologists, occupational therapists, physical therapists, psychologists, special education teachers, and such, these practitioners can provide valuable information on the child's talents, deficits, and responses—and progress, if they have seen the child regularly or repeatedly over time. If the child has already attended regular school, classroom teachers have valuable information about the student's stronger academic areas and specific deficits, as well as socialization and behavioral patterns. Assessors can interview parents, teachers, and service providers and have them complete checklists. Evaluators should also review any test results previously obtained by past or currently involved service providers.

Michigan Grade Level Content Expectations (GLCE)

Michigan's GLCE provides guidance to educators for designing curriculum and instruction, assessing student achievement, and identifying professional development needs. In ELA, each expectation has code letters identifying one of four strands: Reading, Writing, Speaking, and Listening & Viewing. Each expectation is coded to show the specific domain, grade level, and expectation number. Under the Reading strand, domains are Word Recognition/Study, which includes Phonemic Awareness, Phonics, Word Recognition, and Vocabulary; Fluency; Narrative Text; Informational Text; Comprehension; Metacognition; Critical Standards; and Reading Attitude. Writing domains are Genre; Process; Personal Style; Grammar & Usage; Spelling; Handwriting; and Writing Attitude. Speaking domains are Conventions and Discourse. Listening & Viewing domains are Conventions and Response. Michigan's GLCE documents stress to educators: "it is critical...that content knowledge alone is not sufficient for academic success. Students must be able to apply knowledge in new situations...solve problems by generating new ideas, and...make connections between what they learn...[and] the world around them. The art of teaching is what makes the content of learning become a reality."

Reliability and validity

Reliability is consistency of an assessment instrument's data across repeated administrations. For example, reliable test scores are similar when the same test-taker is given the test two/three times at two-week intervals. Internal consistency reliability is consistency of test items with one another by measuring the same quantity/construct. Inter-rater consistency is reliability among individuals scoring the same test. Intra-rater consistency is an individual's consistency in rating responses to various test items. Validity is whether a test measures what it claims/intends to measure. Content validity means a test includes items representing the complete range of possible items. Construct validity means a test's scores measure the construct they are meant to measure, like intelligence. Criterion validity means a test's scores effectively measure a construct according to established criteria. Concurrent validity, a type of criterion validity, means a test measures the criterion and the construct at the same time. Predictive validity, another type of criterion validity, means test scores effectively predict future outcomes, as when aptitude tests predict future subject grades.

Generalizability, compensatory grading, noncompensatory grading, and cut score

Generalizability is related to reliability, i.e., the consistency of test scores over repeated administrations; but it moreover refers to the specific features of a certain test administration. It means the results on one test can be generalized to apply to other tests with similar formats, content, and operations. Generalizability can also refer to whether a test's results can be generalized from an individual or group to the larger population. Compensatory grading is the practice of balancing out lower performance in one area or subject with higher performance in another. Noncompensatory grading does not permit such balancing, but requires a similar standard of achievement in each area or subject. A cut score is a predetermined number used to divide categories of data or results from a test instrument. For example, a cut score can divide the categories of passing and failing scores. It can also divide the category of passing scores from a category of "honors" or "excellent" or "superior" scores.

Standard deviation, standard score, and scaled score

Standard deviation measures variability within a set of numbers. In interpreting assessment results, it measures how much scores among a group of test-takers vary around the mean/average. For example, a bell curve shows a normal distribution of test scores: the high center represents the majority of scores closest to the mean, while the lower sides represent standard deviations above and below it. SD is calculated by obtaining the square root of the sum of deviations of each score and the mean, and dividing this figure by the number of scores in the group. The standard score, or z score, represents the amount whereby an individual score deviates from the mean, measured in SDs. For example, a common SD unit for IQ tests is 15 where the mean is 100. A scaled score is obtained by converting a group of test scores to a scale/distribution with a designated mean and SD. For example, the U.S. Medical Licensing Examination (USMLE) has a mean of 200 and a SD of 20.

Domain and the Item Response Theory

In educational assessment, the term "domain" is the identified scope of expected learning to be assessed. Tests typically present students with samples of assessment tasks. The results of these tests are then interpreted to generalize the performance on the full range of possible assessment tasks that would measure the domain of intended learning. Item Response Theory (IRT) posits that performance on a test item is attributed to three influences: the item itself; the test-taker; and the interaction between the two. In education, when large groups of test-takers are given many test items to produce large data sets, raters can use formulae to separate influences on test items from the test-takers' true ability, skills, or knowledge. However, the kind of assessment that is normally conducted within a given educational program does not afford enough data to calculate parameters according to Item Response Theory that would be stable enough to be meaningful.

Mean, median, and mode

The mean is the average of a group of numbers, e.g., scores within a group of students taking the same test. Among six students, if one scores 50%; one 60%; one 70%; one 80%; one 90%; and one 100%, the sum of scores = 450; divided by 6 (students/scores) yields an average/mean of 75%. The median is the center-most score in a group. For example, if the range of student scores on a test is 65%, 75%, 80%, 85%, and 95%, then 80% = the middle/median. When there is an even number of scores, the median is the average of the two most central scores. For example, with four scores of 50%, 60%, 70%, and 80%, 60% and 70% are averaged for a median of 65%. The mode is the most frequent score in a set. If in a group of students, one scored 100% on a test; one, 95%; two, 90%; three, 85%; four, 80%; three, 75%; two, 70%; and one, 65%, the mode = 80%.

Positive skew, negative skew, and normal distribution

When the majority of a group of numbers, such as test scores, is concentrated toward the high end of the range/distribution with the minority "tail" of scores near the low end, this group of numbers is said to be positively skewed. When the majority of scores is bunched near the lower end of the distribution, with a minority "tail" near the higher end, the set of scores is negatively skewed. A normal curve is called a bell curve because it resembles the shape of a bell, with the largest number of scores collected around the center mean or average score and the numbers of scores descending as they move away from the center and mean. Parametric statistics assume a normal distribution. However, in typical educational assessments, the data obtained as scores on testing instruments are not usually found to be distributed normally.

SEM and Standard Error of the Mean

If an individual student took a lot of tests that were similar in size or length (i.e., the number of items on each test), the assessors can estimate how much that student's scores will vary. This estimate is called the Standard Error of Measurement (SEM). The SEM is calculated using the reliability coefficient that is established for a given test and the Standard Deviation (SD) that has been established for the group of scores that the student achieved. When a group of students takes a test, the assessors can estimate how much the mean or average score of that group would vary if they selected many samples with the same sizes and then calculated the means or averages of their scores. This estimate of variance around the mean of a group's test scores is called the Standard Error of the Mean.

Confidence Interval

Statisticians use the Confidence Interval to express the range wherein a "true" or "real" score is situated. The purpose is to acknowledge and address the fact that the measurement of a student's performance contains "noise," i.e., interfering/confounding variables that influence the measure of pure ability/achievement, akin to static in a radio, phone, or other sound signal. Giving a Confidence Interval shows the probability that a student's true score is within the range defined by that interval. For example, a student might take a test and receive a score of 80%. If that student took several other, similar tests, most likely the student's scores would not all be exactly 80%; they would be similar, but vary. The assessors might give a Confidence Interval of + 2 Standard Deviations, 95% of the time. Computing Confidence Intervals does not use Standard Scores (z scores), but literal scores to show the upper and lower limits of the range of likely scores.

Cut score

Educators use a cut score to determine which scores are passing and which are failing. They set a particular number as the cut score; all scores above it are passing and all scores below the cut score are failing. Using methods developed for multiple-choice tests allows them to adjust for various factors, e.g., the difficulty of a certain test or assessing student population with special needs, rather than arbitrarily assigning the same cut score to all tests. One such method for establishing a cut score is the Nedelsky method: the assessor(s) identify a "borderline" group of students, i.e., those who do not always pass or fail, but tend to score on the borderline of passing/failing. The assessor(s) estimate how many of these "borderline" students will probably answer a given test item correctly. A common number for this group is 10 students. The sum of the percentages of students estimated to respond correctly to each test item is rounded to an integer, yielding the cut score.

Angoff method for determining a pass/fail cut score

To determine which scores on a given test are passing or failing, educators can use several established methods. In the Angoff method, one or more assessors select a group of "borderline" students (i.e., those not always passing or failing but with equal chances of either) and estimate which choice(s) in a multiple-choice test item these students could eliminate as an incorrect answer and what percent of the choices left these students would guess as correct. For example, if they might eliminate one choice of five as wrong, their probability of guessing the right choice from the four choices left is 25% (1/4). The assessors add up the percentages for all of the test items and round the sum to an integer, which would be the cut score for that test. In the modified Angoff procedure, the assessors also estimate how many of the students would fail the test, and if they deem it necessary, they modify their estimations to produce a number of failures they find more reasonable.

Ebel method for determining a pass/fail cut score

Rather than arbitrarily setting the same pass/fail cut score for all tests, several methods exist for determining an appropriate cut score for a particular instrument. The Ebel method considers the importance and difficulty level of each test item in establishing a cut score for a test. First the testers divide all test items into six categories: High, Medium, and Low importance; and High, Medium, and Low difficulty. Then, after selecting a group of "borderline" students who do not always pass or fail tests but are about equally likely to do either, they estimate how many of these students would probably get each item correct in each of these six categories. They add up their estimated percentages for each test item and round the sum to an integer, which is the cut score. The assessors can also then modify their estimations based on data they may obtain from a student class or group's actual test results.

Hofstee method to determine pass/fail cut scores

Several methods have been developed to set a cut score, the score above which all scores are passing and below which all scores are failing, for a particular test with a multiple-choice format. The Hofstee method is also called the compromise method. It addresses the difference between norm-referenced and criterion-referenced tests, i.e., tests that compare individual student scores to the average scores of a normative sample of students found representative of the larger population versus tests that compare student scores to a pre-established criterion of achievement. Educators estimate an acceptable number of students who would fail the test and the largest number of test items a student who fails the test would answer correctly. They then plot the answers to this number of items plus two more on the cumulative score distribution. This allows them to determine how many items students could miss and how many failed test items would affect the number of students who could fail.

Norm-referenced tests and criterion-referenced tests

In reference to testing large groups, like the entire student body of a school, district, or state, the high-stakes standardized tests given are typically norm-referenced tests; that is, they compare students' scores to a normative sample of students deemed representative of the general population. Criterion-referenced tests may or may not be standardized and compare student scores to a predetermined set of criteria for acceptable performance. In the context of educational programs, norm-referenced tests seek to determine the highest or lowest achievement rather than the absolute score achieved. For example, educators might determine the 10 highest student scores on a certain test to reinforce with "best in group" awards. In this context, measures of mastery learning are examples of criterion-referenced or domain-referenced testing. Educators establish a minimum performance level score that equates to passing. Student scores are compared against this score, so the students in a given class could all pass or all fail the test.

Formative assessments versus summative assessments

Formative assessments are given during a lesson, unit, course, or program. Their purpose is to give the teachers and students an idea of how well each student is learning what the teacher has planned and expected for them to learn. The teacher uses the results of formative assessments to explain to each student his/her strengths and weaknesses, and how s/he can build on the strengths and improve the weaknesses, and to report student progress to parents, administrators, and others. Summative assessments are given after a lesson, unit, course, or program has been completed. Their purpose is to determine whether the student has passed the segment of instruction. This determines whether they need to repeat the instruction or can move on to successive segments. Summative assessments apply to lessons or units within a class, to courses in a subject, to promotion from one grade level to the next, and to graduation.

Item analysis

Item analysis is often used to evaluate test items that use multiple-choice formats to show the quality of the test item and of the test overall. Item analysis has an implicit orientation of being norm-referenced rather than criterion- or domain-referenced. That is, it evaluates test items using performance within the group of test-takers rather than an externally preset criterion for expected achievement. Characteristics analyzed in test items include how many high-scoring students got an item correct; how many low-scoring students got the item correct; the test item's discrimination index for separating high- and low-scoring test-takers; the test item's difficulty index; how many test-takers chose each of the answer choices on each test item; the quality of the correct answer choices; and the reliability of the test, i.e., how consistent its results are across separate administrations to the same test-takers.

Discrimination Index and Difficulty Index

The discrimination index is a measure of how well a specific test item can separate students who generally score high on the test from students who generally score low on it. Educators obtain a point biserial correlation between high total scores and low total scores with correct or incorrect item responses. Typically, they use total test scores to select the top 27% and bottom 27% of test-takers to magnify the variation between high and low test performance. When analyzing standardized, norm-referenced tests, the preferred discrimination index is .50. The difficulty index is a simple measure of how difficult a test item is considered. It is obtained by calculating the percentage of all students taking a test who answered a certain test item correctly.

Sensitivity and specificity and the KR20 formula

Sensitivity refers to how well a test identifies every member of a defined group. The more sensitive a test is, the more likely it can include some individuals who should not be in that group. Specificity refers to how well a test identifies only those members of a defined group. The more specific a test is, the more likely it will omit some individuals who should be included in that group. Among many KR formulas used to estimate statistically a test's reliability or consistency, the KR20 is one that assumes that the relative difficulty of items on a test, and the correlations among those items, are basically equal. The KR20 formula deducts the variances of all individual test items from the total test's variance, which produces an estimate of the test's internal consistency reliability. When a test has items of dissimilar difficulty, the Horst's modification can be used to correct for this by estimating the maximal variance possible within a given range of item difficulties for that test.

Modified assessments of students with special needs on standardized tests

Exclusive of actual test items, in some states the test administration instructions may be clarified or simplified. Other than item responses, students may be allowed to highlight or make other marks in their test booklets. Students may be tested in small groups rather than whole class settings. Test administrators may give students additional time within the testing day to complete a test. Individual students may be tested separately with direct examiner supervision. Students with visual impairments may use visual magnifiers for test text, and hearing-impaired students may use audio amplification. Individual study carrels/enclosures may be used as noise buffers for hearing-impaired or distractible students. Special lighting, acoustics, special furniture, or adaptive furnishings may be allowed. Masking or colored overlays may be used to sustain student visual attention. American Sign Language (ASL) or Manually Coded English (MCE) may also be used to give test instructions (but not test items) to deaf, hard-of-hearing, or nonverbal students.

Some states allow students to mark their test responses in their test booklets, and then the school personnel transfer these onto the standardized answer form used by other students to be electronically scored. For students with vision, hearing, manual, or motor impairments, they may dictate their responses to multiple-choice test items aloud or in American Sign Language (ASL) or Manually Coded English (MCE) to a designed scribe who writes, types, or fills in bubbles, circles choices, or otherwise marks the student's answers on a form. For essay questions, some students may be permitted to use word processing software programs, with the spell-check and grammar-check features disabled. Other students may be allowed to dictate their essay answers orally to a voice recorder or scribe, or manually in sign language to an interpreter/scribe, or using speech-to-text computer software. In these cases, students supply all writing conventions of spelling and grammar in their dictation. Assistive devices that allow independent student work may be used.

For blind or visually impaired students or those with visual processing deficits, testers may provide Braille transcriptions of the printed test; large-print versions of the test; or, if the student needs larger type than the fonts used in large-print versions, test items may be enlarged. Students who require additional time and/or shorter testing durations (e.g., those with cognitive impairments, attention deficits, or behavior disorders) may be allowed to take a test normally administered in one sitting over more than one day and/or take supervised breaks during one test section. Medication effects and fluctuating attention and/or performance levels can be addressed by administering tests at the optimal time of day for the student. Examiners may test some students in homes or hospitals. Test items and answer choices may be presented in sign language, audio recordings, or read aloud. On math and science tests, like in fifth grade, some students may be allowed to use calculators and/or concrete math manipulatives.

Modified assessment procedures for ELL or ESL students

Students whose native language is not English are allowed some variations by the U.S. states to participate in standardized testing in the English language on a more equable footing with native English speakers. For example, they may hear the printed test instructions

- 42 -

translated into their native language and read aloud. They may be allowed to ask questions in their native language to clarify test instructions. ESL/ELL students may be granted additional, supervised breaks during a testing day or test portion, providing they complete the portion within the testing day. (Standardized tests typically display a "STOP" sign to indicate the ends of test portions.) Students learning English may be allowed to take tests separately in groups with other ELL/ESL students, under supervision by school personnel cleared for test security, particularly if their regular instruction and/or testing have included similar flexibility. ELL/ESL students taking math and science tests may be permitted access to word lists or glossaries translated from English to their native language, excluding formulae or definitions.

General adaptions to assessments for special-needs students

General testing adaptations include using these oral directions interchangeably: "Find," "Show me," "Point to," and "Give me." Testers should place stimulus cards and manipulatives however the student is best able to perceive these. Concrete materials should be set on surfaces with boundary edges so they cannot roll away or fall down when students use them. Testers should arrange the test environment to eliminate or reduce distractions for students more susceptible to these. For visually impaired students, testers may enlarge stimulus cards as needed. They may replace visual stimuli with Braille, beeping objects or other auditory stimuli, or textured materials if the student is accustomed to using these regularly. Testing teachers can cut out the outlines of shapes or figures from stimulus cards. They may substitute spoken cues like "Tell me" instead of "Show me." As necessary, they may describe the content of pictorial stimuli. They should let students handle concrete objects as is needed. Students who wear corrective glasses should always wear these during assessments.

Teachers can allow students to use augmentative communication devices for receiving and responding to test stimuli. For students who use American Sign Language (ASL) or manually coded English, teachers should use these languages or have an interpreter use them instead of spoken instructions or stimuli whenever appropriate. Nonverbal students should be allowed to give test responses using vocalizations, gestures, or movements instead of speech. Some students may draw pictures instead of writing. (This can also apply to students with dyslexia.) As is appropriate, teachers may accept eye gazes as responses instead of speech or gesture. Students who wear hearing aids must wear them during assessments; teachers should check that they work first. Students with sensorimotor impairments should be given longer times to initiate responses. Teachers should accept changes in facial expressions or muscle tone as observed behaviors. Teachers should stabilize and position students to afford the most controlled possible motions. Teachers should also let students direct others to perform physical tasks.

Technological development of portfolio assessments

Just as physical portfolios show a student's work and creative products accumulated over time, ePortfolios store documents and photos of products and can be shared with others; but given the advent of social networks, they benefit from additional advantages of immediate communication and reinforcement. Digital archives can portray a student's life, from birth through early childhood family learning via scrapbooks, and through formal schooling and into employment and professional development. In portfolios, key processes include collecting products for the digital archive; selecting those demonstrating certain standards or goals by creating hyperlinks for others, which leads to reflecting or metacognition, helping the student construct meaning from the works s/he selected, aided by new storytelling models generated by technology; directing or goal-setting; presenting ePortfolios; and getting feedback on them. Social networking includes processes of connecting with others; listening to or reading posts; responding by commenting on posts; and sharing via linking or tagging. Key processes technology enables include archiving; linking and thinking; digital storytelling; collaborating; and publishing.

Students can be internally motivated (self-directed by inner goals) or externally motivated by outer rewards. The ePortfolios enabled by technology can support students' internal motivation and autonomy by establishing online environments wherein others feel good about participating, keeping systems relatively open, and giving users freedom to participate. Social networks support student autonomy by giving them choices and voices in the content they post and view; opportunities to share and give feedback; and far greater immediacy in all of their interactions. Students can experience academic and personal mastery through social networking, which affords the motivational factors of what Csikszentmihályi called "flow" (energized, positive, task-aligned, spontaneous, single-minded, focused, immersed, joyful, deep, and total engagement in an activity); the ability to showcase their achievements; and the benefits of enhanced self-insight and self-awareness. Via choice and personalization, students find their passions and voices. Constructing ePortfolios also helps students develop senses of purpose by engaging in something beyond themselves, understanding the relevance of what they learn, and seeing the "big picture."

Screening to identify students who need special education services

Screening is the important first step of the assessment process mandated by federal laws. All newborns should be screened for developmental disabilities, and children should continue to be screened through early childhood, preschool, and school years. While more obvious disabilities like spina bifida, cerebral palsy, Down syndrome, autism, multiple disabilities, or severe sensory impairment are detected early, others like learning disabilities, ADHD, and some behavior disorders often go unidentified until school. Public schools typically conduct periodic screenings of large student groups from grades K–3. Very low standardized achievement test scores can lead to referral for formal evaluation—only with written parental consent—to identify possible disabilities. Also, students' parents, teachers, and other school staff may identify students with suspected disabilities, as when they evidence behavioral or academic difficulties in classrooms. Some students are not identified with disabilities until higher grades, due to ineffective screening, referral, assessment, and/or identification procedures; to disabilities acquired later through injury, illness, etc.; or to problems not apparent until school demands surpass student coping skills.

Problems and solutions with school-based screening

While school screenings are vital and the process of identifying students with disabilities has a basic structure, there are no uniform or standardized sets of checklists, procedures, or testing instruments to identify disabilities in most students. The kinds of referral processes and tests utilized vary, both across and within states. According to educational experts, two main problems with screening procedures are over-identification and under-identification of disabilities. Research studies have shown that students have been over-identified with learning disabilities, while students with behavior disorders are under-identified, especially compliant students who are not aggressive or disruptive but have problems like social isolation, depression, or school phobia. Educators have been improving screening procedures to resolve these problems. For example, Walker et al (1990) created the Systematic Screening for Behavioral Disorders with three steps: first, teachers rank students according to designated criteria; then select the three highest ranked students and complete checklists to quantify their observations about them; and school psychologists/counselors observe identified students prior to any formal evaluation referrals.

Prereferral interventions

Prereferral interventions are a frequent practice intended to better the process of identifying students with disabilities by decreasing referrals to special education services and give regular education teachers more assistance and advice. Rather than first referring a student for evaluation to diagnose a possible disability, teachers initially try to address behavior or learning problems in the classroom through modifications. Only if modifications are found inadequate to the student's difficulties, and the teacher believes special services may be required, does s/he initiate the referral process. Most states in the U.S. require or recommend prereferral intervention in some form. One approach uses Teacher Assistance Teams (TATs). TATs usually comprise four members: the referring teacher and three other teachers. These teams provide teachers with a forum to meet, discuss, and brainstorm ideas to instruct students and/or manage them. Another approach is collaborative consultation. Specialists like speech-language pathologists work directly with referring teachers in planning, implementing, and evaluating instruction for students identified in regular education classrooms.

Identification through Child Find, referral, or request for evaluation

Under the federal IDEA law, each U.S. state is held responsible for locating, identifying, and evaluating all children in that state as having disabilities and in need of special education and related services. To carry out this mandate, the states engage in Child Find processes. This is one way that children are identified with disabilities. The state's Child Find system may ask a child's parents for permission to evaluate the child, or parents can contact the Child Find system themselves and request evaluation of their child. Another way children are identified is by referral. A teacher or other school professional suspecting a student might have a disability may request, in writing or orally, the student's evaluation. Parents must give consent before the evaluation can be made. The law also stipulates that a requested evaluation be within a reasonable time after receiving parental consent. Parents who suspect disability in their child may also request that the school evaluate the child.

Evaluation and eligibility determination

After screenings and prereferral interventions have been completed and a student is referred for formal evaluation or evaluation is requested, professionals must evaluate all developmental/learning areas related to the disability suspected. Test results are applied to decisions regarding eligibility for special education and related services, and an appropriate educational program. If parents disagree with evaluation results, they have the right under the IDEA to arrange an Independent Educational Evaluation (IEE) and to request payment for this evaluation by the school system. Once evaluation results have been collected and reported, parents meet with teachers and other qualified professionals to review them. They decide together whether the student meets the IDEA definition of a "child with a disability." Parents are entitled under the law to request a hearing challenging the eligibility decision if they disagree. If the child is found eligible for special education and related services, an IEP team must meet within 30 calendar days of eligibility determination to write an IEP.

First IEP meeting after eligibility is determined

After a student is determined eligible for special education and related services according to the IDEA, the school must schedule the first meeting to write an Individualized Education Program (IEP) for the student. The IDEA mandates that ALL students that receive special education and related services must have an IEP written for them. By this law, the school system must contact the parents and all others who are to participate in the IEP process. They must inform the parents early enough to ensure they are able to arrange to attend the meeting. They must schedule the meeting at a place and time with which the parents and the school agree. They must inform the parents of the purpose of this meeting and its location, date, and time. They must also inform the parents who else will be attending the meeting. The school staff is also to inform the parents that they may invite any other people to the IEP meeting who have special expertise or knowledge about their child.

In the first IEP meeting for a student, the IEP team includes the student, the parents, the student's teacher(s), specialists, other school personnel who interact with the student; outside consultants if invited; and any others with knowledge about the student, invited by the parents. If a group other than this IEP team decides placement for the student, the parents must also be included in that group. Parents must give consent before initial provision of special education and related services. With this consent, services must commence as soon as possible following the first IEP meeting. When parents disagree with the content of the IEP and/or their child's placement, they can discuss this with other IEP team members and work toward solutions. If the parents still disagree, they may request mediation or the school can offer mediation services. Parents also have the right to file complaints with the state education agency and to request a due process hearing. Mediation must be made available at this hearing.

IEP implementation

Once the IEP team has met and developed an IEP for a student and the parents agree with it, the school must give them a copy of the IEP. Each teacher and service provider working with the student can access the student's IEP and must know his/her specific duties in implementing the IEP. The school must ensure that the IEP is implemented as it is written, including providing all accommodations, modifications, and supports to the student as specified in the IEP document. As outlined in the IEP, the school must measure the student's progress toward yearly IEP goals. The school regularly informs the parents of their child's progress and whether it is sufficient for meeting the annual goals. Progress reports must be provided at least as frequently as those reporting nondisabled students' progress. IEPs are reviewed at least annually—more if the parents or the school request it. The IEP is revised if needed. Parents must be invited to review meetings, can suggest changes, and agree/disagree with IEP goals and/or placement.

Legal requirements for reevaluation in IEP process

All students receiving special education and related services are required by law to have an Individualized Education Plan (IEP). It is developed by the IEP team, which includes the student, parents, teachers, other school employees, other professionals, and any others invited by parents or schools who have contributions relevant to the student and his/her education. The student has received a formal evaluation to determine eligibility. The IEP is reviewed at least annually or more often if the school or parents request it and is revised as needed. Additionally, the student must be reevaluated at least every three years. Educators often call such reevaluation a "triennial." Reevaluation is made to determine whether the student still meets the IDEA definition of a "child with a disability" or not, and to reexamine the educational needs of the student. The three-year interval is a minimum, though: if circumstances indicate it, and/or if the parents or teachers request a new evaluation, the student must be reevaluated sooner than after three years.

Legally required information in IEP

Current performance, annual goals, and special education and related services
The IDEA requires the IEP to state the student's "present levels of educational performance," i.e. the student's current progress in school. Results of evaluations made to determine eligibility for special services; classroom tests and in-class and homework assignments; and observations contributed by parents, teachers, related service providers, and other school personnel provide the information for the statement of the student's current school performance. This statement includes the impacts of the student's disability on his/her progress and engagement in the school's general education curriculum. Annual goals are those the student can reasonably attain within a school year. These are subdivided into short-term objectives, or benchmarks. Goals can be academic, behavioral, social, or physical. Goals must be measurable to show if the student has met them. The IEP must name all special education and related services to be provided to or on behalf of the student, including supplementary services and aids; changes to the program; and training, professional development, or other provisions supporting school staff in providing services to the student.

Student's participation with nondisabled students, participation in statewide and district-wide testing; and dates and locations of services
All students identified with disabilities and eligible for special education and related services must have IEPs (Individualized Education Programs). The IEP must include an explanation of the degree, if any, to which the student will NOT be participating with nondisabled students in regular classrooms and other school activities. Regarding statewide and district-wide standardized achievement tests regularly given by school systems to students at certain age or grade levels, the IEP must identify which modifications in test administration the student will need. Moreover, if any such test is deemed inappropriate for a particular student, the student's IEP must explain why and state what alternative testing will be substituted. The student's IEP must also state when the student's special education and related services will start, how often services will be provided, in what locations services will be given, and the duration of the services.

Transition services, student's reaching the age of majority, and progress measurement
While a student reaches the age of 14—or sooner when applicable—the student's IEP must include in its pertinent sections which courses the student must take to attain his/her

postschool goals. Every IEP following this must also contain a statement of the student's needs in transition services. Transition may be to postsecondary education; job training; and/or community living. When the student is 16 years old—or before if appropriate—the IEP must define which transition services the student will need as preparation for exiting the current school program/system. At least one year before the student reaches the age of majority, his/her IEP must state the student has been informed of any rights that will transfer from parents/caregivers to him/her. This only applies in states where rights are transferred when minor children reach majority age. Law requires the IEP to state how the school will measure the student's educational progress and how it will inform the student's parents of their child's progress.

Additional content school systems and states may include in IEPs

While the IDEA federally mandates certain content in students' IEPs, individual states and school systems have much flexibility regarding what other information they require. Since federal law dictates that school districts document their compliance with federal requirements, some states and school systems choose to add information in their students' IEPs that serves to document their compliance with both federal and state laws. In general, some examples of additional elements IEPs can contain that document this compliance include: documentation that the school held the meeting(s) for writing, reviewing, and revising when necessary the student's IEP on a timely basis; documentation that the school furnished the student's parents with a copy of their legally mandated procedural safeguards and rights; documentation that the school has placed the student in the least restrictive environment possible where s/he can experience adequate learning and progress; and documentation that the school received parental consent to provide their child with evaluations, special education, and related services.

Key members of the IEP team

Members of a student's IEP team are not limited to, but include: the student; the parents; the special education teacher(s); specialist(s) or other service provider(s); the regular education teacher(s); someone able to interpret evaluation results; a representative of the school system; a representative of a transition services agency; and others having special expertise/knowledge about the student. (Sometimes an individual member fulfills more than one of these functions.) Parents are important team members for knowledge of their child, including his/her strengths and needs and their ideas about how to improve his/her education. Parents can contribute insights about their child's learning style and processes, what academic and life areas are of particular interest to their child, and other things only parents know about their children. Parents can consider other team members' recommendations about areas to focus on in school and can share their own suggestions. Additionally, parents can report to the school whether their child is applying skills s/he has learned in school, at home, and in other settings outside school.

The IEP team member who can interpret evaluation results can not only explain to other members what test results signify, e.g., the type of disability and deficit areas, but moreover how to design instruction appropriate to the student and characteristics identified by evaluation results. Skillfully interpreting test results informs the team how the student is currently faring in school and helps them pinpoint areas of particular student needs. This member's role is not only understanding and explaining test results, but furthermore explaining the instructional implications of those results and helping plan accordingly suitable instruction. The school system representative contributes extensive knowledge about teaching students with disabilities and about the special education services available in the school system. This member can discuss the school resources the student and educators will need. It is also important for this individual to have the authority for committing school system resources, and the ability for assuring all services specified in the IEP are actually provided to the student and staff.

If a special education student participates in regular education at all (which is increasingly the case these days), at least one of the student's regular education teachers must be included in the IEP team. This teacher can inform other team members about the regular classroom's general curriculum, and also what kinds of services, changes in the educational program, and/or aids would help the student to learn and succeed best. S/he can also suggest strategies for managing classroom behavior if this is an issue. The regular education teacher can also talk with the rest of the team about which supports the school staff will need to help the student progress toward annual IEP goals, engage in regular curriculum and succeed in it, participate in extracurricular activities, and be included in instruction with both nondisabled and disabled peers. Such school staff supports can include additional training, professional development, etc., not only for teachers but also administrators, cafeteria staff, bus drivers, and all others providing services to students with disabilities..

Informed by her/his training and experience in special education, the special education teacher contributes to the IEP team by discussing various topics. These include how to make adaptations and modifications to the general education curriculum that will enable the student to learn in the regular education setting; which supplementary services and aids the student is likely to require for succeeding in regular classrooms and other places; techniques for modification of assessments that enables the student to better demonstrate what s/he has learned; and additional elements of individualizing the instruction according to the unique needs of the student. Special educators not only help write IEPs; they are also responsible for working with students to implement them. They may do this in special education classes or resource rooms; team-teach with regular education teachers; and collaborate with regular education teachers and other school personnel, contributing expertise to meet the student's individual needs.

Parents and/or school system employees can invite individuals to participate as members of a student's IEP team based on their especial expertise and/or knowledge about the student. For instance, parents may know a professional with specific expertise in the student's particular disability; an advocate who has a relationship with the student; or a vocational educator who has been working with the student on employment skills. Such individuals are able to discuss the student's individual strengths and needs. The school system may also invite individuals, like paraprofessionals or professionals specializing in related services, who can contribute special expertise and/or knowledge about the student. A significant aspect of IEP development is the related services a student often needs; therefore, professionals specializing in such related services are frequently members or participants in the IEP team. These professionals can include physical therapists; occupational therapists; adaptive physical education instructors; orientation and mobility specialists; ASL interpreters; speech-language pathologists; psychologists; and others.

Material reviewed to determine special education and services needed

To develop the IEP, the team reviews evaluation results including individual tests given to the student to determine eligibility for services; classroom tests the student has taken; and the observations of parents, teachers, related service providers, paraprofessionals, administrators, and others involved. These help the team characterize the "present levels of educational performance" of the student, i.e., how s/he is currently functioning in school. They develop yearly goals targeting areas of educational need identified through this information. Information specific to the student they discuss includes the student's strongest assets; recent evaluation and/or re-evaluation results; parents' ideas to improve the student's education; and the student's performance on district-wide and statewide standardized examinations. The team's discussion of what the student needs should be guided by how they can help the student progress toward meeting yearly goals; engage in the general education curriculum and make progress in it; be included in participation and education with other students, both with and without disabilities; and participate in nonacademic and extracurricular activities.

Legal requirements regarding a student's placement

Once an IEP team has developed and written a student's IEP, where this program will be implemented—i.e., the student's placement—must also be decided. In some U.S. states, the IEP team is also the group that makes placement decisions. In others, a different group may decide student placements. However, in every instance the parents have the legal right to participate as members of the group deciding placement. Placement decisions must abide by the IDEA's requirements for the Least Restrictive Environment (LRE): students with disabilities must be educated together with students without disabilities to the maximum degree possible and fitting. In addition, the IDEA specifies that students with disabilities may only be removed from the regular school setting—to special classes or separate schools—if the severity and/or nature of the student's disability makes education in regular classes, including the use of supplementary services and aids, impossible to attain with satisfactory results.

Integrating affective, social, and life skills into academic curricula

Many students with disabilities need special education and support to learn daily living skills. With proper instruction, they can obtain and keep meaningful jobs and live in the community; but without specialized instruction, they frequently lose jobs and/or home placements. Life skills include proper attire, grooming, and hygiene; acceptable table manners; financial decision-making; and utilizing transportation to employment. Instruction in financial skills is required by some states, including counting money and making change; managing bank accounts; keeping personal budgets and records; making personal financial decisions; spending and using credit responsibly; estimating and paying taxes; paying bills; and renting/leasing. Household management includes housekeeping; meal preparation; doing/hiring home maintenance/repair; and new appliance warranty registration. Personal care includes obtaining health care, eschewing substance abuse; recognizing common illnesses, knowing prevention and treatment; and nutrition, physical fitness, and weight maintenance. Safety awareness includes recognizing safety/hazard signs, rules, and procedures; unfamiliar sounds and/or smells; and knowing emergency evacuation procedures. Buying, storing, planning, preparing, and eating balanced, appropriate meals are included.

In addition to skills in dress, hygiene, other personal care, finance, household management, safety awareness, and food preparation, students with disabilities must also receive instruction, integrated into academic curricula in school, in how to purchase and care for clothing. They must be instructed in responsible citizenship, including knowing their own civil rights and responsibilities; obtaining legal aid; reporting crimes; for males, registering with Selective Service at age 18; knowing and obeying laws; knowing about federal, state, and local governments; and voting. Disabled students must also learn about community resources available; how to select and plan leisure activities, appreciate their importance, and participate in them; to plan vacation activities and social events; and practice music, arts, crafts, hobbies, and sports. Students must also be instructed in community navigation, including knowing right from left and front from back; safety and traffic rules; carpooling and other transportation; reading maps; and when applicable, learning to drive and obtaining a driver's license and automobile insurance. Special and regular educators, families, and peers provide instruction.

Special student factors

The law requires a number of "special factors" for the IEP team to consider as applicable with individual students. If a student's behavior impedes his/her and/or other students' learning, the team must consider effective, positive behavioral supports and intervention techniques to manage, control, or change the behavior. If the student has limited English-language proficiency, the team must consider the student's linguistic need relative to his/her IEP. If a student is blind or visually impaired, the team must provide Braille texts or instruction in Braille, or determine through evaluations the student does not need such instruction. In the latter case, the team must specify any other methods and/or devices the student needs and provide these. The team must consider any communication needs a student may have. For deaf or hard-of-hearing students, the team must consider their communication and linguistic needs, including opportunities for communicating directly with peers and staff in ASL or their other customary communication method(s). The team must also consider any student needs for assistive technology services and/or devices.

Different program placement and integration into placement

A student's IEP may be implemented in various placement settings according to the individual student's needs. Settings include placement in the regular education class, with supplementary services and aids the student needs; in a special class for all or part of the school day, with other students all also receiving special education and related services; in a special school dedicated to students needing special education and related services; in a hospital; in an institutional facility; and other settings. To fulfill its legal requirements to make sure a student is placed appropriately, a school system can take various actions. For example, it may furnish the student with a suitable program as part of the school system. Or it may contract with an outside agency that can provide the student with an applicable program. Or it may make some other arrangements and/or make use of other mechanisms available to pay for or otherwise provide the student a program appropriate and consistent with the terms of the IDEA.

Prioritizing areas of the general education curriculum for students with disabilities

The IDEA and NCLB require all students' access to general education curriculum. Educators can help disabled students by connecting academic content to real-life activities.

Achievement standards include the same academic content, but utilize alternate performance indicators still fitting content standards for reading and math. While alternative assessment methods and definitions of achievement standards vary considerably across states, educators in all states must provide instruction effective in helping students with disabilities meet standards. Teachers in some states select which responses are assessed to document progress toward state standards—e.g., portfolio assessments; specific choice-making; sight words; task analyses; generalized responses, like requests; problem-solving; and self-initiation responses. Systematic prompting with feedback, reinforcement, correction, and fading is an instructional support method. In general education settings, systematic instruction to small mixed-ability groups; cooperative learning groups; trials embedded in general education lectures/lessons; observational learning; peer tutors; and self-instruction and problem-solving materials are options. Assistive technology aids symbol use, and can reduce behavior problems and increase social interaction. Special and general educator planning collaboration is vital.

Promoting Development and Learning in Students with Cognitive Impairments

Impact of teachers' attitudes and behaviors on student achievement outcomes

Research studies show that when teachers establish supportive relationships with their students; communicate clearly and consistently enforce high expectations of their students academically and behaviorally; and deliver a high quality of pedagogy and instruction to their students, the students are more likely to develop attitudes and behaviors of engagement in their learning, and perceptions of their own academic competence. These student attitudes and behaviors are found in turn to augment student achievement in key academic areas like reading and math. Experts define students' engagement as how much inherent interest they demonstrate in school, and the quantity and quality of their participation in schoolwork. This engagement and participation include both attitudes, like positive values about learning, motivation, interest, enthusiasm, and pride in succeeding, and also behaviors like attention, effort, and persistence. Therefore, students who are engaged pursue activities in and out of classrooms that further learning and/or succeeding. Additionally, they demonstrate curiosity, desire for more knowledge, and emotionally positive responses to school and learning.

Expectations and student behavior

Researchers have found that teachers are often unprepared for problem behaviors from both nondisabled and disabled students in urban school settings. Some reasons for such problem behaviors include the higher proportions in urban school populations of students from lower socioeconomic levels; of students from families who do not speak English; and of students with special needs. Some researchers have experimented with elementary-level urban schools by introducing a "Good Behavior" game. Teachers were directed to identify acceptable and unacceptable behaviors clearly to their students. Then they were to observe the students during specified periods of time and count the numbers of unacceptable behaviors. The individual student or group of students receiving the smallest number of recorded unacceptable behaviors would win the game. The researchers found that using this technique both increased on-task behaviors and decreased disruptive behaviors in the students. This approach is considered to be generalizable to schools in nonurban settings.

Factors in school that influence students' motivation to learn

One factor that is found to increase students' motivation to learn is a sense of belonging in their school settings and a sense of having caring relationships. This includes the students' feeling that their families and friends support them and their education, and in school particularly, that their teachers are supportive. Individualizing and personalizing their instruction is one way that teachers accomplish this. Teachers also create caring, supportive social environments in school by demonstrating interest in their students' lives, inside and outside school. Students experiencing such positive interpersonal relationships are found to display more positive attitudes and values regarding school, and more satisfaction with it, and to attend school more, learn more, and report more academic engagement. Another factor is clearly defined, high, consistent, and realistically attainable teacher expectations of student performance. A third factor promoting students' cognitive engagement is teachers' use of active pedagogical strategies challenging students to tackle new ideas, explain their thinking, defend their decisions, and/or explore alternate methods and solutions, especially through peer collaboration.

Student activities that promote student engagement

Educational research has found that students are more likely to experience and demonstrate greater classroom engagement over the long term of their education when teachers assign them to such hands-on, authentic activities as constructing models; planning, implementing, completing, and reporting on projects; participating in role-play exercises; participating in debates on topics relevant to school subjects and activities; and planning and conducting experiments, making conclusions about them, and reporting their results to their classmates and teachers. Studies have also shown that teachers can make the lessons that they teach more relevant and meaningful to students when these lessons draw from and build upon the students' existing background knowledge, cultural backgrounds, and experiences in the real world and life. When the material that they study is personally interesting to students and related to their lives, they both learn more effectively and also enjoy the learning process more.

Establishing rapport in early elementary grades

Teachers report warm lighting helps create a cozy, "at-home" atmosphere. Many elementary teachers assign a theme for the school year, like bugs, birds, fish, or rocks. They display posters illustrating the theme, including catchphrases expressing their learning strategies; incorporate the theme in first-day handouts, student folders, and parent letters; devise activities around the theme, like reading books to the class about the theme and assigning student pairs/small groups to design an original bug. On first days, teachers assign activities enabling students to move around, become comfortable with the classroom, get acquainted with each other, work collaboratively, and think creatively. They use games—searching for all classmates' names in puzzles or physically finding each classmate and collecting their signatures. Teachers use "brainteasers" to engage students in creative problem-solving. They take inventories of student interests on first days. And they assign students artistic activities—like cutting out and illustrating paper "T-shirts" identifying their preferences, interests, future dreams, past experiences, and adjectives describing themselves.

Modeling to teach eye contact, vocal tone, and pronunciation

Many autistic students avoid eye contact, as do some cognitively impaired students and even nondisabled younger students. Often they do not understand its importance and have no practice using it. Some teachers with teaching assistants or aides find it helps to model through conversations with them: the teacher says to the assistant that s/he noticed how the assistant's eyes were looking right at a student's eyes when they were talking; that this showed the student the assistant was listening, and the assistant could see the student was also listening; and praises the assistant for "good eye contact." The assistant replies that good eye contact during conversation is good manners. The same technique can be used to describe appropriate vocal tones for conversations and correct pronunciation. The teacher can follow up by asking students to demonstrate good eye contact when greeting another student. They observe and provide prompts as needed. This is most effective when the teacher immediately rewards the interaction with verbal praise, plus applause from the class.

Successfully relating to and instructing high school students

Experienced high school teachers find that classroom success centers on three crucial areas: establishing rapport with the students; setting the teacher's rules and expectations for the class; and having strategies to promote students' motivation to learn. While teacher education students and new teachers observing experienced teachers may feel they seem to do it by some kind of magic, the experienced teachers say that strategic planning is actually at the heart of establishing a rapport and developing good working relationships with their students. For example, a high school teacher can help to build rapport with a new class of students by presenting oneself as having a "stern yet caring" (as one teacher puts it) presence; set class rules and conduct other activities together *with* the students rather than unilaterally, which helps to establish a classroom community; and communicating one's expectations to the students clearly on the very first day of school.

Engaging disabled and younger students in paying attention to directions

Some experienced teachers use techniques like rhythmic clapping and/or chanting to engage student attention. For example, the teacher demonstrates a loud, rhythmic hand clap and tells the students that when they hear the teacher do this, they should stop what they are doing and imitate the hand clap. The teacher tells the students the clap means s/he has something important to share with them and to copy clapping when the teacher's hands go down, and s/he will know they are done when they make eye contact ("I see you looking at my eyes"). Teachers can chant directions, like "If you hear me, put your hands on your shoulders....If you hear me, put your hands on your hips....If you me, put your hands on your tummy...." Teachers enhance students' attention by modulating their voices. For students who do not pay attention, teachers instruct them aloud to be sure their hands are empty and they are looking at the teacher's eyes. Teachers may need to wait for all students to focus.

Establishing rapport with sixth-grade students

One way a sixth-grade teacher can get acquainted with new students is to give them surveys about their interests and surveys of Gardner's Multiple Intelligences to get ideas of students' preferences, strengths, needs, and learning styles. To assess student writing abilities and styles, a pre-assessment can involve writing a letter to the teacher about themselves. The teacher gives no pre-instructions on the steps of writing to discern what they already know how to do independently. The teacher may use her/his district's model for assessing writing. As icebreakers, teachers can assign as homework writing and illustrating a "Me" page, guided by teacher-given questions. They can have each student create a poster using the letters in their first name, filling the page with large "bubble" letters, and filling each letter with information, photos, or drawings about themselves. Then the teacher can display these in the classroom, integrating technology by adding printed digital photos of students to their posters. They can have students create PowerPoints and revise them at the end of the school year to add what they have learned.

Class rules for disabled and nondisabled high school students

The high school teacher can first establish basic, vital "ground rules" based on what the teacher needs in the classroom. For example, students must arrive on time and be prepared; respect both classmates and classroom materials; and follow directions the first time the teacher gives them. After conveying these rules, the teacher can involve students in collaborating to create class rules. This helps build a class community. The teacher can integrate the opinions and viewpoints of students by asking them simple questions, like why they are there and what they need to achieve their goals. The teacher records student answers, incorporating these in expanding on the ground rules. Involving students gives them a sense of a democratic class community instead of a dictatorship and stimulates processes of critical thinking. Teachers should also give students lists of daily materials needed and examples of acceptable versus unacceptable work, and inform students how they will assess their work (rubrics, etc.). Teachers should communicate their expectations orally, in print/writing, and visually.

Motivating high school students to read

Some high school teachers experienced in teaching teens who struggle with reading meet such challenges by getting students excited about reading. They find books their students can relate to and enjoy, and they can begin the school year by reading these books aloud to students. Only after they have stimulated student enjoyment and enthusiasm for reading do they assess students' current reading levels, using instruments like the Scholastic Reading Inventory. Teachers can use a Book Pass activity to help students become familiar with books in their class library and select books with topics interesting to them at suitable levels for independent reading. Small groups (like five each) designate one student timekeeper. Seated in circles, each group member previews the front and back of the book and begins reading that book. The timekeeper announces when 2 to 3 minutes elapse; students write down the book title, pages read, comments, and whether they would like reading it further. Students then pass the books to their right, repeating with another book. They finish with group sharing of individual book comments.

Safe, supportive, and positive elementary classroom and school climate

Elementary school teachers realize that students will be more engaged in school and learning if it is fun and they are happy. Some teachers help students consolidate what they just learned and/or take a break from schoolwork with a group singing period in the classroom. A few weeks into the school year, once students have gotten to know each other and developed into a cohesive group, some teachers have them vote for an alliterative class name reflecting their interests, ambitions, and/or attitudes. The teacher calls them by this group name when they are lining up to leave the room and at other key moments to reinforce their feelings of belonging and ownership. To encourage and reinforce student responsibility, some elementary teachers assign a job to each student for the week, posting these on a chart on the wall, and all of the students take turns assuming different weekly job rotations.

Communicating expectations of students and regular routines

Some schools use an acronym like BEST, representing Be respectful, Enjoy learning, Stay safe, and Totally responsible, to help students remember these principles. Some teachers have students negotiate their classroom expectations, keeping them generally consistent with school expectations, and on reaching consensus, they display pictures and words on the walls reflecting these. They also discuss choices and how expectations keep everyone safe. They set routines, posting their daily schedule on the wall and discussing it. Some teachers institute weekly lessons involving behavioral tasks explicitly teaching behavioral expectations aligned with school values, and they post these on the wall. Some teachers use a token economy. For example, each student gets a smiley face on a chart for making good choices; upon accumulating 10, the student can select a prize, which the teacher reports schoolwide to record all recognition of positive behaviors. When students do not meet expectations, some teachers explicitly model and teach expected behavior, like teaching how to apologize sincerely for hitting/kicking, with the victim choosing whether to accept the apology.

Addressing and preventing bullying

In April 2013, the U.S. Department of Justice arrived at a settlement agreement with the Metropolitan School District of Decatur Township, Indiana. This concluded a review of district practices and policies regarding bullying and harassment, prompted by 2011 reports of possible racial targeting at one school. The district arranged to collaborate with the federally funded Great Lakes Equity Center at Indiana University-Purdue University Indianapolis on actions against bullying for disability, race, national origin, color, gender, or religion and promoting safe, supportive learning environments for all students. Actions include creating a district-wide antiharassment task force to review and revise district harassment/bullying and disciplinary policy and procedures; creating a coherent process to receive, investigate, and monitor bullying/harassment complaints, and track repeating instances involving groups/individuals in special classes; and give students and staff at two district schools school climate assessments, training, and professional development. A Civil Rights Division spokesperson said these affirmative steps provide statewide and nationwide examples. Nationwide work against school bullying also aligns with federal civil rights legislation.

Icebreakers to use to get acquainted with high school students

Experienced high school teachers find adolescents are primarily concerned with adjusting to the new setting and getting acquainted with new classmates, and teachers need to start the year by familiarizing themselves well with new students. To help both teacher and students get acquainted, teachers can use icebreaker activities. One involves "matching" index cards based on common interests of the school's student body. For example, teachers make card pairs like Bill Gates and Microsoft; Russell Simmons and Def Jam Records, etc. Each student gets one card and finds the student with a matching card. Then they interview each other. Teachers can suggest questions, like the last school they attended, their favorite book genre, pet peeves, favorite things, embarrassing incidents, hobbies, etc. Following interviews, each student presents information about his/her "match" to the class. Another activity groups and numbers students in fours; each student writes down adjectives describing themselves and alliterative with their names (e.g., "Shy Shannon" or "Bookish Brad"), and take turns introducing themselves and another student using these.

Integrating technology to motivate learning

To prepare and motivate adolescents to learn right away, high school teachers can integrate technology, yet need no more than a video camera and books when they assign projects the first week of school. For example, the teacher can ask the students to choose a book they have recently read and/or is their favorite. The teacher can lead a class discussion about characteristics in TV commercials that make the viewer remember the commercials best, like musical jingles; vivid visual imagery; strong slogans or tag lines; or humorous/incongruous situations. The teacher creates a model for students with a sample commercial. The teacher can then have the students make their own commercials advertising their chosen books. Another example of a project is to assign students to make their autobiographies, using videos about five minutes long. The teacher can guide the students to incorporate details related to their early childhoods; pets, friends, their home lives; their hobbies, what things interest them most, and what their major goals in life are.

Promoting parental support for children's education

Some teachers implement a practice of using a communication book for each student. These books are sent back and forth between the school and the students' homes for the teacher and parents to write correspondence to one another. Before calling the roll every morning, the teacher checks the communication books for new entries. (This practice likely works best with smaller class sizes.) Some elementary school teachers also invite all students' parents to visit their classrooms in the morning to help by reading or telling stories to the children to get them settled down and ready for the day. Some elementary school teachers regularly send notes to parents with students. For example, one teacher noticed her young students became hungry at midmorning, and the class agreed to schedule a snack period. She sent parents notes asking them to send healthy snack foods, including a list of appropriate, easy-to-prepare snacks. This teacher reported their snack time soon ran smoothly, with children usually eating and doing schoolwork concurrently.

Physical education for disabled students

Federal laws
The IDEA and other federal legislation for students with disabilities mandate that these students be provided physical education. Federal law defines physical education as the development of physical and motor skills; fundamental motor skills and patterns like catching, throwing, walking, running, etc.; and skills in individual and group sports, including intramural and lifetime sports, and in dance and aquatics. The IDEA mandates instruction in the least restrictive environment (LRE) possible. Regarding PE, this involves adaptations and/or modifications to curriculum and/or instruction as it does regarding academic education. In PE, adaptations/modifications assure each student's success in a safe environment. A student's IEP defines placement, which can include one or several options among the general physical education setting alone; this setting but with aid from teaching assistants or peers; a separate PE class setting with peers; a separate PE class setting with assistants; and/or settings with 1:1 student-instructor activities.

Potential modifications to games
To level the competition, PE teachers can modify activities. They can let special-needs students hit or kick instead of pitching a ball. In volleyball games, they can let students catch and throw the ball and/or let it bounce. Teachers can permit longer time periods equal to

student ability for moving to a goal/base. When possible, they can schedule games inside the gym on smooth floors to facilitate movement instead of outdoors in a field. When modifying rules for disabled students, teachers can involve them in the decision-making process. Teachers can reduce distances by moving bases closer together; letting students get closer to the net/goal/target; and letting them serve from midcourt in volleyball/badminton/tennis. Teachers can provide more scoring opportunities by substituting four for three strikes/ten arrows for six/three for two foul shots/etc. They can assign disabled students to be pitchers/goalies/first basemen, or other positions requiring less mobility. Adaptive equipment they can provide includes bigger bats/racquets; bigger/lighter/softer balls; and bigger baskets/goals/bases.

Benefits of inclusive educational programs

Educational research has found that both students with disabilities and their nondisabled peers obtain significant benefits from inclusive educational programs. For example, students with disabilities experience more stimulating learning environments via inclusion. They benefit from nondisabled role models of adaptive, communication, and social skills and behaviors. They have more opportunities for making new friends and sharing new experiences with them. They gain greater peer acceptance from being included, and they have a greater sense of membership in a regular class and in the school. Students without disabilities benefit by learning greater acceptance of individual differences among people. They learn to feel more comfort around students with various disabilities. They learn to help their disabled peers, which generalizes to learning to be more helpful to others. They gain leadership skills by providing examples, help, and guidance. And they gain greater self-esteem through modeling helpful leadership behaviors. Thus, inclusive education benefits all students.

Adapting the physical environment to facilitate learning

For students whose cognitive levels, attention spans, or other differences make large assignments intimidating, teachers can divide these into small, more achievable "chunks" so they are more willing to tackle them and experience some success daily. For students having difficulty taking notes from the blackboard, teachers can offer paper handouts/notes. Distractible students can be seated away from windows, noisy, high-traffic areas, and classmates who encourage chatting. Teachers must implement all adaptations in student IEPs, monitor their effectiveness, and discuss changes with the team if adaptations are not enabling best student performance. With students needing constant reminding of how to follow class practices, teachers can make an enlarged checklist of expectations for their daily assignments/routines and tape it to their binder/desktop, enabling more independent work tracking. Scheduling morning periods daily to check student homework and planners clarifies expectations and allows time to resolve problems and still have productive days. Assignments and assessments can use computers/scribes/time extensions/oral responses as alternatives for students with writing/printing difficulties.

Arranging physical space to accommodate students

Teachers must consider all learning community members' needs, including students, teachers, specialists, paraprofessionals, and volunteers. When community members change, last year's arrangement may not work. Teachers must also consider size and layout of their classroom/space, including attached equipment/furnishings, classroom location in the school, and instructional materials. Depending on curriculum and teaching philosophy and approach, teachers may want to arrange space for large and small groups, teams, cooperative learning groups, and individual instruction. If any student(s) use wheelchairs, teachers must consider accommodating their maneuvering in the room. They must consider preventing distractions for ADHD students. They may lower chalkboards, bulletin boards, and pencil sharpeners, and add bathroom grab bars for wheelchair students, and they may procure more electrical outlets for computers, language masters, and tape recorders for students with LDs or visual impairment. They may place carpet in areas for students needing to sit/lie on the floor periodically. Insurmountable obstacles may dictate extensive remodeling or relocation to different classrooms. Advance planning is hence necessary to allow budgeting and work without interrupting school-year instruction.

Teachers should allocate areas within their classroom for individualized teaching, and also small and large groups. The teacher and/or learning specialist might need a small-group instruction space. Teaching stations, learning centers, and areas for partner/pair work are good whenever possible. Teachers need to separate/designate noisy and quiet areas, and spaces free of distractions. According to educational research, horizontal and vertical paths must allow teachers to reach any student within eight steps. Wheelchairs require at least 36" to maneuver. Student coats and backpacks must be placed to avoid blocking traffic. Some experts suggest having students turn their desks so the lids open away from them, to keep them from accumulating unwanted/forgotten things inside. If a classroom faces the playground, a busy road, student cafeteria lines, and/or steady streams of traffic—especially since classroom relocation, even when available, can take extreme effort and a whole year—teachers can adapt existing spaces by putting curtains over windows, closing the door, and hanging visual displays from the ceiling that absorb sound.

Instructional accommodations and modifications

Accommodations are changes in HOW students learn and are assessed, while modifications are changes in WHAT students are expected to learn. Accommodations can involve teaching methods, materials, assignments, tests, the learning environment, scheduling, time demands, and special communications systems, and they need not change school learning goals. Modifications can involve partial program or course completion; lower than grade-level curriculum expectations; alternative curriculum goals; and alternate assessments. The IDEA mandates that schools give students with disabilities the chance to be included and progress in the general education curriculum, which can require accommodations and/or modifications to accomplish. The IDEA also requires all students receiving special education and related services to have IEPs Section 504 of the Rehabilitation Act that requires that schools provide accommodations to students with disabilities even if they do not have IEPs. The Americans with Disabilities Act (ADA) bans discrimination against the disabled. State laws follow the federal laws in allowing accommodations and modifications for students with disabilities.

Effective use of common spaces

While teachers have little or no control over their school building's commonly shared spaces, they can instruct their students to work with these. For example, they can teach them the common courtesies of walking quietly on the right side of the hall, and of speaking quietly in the library and cafeteria, auditorium, or cafeteria. This will help students adjust to large spaces inside the building. Teachers can also instruct all students to allow sufficient space for students using wheelchairs to go around corners and not to crowd wheelchairs. This not only helps the students in wheelchairs; it also prevents ambulatory students from being injured by coming too close to wheelchairs. Students in both special and general education programs must be taught to take special care in adhering to rules and guidelines on the playground and in the school gymnasium. Students make successful adaptations to school building spaces when they have learned how to navigate from one place to another, and how to behave in each school area.

Accommodations for students with difficulties with self-control

Some students with disabilities can require alterations in the learning environment to assist them in managing their behavior. For some, behavior management plans and/or counseling services may be required. There are also classroom accommodations educators can make for students whether or not they have such behavior management plans and/or counseling services. For example, teachers can let students use study carrels or other enclosures to work independently with less distraction. Teachers can assign work that students are able to finish in shorter time durations. Teachers can also allow students to use timers to help them monitor how much more time they have to finish assignments and how much more time they need to complete their work. For students needing structure to promote behavioral self-control, teachers can positively reinforce following classroom rules, list consequences for breaking rules, and ensure students' knowledge of rules and consequences.

In addition to posting lists of classroom rules and consequences for breaking them and making sure all students know these, teachers can also make sure to supply students with activities to pursue during free time periods. Students requiring structure are apt to act out during unassigned times without the direction of something specific to do. To prepare students for transitions such as beginning new lessons, going to lunch, moving to other school areas, or changing classes, teachers should follow regular routines and give students prompts about the changes. Teachers may seat some students next to trained peers, teacher's aides, or volunteers to help them attend to lessons. They can also designate "study buddies" who know how to interact effectively with some students to help them when the teacher is otherwise occupied. For pupils who lack behavioral self-control without personal support and attention, the teacher can also conduct 1:1 instruction with certain students and work with others in small groups to address their needs.

Crisis intervention and prevention

In immediate responses to crises in schools, educators should concentrate on restoring equilibrium for students. Their demeanor should be calm, authoritative, and nurturing; their behaviors direct, informative, and oriented to problem-solving. Educators should address student denial by providing them with accurate information and realistic explanations about what happened and what they can expect. Reassurance should never be untrue or unrealistic. Educators should encourage students to face the factual aspects of a crisis. They should invite students to cope with their emotional responses, and discuss with them their responses and defense mechanisms. They should communicate to students a sense of positive expectations and hope, in that although crises bring changes, they have means of coping with these. Educators can shift students' positions from victims to actors by helping them plan appropriate, realistic, and salutary actions to follow after they separate, building upon demonstrated student coping skills and techniques, and when appropriate, engage them in helping restore equilibrium. They should link students with peers, family, and staff for immediate social support.

Three main elements of responding to and preventing crises in schools are: Communication; Direction and Coordination; and Health and Safety. During a crisis, educators communicate: they sound alarms if needed; clarify next steps; give information about the occurrence and first-aid station locations, etc.; control rumors about the event; interact with the media as needed, and with the school district and community; respond to parent concerns; and keep track of the students and staff. Direction and coordination during a crisis include monitoring and solving problems and directing emergency operations centers. Health and safety during the emergency include directing evacuation, security, search and rescue operations; providing first aid for medical and psychological injuries; and reducing hazards to students and staff. Immediately after a crisis, communication includes dispelling rumors, clarifying crisis sources and impacts, and supplying information on medical and psychological resources available. Direction and coordination include continuing problem monitoring and solving. Health and safety include continuing activities begun during the crisis.

In the days and/or weeks following a school crisis, educators continue communication by supplying information and counseling to promote closure to students, school personnel, parents, and other school district and community members. They continue direction and coordination by monitoring and solving problems ensuing from the crisis. They continue health and safety by supplying case management, direct services, and/or referral for longer term treatments as needed to those involved. In efforts to prevent future crises, educators demonstrate communication by conducting debriefing meetings with school staff, parents, other community members, district personnel, and students as appropriate to make clear any deficits in their response to the recent crisis. They demonstrate direction and coordination by applying debriefing analysis to plan possible prevention of additional crises; limit the impacts of inevitable occurrences; and improve crisis response procedures and resources. They provide health and safety education to students, parents, and staff.

Difficulties in reading and following instructional methods

Many students with various disabilities have difficulties in the classroom due to problems they experience with following the instructional methods and reading and applying the textbooks and other printed or written learning materials used in regular education programs. Educators can help these students to work around such difficulties by providing them with accommodations. One of the most important skills to enable success in school is being able to read. However, many students who have disabilities are not reading at their grade level because of various impediments to their reading skills. Some are still in the process of acquiring fundamental skills in phonics (i.e., the relationship between speech sounds and the alphabetic letters that represent them) and word recognition. Some students are still in the process of learning how to apply techniques to assist them in comprehension of printed words, phrases, and sentences. In addition, plenty of textbooks, worksheets, and similar learning materials are not well-organized or clearly articulated, constituting further challenges to these students.

Accommodations for students with trouble understanding oral presentations

Some students with disabilities have trouble deciphering what they are meant to learn from an oral lecture or discussion on an academic topic. Teachers can make such accommodations as visual aids, like supporting their oral presentations with overhead projectors, large charts, or blackboards. They can give students an overview of a lesson's content before presenting it, and also introduce students to new vocabulary words prior to the lesson. Immediately following an oral lesson or lecture, teachers can give a printed summary of its important points, accompanied by a list of questions for them to answer. To help students with difficulties following ideas in oral lectures and discussions, teachers can break up lectures with discussions or other activities in small groups, and also maintain student engagement by inviting their questions. They can identify the primary parts of steps in the information. They can write important ideas on chalkboards/whiteboards, emphasizing parts using different colors.

When students with various disabilities have trouble with taking notes on the teacher's oral lectures or lessons, the teacher can distribute printed copies of their lecture notes to accompany the oral presentation. They can allow these students to record orally presented class lessons, lectures, and discussions for their review and study. Teachers should repeat important concepts, paraphrase them to express them in more than one set of words, and provide students with summaries of all the most important points. It is especially helpful if teachers repeat, paraphrase, and summarize at the end of a lesson, lecture, or class discussion. Teachers can help students with taking notes by giving them copies of their overhead projector documents, diagrams, and/or outlines of their lectures. To reinforce the information in oral presentations, teachers should supplement them with charts, diagrams, written/printed text, and/or pictures, and repeat as frequently as needed. Also, for deaf or hard-of-hearing students, teachers should procure a sign-language interpreter or a note-taker.

Accommodations for students with trouble learning math

Some students who have various disabilities have deficient skills in basic arithmetic and may still depend on counting on their fingers beyond the usual age. Some students with disabilities have major problems with remembering fundamental facts related to math. For students who have trouble with understanding mathematical concepts and solving math problems, teachers can provide accommodations such as giving them concrete objects and materials to assist in learning math concepts. Many students who cannot understand abstract ideas solely through mental processes can succeed better when they can process them using concrete, tangible things they can see, touch, and manipulate. Teachers can also highlight or color-code the important words in mathematical word problems for students. They can allow students to utilize charts to plan how they will solve math problems. And they can permit students to use basic fact charts and/or calculators to follow formulas and compute numbers for solving math problems.

Accommodations for students with trouble reading

One common problem for students with disabilities is isolating the main ideas in a book they are reading and/or which parts are important to remember. Teachers can highlight the important concepts and instruct students to read these first. They can give study guides to students for independent reading. They can offer students books on the same subjects at lower grade levels to make the main ideas easier to identify. Some students comprehend information when they hear it, but cannot read it. Teachers can supply books on tape/recorded versions; videos or movies of the information; computer text-to-speech software programs; and/or assign classmates to read printed materials aloud to students. Students with blindness or visual impairments may need specially produced materials and/or equipment to access class information. Teachers can supply books on tape or texts with large print; books and other materials in Braille or embossed formats; and give students equipment like magnifying devices or optical enhancers.

Accommodations for students who have trouble with handwriting

Students with a number of different disabilities can have difficulty with the fine motor control involved in handwriting. In general, the same kinds of classroom accommodations are required to address disabled student needs for both written assignments and written tests. For example, if a student needs to complete a written assignment using a word processor, s/he will also need the word processor to complete a written test. For students having difficulties with fine motor control, teachers can allow them to write straight into their workbooks instead of on separate paper or on photocopies of the workbook pages. They can permit students to type on typewriters, word processors, or computer keyboards. They can arrange for students to dictate their assignment and/or test responses to scribes, like classmates or teaching assistants, who write down their dictations. Teachers can also allow and provide adaptive equipment for students, such as special pen/pencil holders or grips, pens with erasable ink, and special paper featuring raised/embossed lines or color-coded line ruling.

Accommodations for students who have trouble with expressive language

Many students with disabilities may have good ideas, but have difficulties with expressing these in writing and/or speech. Teachers can provide them with accommodations that can facilitate their use of expressive language. For example, they can allow students to use a thesaurus to look up words that express the ideas they want to convey, and to find additional synonyms and antonyms for words if their actual vocabularies and/or their access to retrieving words they know are limited. Teachers can allow and provide to students specialized word-processing software programs that predict the words that students are trying to express. They can allow students to make use of electronic spelling aids and/or spelling dictionaries to support correct orthography. Teachers should also grade the content of written assignments separately from the writing mechanics in academic subjects (other than English composition, grammar, or spelling). They should additionally allow students with disabilities to correct their grammatical and spelling errors when they are completing written assignments or assessments.

Accommodations for students who have trouble completing assigned work

Some students with disabilities can do the same work as others, but much more slowly. This can cause them to run out of time to finish assignments. Other students have trouble remembering to assemble the materials and resources they will need to complete assignments. For students who have trouble keeping track of their class assignments, teachers can provide accommodations by dividing longer assignments into portions and giving students separate due dates for each portion. Teachers can instruct students to mark their assignments' due dates on a calendar they can see. To accommodate students who work more slowly than others, teachers can assign a smaller total amount of work, while still ensuring that the items or tasks they choose are those necessary for meeting all the learning objectives they have identified. Teachers can allow these students to use instructional materials and resources outside of class. Until students can complete assignments on time, teachers can provide them with reinforcement via partial credit for incomplete or late work.

Accommodations on tests

Five main categories wherein accommodations are permitted on standardized tests are presentation, response, schedule, setting, and assistive technology. Insofar as they are legally allowed on standardized tests, students with disabilities generally need the same kinds of accommodations for classroom and standardized assessments. Accommodations enable students to demonstrate their mastery of skills and knowledge without their disabilities interfering. For students with reading deficits, teachers can read test items aloud to them (excluding reading skills tests). They can supply text-to-speech software to present students with test directions and/or nonreading test items. They can let students read test items to themselves instead of presenting them orally. They can supply Braille or large-print test forms, and/or visual magnifiers, auditory amplifiers, or other assistive technology. To aid in focusing visually on tests, teachers can have students use positioning tools, pointers, blank cards, templates, colored, blank overlays, or transparencies. To decrease auditory distraction, they can give students headphones and "white noise" machines.

Accommodating students who have trouble following directions

In general, teachers speak, write, or demonstrate to students what they want them to do in school. Some students with disabilities have difficulty attending to spoken, written, or demonstrated information; some with remembering it; and some with both attending and retaining it. Moreover, some students with disabilities have difficulty comprehending and/or applying directions. When students find it hard to remember what they were instructed to do, teachers can provide accommodations by asking them to repeat the instructions in their own words or to demonstrate physically what they were instructed to do. They can also teach these students how to use personal planners or assignment notebooks for keeping track of assignments and tests. When students have difficulty comprehending the teacher's instructions, the teacher can provide accommodations by giving directions broken down into consecutive steps, and furnishing pictures or outlines of them. They can demonstrate for students how to complete sample tasks or problems, and combine oral instructions with pictures, diagrams, and/or printed words.

When students with disabilities are taking classroom and/or standardized tests, they can often have difficulty with accessing, understanding, and/or following the directions in the tests. Teachers can provide classroom accommodations to these students to facilitate test-taking. For example, they can provide answer forms or test forms with visual symbols, like stop signs, arrows, etc., to guide students in following directions. Some standardized tests already include such symbols for all students. When test directions are presented orally, teachers can provide sign language interpreters for deaf or hard-of-hearing students. When test directions and writing prompts are presented in print, teachers can read these aloud for students with visual impairments, cognitive disabilities, and reading-related learning disabilities. For students who need it, teachers can reread test directions or further explain their meaning. Teachers can also highlight or underline the most important words in test directions and/or test items for students with disabilities.

Accommodating students who have problems with organization

Students with attention deficits, cognitive impairments, and other disabilities can be distracted more easily than usual, causing them to confuse or forget the teacher's instructions. Students who find it hard to pay attention to more than one thing at a time frequently encounter difficulty completing complex assignments. Compounding these, some instructional materials are unclear by nature, and materials with excessive details can cause disabled students great confusion. Additionally, many disabled students have trouble storing, finding, and keeping track of classroom materials. Teachers can provide accommodations for confusion with complexity in materials and instructions by color-coding different materials or tasks to help students identify them. They should arrange tasks in clear, uncluttered formats with obvious beginning points and step sequences. To help students keep their materials organized, teachers can provide them with special binders or folders with dividers and different colors for each subject and unit. Teachers can also provide students with checklists of the materials they need for each class, which students keep in/on their binders, desks, or lockers.

Accommodations for students who have difficulty understanding test directions

When students with disabilities are not sure what to do on tests, teachers should avoid hinting at right/wrong answers but still accommodate them verbally by encouraging them (e.g., to answer each question and continue working), and they should give them additional examples of test items for practice to ensure they know what to do during actual testing. Most standardized tests prohibit accommodations in presentation that alter the assessed skill; for example, if a test measures reading skills, teachers cannot read items aloud to students. However, certain accommodations are permissible for classroom assessments. For students having difficulty switching among task types, teachers can group similar items and place easiest items first on tests. They can divide matching tasks into smaller groups of 4 to 5 items each. For essay/fill-in-the-blank items, they can provide applicable word lists. Whenever memorization is not required, teachers can let students take open-book tests. On multiple-choice tests, teachers can remove one choice from each question. Teachers can select test questions covering all content required but give fewer total questions.

Accommodations for students who have trouble sustaining attention on tests

When administering state standardized tests, teachers may provide some accommodations to disabled students who struggle to maintain their attention and energy during testing. For example, teachers may monitor student answer sheets to see whether they are putting their responses in the right places. When student responses to extended-response items are partly correct, teachers may give partial credit as designated by the rubrics for these items on state standardized achievement tests. In classroom assessments, teachers may furnish students with prepared outlines, charts, diagrams, and/or webs to help them plan essay or open-ended question responses. Students may demonstrate their skills and knowledge via alternate formats like role-plays, oral interviews, or physical demonstrations. They may be allowed references like thesauruses, dictionaries, or almanacs. They may be allowed concrete manipulatives to do and/or check calculations. Students may retake tests and get credit for improving. Also, some state standardized tests even allow certain grades to retake them.

Accommodations students may need regarding location of test

Some students with special needs are so easily distracted that they cannot perform to their ability if they take a test in a large group. Accommodations to address this problem include administering the test to the student in isolation or in a smaller group; allowing the student to take the test in a study carrel or other enclosure; or having the student take the test in another room free of distractions. Other students have physical or sensory disabilities that have an impact on their ability to take a test. In such cases, schools and teachers need to allow these students to use whatever adaptive equipment or furniture they require to be able to participate in the assessment. One important consideration in allowing the use of assistive technology is that it does not alter the performance of the actual skills being tested. For example, if a test measures skills in reading printed language, a student could not use text-to-speech software for that particular test.

Accommodations students may need for providing test answers

Students with various disabilities can have difficulty handwriting test answers, circling or checking multiple-choice answers, filling in bubbles, or solving problems and explaining their solutions. Accommodations often allowed on standardized tests in some states include giving additional space for students to handwrite their answers; allowing students to answer questions orally instead of in writing, to dictate their answers into a sound recorder, or to a scribe or test proctor; or allowing the student to sign his or her test responses to a sign-language interpreter. Students may also be permitted to use word processors or computer or typewriter keyboards to answer test questions, although state standardized tests typically prohibit their using spell-check and grammar-check software when typing. Students may write into their test booklets instead of on separate sheets, create Braille answers on separate paper, or record their answers using speech-to-text software programs. Students are also often allowed to use outlines, charts, and/or diagrams for planning essay or open-ended question responses on tests.

Assistive technology
Students with various disabilities may need assistive technology to acquire the information they are expected to learn and/or to communicate what they have learned. As long as the purpose of assessment is not defeated, the skills being assessed are not changed, and the student's responses still reflect his or her independent efforts, students can generally use the same assistive technology they use during classroom instruction to complete assessments. For example, a student with a disability might be given an accommodation allowing him or her to use an adaptive calculator for solving mathematics problems on a test. Some state standardized achievement tests allow students in seventh through tenth grades, for example, to use calculators. Another example involves completing answers to essay questions and/or long explanations or answers to questions on tests. Students with disabilities may be permitted to use assistive technology, such as voice recorders to dictate their responses, or word processors to type them.

Accommodations regarding test schedule

Some students with disabilities need additional time to finish taking a test. Students who work very slowly, those who can work for only briefer periods at a time, and those using certain types of assistive technology may need alterations in testing schedules. Accommodations when administering typical state standardized tests include allowing longer times for students to take the test; dividing a test into smaller portions and allowing students to take each portion on a different day if necessary; permitting students to take short breaks during the testing period; and allowing students to take a test at different times of day if physical conditions and/or medications affect their alertness and attention. Teachers may provide additional accommodations not allowed on standardized tests for classroom assessments. For example, the teacher can give disabled students fewer test questions, as long as they still cover all the same skills and content being assessed. Teachers may also let students review and correct their test answers from the day before.

Unusual or unique test accommodations required by some students

Some students can have disabilities that necessitate more unusual accommodations in order to participate in state standardized achievement testing. Testing accommodations identified as unique usually entail some changes in the existing assessment materials. Typically, states will allow such unique assessment accommodations if their Commissioner of Education has previously approved their use. Parents and teachers can look to the program of educational services to exceptional students in their school district to assist them with making a request for approval of such accommodations. Several examples of unique or unusual accommodations that may be approved for students with disabilities to participate in standardized assessments include: test forms with fewer items on each page; test forms with more space separating each item from the next; test forms with modified or tabbed pages to enable students to turn pages more easily; and having test question and response forms attached to the student's work area to prevent their falling, sliding, or shifting to facilitate reading and writing or marking on them.

Adapting class schedules and time constraints

Many students with disabilities learn and/or work at slower speeds than their nondisabled peers. Others perform better without the pressure of rigorous schedules. Teachers can provide them with time- and schedule-related accommodations. For example, some high school students may be given an Incomplete course grade and finish the course in summer school or the next semester. On practice assignments with multiple similar items, students who have the cognitive ability to learn without excessive repetition but need additional time and/or perform poorly under time pressure may be permitted to complete only every other item. Another educator consideration regarding students with disabilities is that in middle school and high school programs, it is particularly critical to assign these students to classes appropriate for them. Teachers of special education are advised that they may facilitate this process by working with their school administrators to ensure that the schedules of assigned classes are able to accommodate the special needs of any students who have disabilities.

Some students who have disabilities can handle the same course content as their peers, but they need more time to do so, or they need their work to be broken up into shorter time periods with breaks in between. Some students with disabilities suffer deterioration in their performance when they feel pressured by time limits. Some also require more time to complete assignments and assessments due to the adaptive equipment they must use in order to participate. Some strategies teachers can use include keeping schedules flexible to allow students with disabilities more time to finish a course. This can include completing the requirements in summer school. Teachers can allow students with disabilities extra time to complete their classwork and take tests. They can assign work further in advance to allow students with disabilities a chance to begin their assignments earlier. Teachers can also supply students with clear schedules of all units, assignments, and tests, and include periodic checkpoints within these schedules to help students monitor their progress.

NIMAS

The IDEA incorporates the National Instructional Materials Accessibility Standard or NIMAS. The stated purpose of this standard is to "facilitate the provision of accessible, alternate-format versions of print textbooks to pre-K–12 students with disabilities." This standard provides information to assist school IEP teams in deciding how they can electronically provide access to textbooks and other reading materials to students who have dyslexia and other LDs with reading. Parents who have children with reading disabilities should look at their children's IEPs and/or 504 plans to discover whether they contain anything about eligibility for accessible instructional materials, or AIM. If a student was determined not to be eligible for AIM, parents have the legal right to talk with their school personnel about why not. Parents can advocate for their children with schools by initiating conversations about how their children learn best, and how alternative formats, digital software, and/or readers can sometimes strikingly improve their learning and their motivation and confidence in it.

AIM

AIM stands for Accessible Instructional Materials. Many students with disabilities find reading impossible or difficult because of various disabilities affecting being able to read standard printed materials. AIMs consist of textbooks and other printed educational materials published in special digital formats. These formats provide accommodation to individuals who are blind, visually impaired, have various physical disabilities, and have reading-related learning disabilities (LDs) including dyslexia. Using digital formats enables students with reading and/or print disabilities to hear and see the text simultaneously using a computer, tablet, or other digital device. AIM includes formats like Braille, large print, audio, and digital text. The standard format for digital text files is named DAISY, for Digital Accessible Information System. DAISY allows users to listen to recordings of human voices or electronic speech synthesizers for audio versions of print materials. Accompanying reading software presents text visually at the same time. Today, most young students are comfortable and familiar with electronic voices and adapt easily to using them for reading.

Resources providing accessible text formats

Two organizations whose specialty is providing accessible text formats are Bookshare at bookshare.org and Learning Ally at learningally.org. Bookshare is an online library of over 150,000 digital versions of copyrighted textbooks and other books. Learning Ally is an online library of more than 70,000 audio versions of literary works and textbooks, with both recordings of human voices and digitally synthesized voices reading the material.

These organizations both have approval from the U.S. Department of Education for providing accessible instructional materials (AIM) to school districts and individual schools. Schools and/or districts can request digital formats or files from these groups for qualifying students with reading or print disabilities. Due to their cooperative missions, qualified members of either organization can more easily gain membership in the other. Some school districts or schools even pay for memberships in both organizations or either one for students who are found eligible.

Research evidence regarding text-to-speech technology

Studies suggest that reading technologies that use audio or digital formats can enhance the reading process for students with learning disabilities. When students simultaneously see words and sentences highlighted on the screens of computers, tablets, or other devices and hear them read aloud via text-to-speech (TTS) programs, this is described as "multisensory" or "multimodal" reading. With digital education widespread today, students may learn at home or while on the go as well as in the classroom. In this environment, AT programs are compatible with student learning processes. Some high-quality programs include Read Write Gold by TextHelp; Read: OutLoud by Don Johnston; and Kurzweil 3000 by Cambium. For iPads and other Apple devices, the large online digital library Bookshare offers an application ("app") called Read2Go, which enables its members to download and read its digital books on their devices. Students can digitally navigate through books' tables of contents, chapters, pages, and paragraphs.

Challenges in converting elements in print books to digital formats

According to the National Center for Learning Disabilities, certain visual images in printed books—for example, mathematical concepts, charts, and graphs—cannot be accurately represented using text-to-speech software programs. This presents a limitation to what students with reading or other disabilities can access compared to the original printed book versions. However, progress in technology is addressing this need. The organization Benetech is the parent group of the extensive online library known as Bookshare (bookshare.org). Benetech has a division called the DIAGRAM Center. At the DIAGRAM Center, designers of digital technology have created a new web application tool named POET. POET is an open-source application that enables crowd sourcing of verbal descriptions of visual images. In addition, it facilitates the process of creating descriptions of visual images for Digital Accessible Information System or DAISY file format, the standard format for digital text files. The progress of this and similar technology developments afford increased access to text for students with disabilities.

Research findings concerning instruction of literacy, math, and science

Comprehensive literature reviews find nearly twice as much research exists about teaching literacy as math, and four times more about math than science. One commonality among these areas is that using behavior analysis principles is effective for teaching them all to severely developmentally disabled students. For example, using task analysis to break down the instruction of multistep (chained) tasks and using time delay for teaching separate tasks are both highly effective for teaching academic content. These techniques are used in systematic instruction, which studies show is an effective overall teaching strategy for these students. Systematic instruction has been used to teach feeding, toileting, dressing, safety, and many other functional skills, and academic skills as well. Systematic instruction procedures define observable, measurable target skills; collect intervention data to prove new skill acquisition; apply behavioral principles and techniques like systematic prompts and fading, error correction, and differential reinforcement to aid transfer of learned skills; and effect behavioral changes that can be generalized across skills, materials, people, and contexts.

Digital books

Today, students can download and read books digitally on tablets, other devices, and computers from online digital libraries, which even offer apps (applications) for downloading to digital devices. Students can interact with, manipulate, and change settings in digital reading matter, including the sizes and colors of the fonts, both in the text and in hypertext links; choosing between male or female voices in audio versions of text; adjusting the speed of the readers' speech in audio text; turning on and off the read-aloud function in books with both visual and audio text; setting bookmarks in books; and changing the appearances of background displays in digital books. Some software programs and portable devices incorporate graphic organizers to aid comprehension and studying; note-taking tools to aid in essay writing; built-in scanners to copy and upload/download documents and pictures; support tools for outline writing; dictionaries, spell-checkers; keyword searches; bibliographers; voice recorders, voice recognition; and Acapela Voices, which reads text aloud translated into Spanish and other languages for ESL/ELL students.

Effective instruction in reading

According to the National Reading Panel, three main components of effective instruction in reading are (1) phonemic awareness, phonics, and alphabet knowledge; (2) vocabulary, text comprehension, and reading fluency; and (3) reading comprehension strategies. When the National Center for Learning Disabilities surveyed teachers and assistive technology (AT) specialists about digital technologies and digital books, the consensus of their responses identified a number of benefits. These included that digital reading technology affords a whole new world of learning potential for students, and that it affords flexibility among more learning options according to student preferences and learning styles. Teachers and AT specialists also find that digital reading options further the personal achievement, independence, and socialization skills of students. They say digital reading does much to aid students who struggle with decoding printed words. It keeps students' attention for longer time spans. It helps students read at their grade levels. It encourages students to take notes and make annotations to texts. And it corrects students' spelling errors.

Evidence-based strategies for teaching science

Recent educational research studies have shown that teachers, when trained in a specific task analysis, could teach developmentally disabled students to conduct science experiments. Some researchers have used graphic organizers to teach science core content to students with autism in middle school. Others taught science vocabulary and concepts to similar students using explicit instruction of descriptors. And some have taught the steps of scientific inquiry lessons, and science concepts that the learners generalized to new materials, to students with moderate intellectual disabilities. Research has shown that time delay and similar strategies for special educators to teach math and science vocabulary across multiple academic content areas is effective with high school students having moderate and severe developmental disabilities. Other researchers have recently investigated teaching early science concepts and vocabulary to elementary school students with severe DDs. They find even at lower ages/grades and more severe disabilities, students learned comprehension of both scientific vocabulary and concepts, meeting the criteria of state standards for progress through science lessons in the general education curriculum.

ESL classes

American classrooms where students are learning English as a new language demand much more interaction between students and teachers than other classrooms generally do. Many activities assigned in ESL classes involve group work, which necessitates moving desks, getting up, and moving around, which must be kept in mind for disabled students. Teachers should also be sensitive to the diversity of most ESL classes, which often include students from different countries and of various ages. ESL teachers can help by educating themselves in advance about any specific disabilities incoming students to their classes have. They should ensure their classes are inclusive, by providing accommodations and/or services needed by disabled students, and communicating this to students clearly in their course syllabi and in other ways. They should discuss with disabled students how their needs and accommodations might change, and any help or adjustments such changes could necessitate.

Approach to having disabled students in ESL classroom

ESL teachers with disabled students should discuss their needs and accommodations with the students. They should also discuss these with their teaching assistants, aides, school office staff, and other support staff, and also request that they help with accommodations for these students. Teachers must observe privacy regulations and not disclose disability information with faculty, staff, or other students, except in regard to accommodations that are needed. In the United States, the law requires schools, agencies, and other organizations to provide the same accommodations to international students with disabilities as they do to U.S. citizens; ESL teachers in America should comply with this legal requirement. All world nations have organizations that provide access to local resources for people with disabilities. ESL teachers with disabled students can contact these groups for resources and advice. Regardless of the type of disability, teachers should concentrate on the individual student's abilities and strengths.

Depending on the type and extent of a disability and the classroom situation, students with various disabilities can find everyday classroom activities difficult, e.g., active learning that involves getting up and engaging in different physical actions; making physical and oral presentations; or participating in group or class discussions. ESL teachers can exercise their creativity by adapting the activities they design and assign to allow more universal student access, while still attaining the same learning goals. When an ESL teacher has a student with a disability in the class, the teacher should communicate the same expectations and standards for academic achievement and personal behavior that s/he has for all students. The majority of students with disabilities appreciate being treated with the same educational standards and teacher expectations as a sign of respect from the teacher. ESL teachers should also ask their disabled students regularly for feedback about what things in class work and do not work for them, and how things that do not work may be adjusted or modified.

Communication skills and instruction for blind or visually impaired students

While teachers routinely use visual aids like pictures, flash cards, graphs, charts, and pointing at objects in the room while saying "this" or "that," they must realize these are not accessible to blind or visually impaired students. They must provide them with additional tactile versions and/or verbal descriptions. Students with low vision may not be able to see writing on blackboards/whiteboards, in workbooks, etc. They should be seated at the front of the room and allowed to bring their own magnifying devices. Before class, teachers can provide handouts to these students in Braille, large print, audio formats, or electronic formats depending on their preferred format, and/or give students additional prompts during class. When presenting visual information, teachers should spell new vocabulary words aloud; print using large, clear letters; use larger sized fonts in overheads and handouts; and read aloud as they write, which benefits all students. When drawing or displaying pictures, teachers should verbally describe their contents.

Equal access to classroom content for students with low vision or blindness

When school assignments involve large amounts of reading, students with low vision often experience eye fatigue and need to rest their eyes frequently. Teachers can permit them breaks during class and/or give them extensions on due dates for reading assignments. Teachers should ensure student access to alternative media formats like Braille, audio recordings, or large print. Some students bring laptops or other computerized devices with text-to-speech, large print, or Braille conversion software; teachers should provide their teaching content in electronic formats for these students. They should also discuss with them whether any websites the teacher uses as lesson supplements are incompatible with students' special software, and consider adjusting their curriculum to use compatible sites. Teachers should also keep classroom layout consistent to facilitate student orientation and navigation. Teachers sharing classrooms can try to enlist the other teachers' cooperation and assistance. Tactile and/or audio rather than visual cues more effectively get these students' attention. Teachers can also instruct other students to say their names before speaking during group discussions.

Considerations for students with mobility disabilities

When assigning group activities, teachers may need more flexibility and time for assembling groups and moving furniture. Teachers should consider this in assigning groups/pairs, without restricting variety among student partners/classmates. Students with limited/no use of their arms cannot perform common classroom behaviors like jotting down new vocabulary words, looking words up in dictionaries or encyclopedias, or even raising their hands. Teachers need to provide them with alternative methods, like a scribe to take notes, orally saying "yes"/"no" instead of raising hands, etc. Teachers can collaborate with students on alternative means to get teacher attention. Students in wheelchairs may arrive late and/or need to leave early because of weather, transportation service, architectural barriers, or other factors outside their control. Teachers should discuss with students whether their disability requiring accommodation or behavioral factors cause late arrivals/early departures, defining expectations and resolving issues accordingly. Teachers should ensure other students realize wheelchairs/other adaptive equipment constitute personal space and respect it. Teachers and students should sit when interacting with students of shorter stature or students in wheelchairs.

Instructional considerations for deaf and hard-of-hearing students

Some deaf/hard-of-hearing students learn written English and speech reading to understand hearing people, but communicate using sign language and do not learn speech. Others want to learn speech and have pronunciation difficulties due to their hearing loss. For students who want to use spoken English, teachers can find technological help. For example, microphones equipped with FM systems not only amplify speech sounds, but also send them directly to the student's hearing aids. Teachers can also repeat what other students say if they are out of microphone range, which benefits all students. For deaf students who communicate using sign language, teachers can engage the services of sign language interpreters; they can additionally learn several simpler signs themselves to facilitate basic communication with these students. Interpreting can be challenging for international students, because sign language is not universal but varies among countries. In this case, speech-to-text services may be better. Teachers should always directly address the student rather than the sign language interpreter/STT assistant.

Even deaf/HOH students who use spoken English are apt to have problems during class activities involving faster reaction times, like listen-and-repeat exercises. Teachers can give them more time to repeat, and also try to eliminate background noises—including cross-talk from other students—as possible. Fire alarms, other audio emergency signals, and PA speaker announcements are not usually accessible to deaf students. Teachers can accommodate them by flicking the overhead lights on and off, waving a hand, or touching them on the shoulder to get their attention before announcements or during alarms. Viewing videos of movies and TV programs is an activity often used and enjoyed in classrooms in general and even more so in ESL classes. However, teachers should be sure the videos include English closed captions or subtitles. This benefits comprehension for both deaf/HOH and ESL students. If captions/subtitles are unavailable for a video, teachers can procure sign language interpreters or speech-to-text note-takers. HOH students often comprehend video images better than audio practice.

Teachers should seek means of utilizing visual aids as supplements to all their lessons. They should wait to allow time for students to view both the signs of a sign language interpreter or the text of speech-to-text software programs, and also the visual aid the teacher presents. Teachers should be mindful whether they are standing between the student and interpreter. Teachers can also use color-coding, e.g., different pen colors to represent different parts of a sentence—like red for subjects or blue for verbs. They can use geometric shapes to adapt concepts visually and use their fingers to represent different subjects or different tenses when conjugating verbs. Since some deaf/hard-of-hearing students speech read, teachers should not stand in front of windows or other places that interfere with this. Seating in front of the room or circular seating wherein students can see both the teacher and classmates can help hearing-impaired students always see who is speaking. Decreasing background noise from open windows, large groups, fans, or cross-talk helps students follow class discussions.

Considerations for students with chronic health and mental health disabilities

Some students have different conditions like diabetes, asthma, seizure disorder, multiple sclerosis, arthritis, or anxiety, depression, obsessive-compulsive disorder, or bipolar disorder. Individual differences in symptoms complicate such chronic disabilities. Due to the condition, medication side effects, and/or the environment, students may feel/perform better/worse at certain times of the day/on certain days. This can influence attendance, attention, and memory. Teachers should permit students flexibility in taking breaks, extend time for finishing assignments, allow note-takers, adjust schedules, and let students make up missed tests as necessary. Some students with chronic conditions need rest at home for days/weeks, but may be able to study and do homework there. Teachers can design and adhere to a good syllabus to inform students what to do if they miss classes. Some students have sensitivities to sensory stimuli like temperature changes, lights, or sounds, or they have other conditions affecting classroom participation and/or social interactions. Teachers should make time to acquaint themselves with each student's unique circumstances and which accommodations help them most.

Teaching communication skills to students with speech disabilities

Some students have difficulty controlling their speech muscles secondary to cerebral palsy; some progressive illnesses cause speech problems; and traumatic brain injuries can cause aphasia, a language processing problem. Some students stutter, and some have voice disorders secondary to cleft palate/lip, vocal nodules/polyps, etc. Students who cannot speak functionally use electronic voice synthesizers or visual-manual communication boards/books. Others can speak, but less quickly, clearly and/or fluently than normal. Many students have milder articulation disorders that still affect their communication. Teachers not understanding a student should not say/pretend they do, but allow them to repeat; they are accustomed to it. Teachers should not finish their sentences for them, but give them time for self-expression, promoting self-confidence. Teachers must adjust their expectations for oral assignments/tests. They can also seek alternative means for students to attain class goals, e.g., hand-raising, writing, or group-texting question answers and slower discussion speeds. For students with communications assistants, teachers should address the student, not the assistant.

Teaching strategies for students with cognitive and learning disabilities

Students with learning and cognitive disabilities are increasingly common in today's classrooms and quite common in ESL classrooms where they can substantially affect how students learn English. Standard instructional methods for language are usually less effective for students with learning disabilities, autism spectrum disorders (ASDs), and various other neurological deficits. Teachers are responsible for modifying their teaching styles to facilitate learning, and ESL teachers to facilitate learning a new language. In ESL, students with LDs must not only process words and symbols; they also contend with various difficulties remembering/retrieving words, articulating speech sounds, fluency, organizing thoughts, constructing sentences, and thinking abstractly. Teachers should focus not on student deficits, but strategies many students have developed independently to compensate. Teachers can provide accommodations like more time for activities and tests; note-takers; and tutors. Neurological deficits that affect social skills, as with ASDs, can make group/pair activities challenging. Teachers should provide structure and lead classes deliberately, clarifying the goals and purposes of each segment of the class.

An ESL teacher may find that students with traumatic brain injuries or ADHD encounter difficulty in class, especially if the teacher presents information using only one format, modality, or approach. Teachers should use multimodal teaching approaches and alternative assessment formats. Utilizing a variety of instructional methods, e.g., lectures, games, small group assignments, or paired work, will make it easier for these students to find which technique(s) are most effective for them. Students with LDs often perform better in one modality and worse in another, e.g., excelling at spoken skills but struggling with written skills. Teachers can accommodate these students by offering them a variety of ways to demonstrate their learning, like doing assignments in artistic or oral formats. Teachers should also realize that individual differences give every student's neurological deficit a unique presentation, so they must discover solutions case by case. ESL teachers need to understand students' abilities/skills in their native languages to differentiate errors due to disabilities from those naturally due to learning a second language.

Self-confidence in disabled students

Many students with disabilities are aware of their disability, which can undermine their self-confidence. They often feel they are different and do not fit in socially and have experienced rejection, ridicule, and bullying by other students. Additionally, experiencing failure at tasks their nondisabled peers complete easily can lower their self-esteem. Teachers can offer explicit instruction, asking students to identify good qualities they possess; help them develop positive affirmations they can understand, repeat, and believe; and provide plentiful positive reinforcement for every small success and for admirable efforts regardless of outcome. They can have students describe how they think others see them, and collaborate to develop strategies to improve their own and others' images of them. They can teach students to accept and offer praise and criticism appropriately with others. Students may also need training in wearing clothing appropriate to different social situations and answering and using telephones properly. The more students master such social skills, the more self-confidence they will develop.

Personal and social skills

For all people with and without disabilities, it can be challenging to get along with others. One of the commonest reasons that adults are fired from jobs and students have problems in school is inadequate social and personal skills. Students with various disabilities that affect learning often do not learn through observation and imitation as others do. Teachers need to instruct them explicitly in areas like self-awareness. They must teach them to identify their own physical and psychological needs, abilities, interests, and emotions by asking them questions; showing them how to point to pictures representing various feelings, actions, events; or teaching them descriptive vocabulary. Teachers need to guide students to learn to identify and demonstrate knowledge of their physical beings and their relationship to and interaction with space, objects, and other people. They need to help students properly utilize, care for, and maintain hearing aids, glasses, braces, crutches, wheelchairs, or walkers. Teachers can also help disabled students learn appropriate strategies for coping with life stressors.

For students with disabilities to interact well with their classmates and others, one key area is in social conversations as well as in class discussions. Students must learn both to listen to others, which includes not only refraining from interrupting them, but also listening attentively to what they say, and to respond appropriately to what others say. Students with intellectual disabilities may, for example, change the subject completely instead of saying something that continues the topic. Teachers can give explicit instruction. For example, they can ask the student to repeat or paraphrase what another student just said; then ask her/him what possible things s/he could say in return on the same topic; have her/him demonstrate; and give positive reinforcement. Another area is forming and maintaining close relationships and friendships with others. Teachers can counsel students by asking them who shares particular interests, activities, and/or personal characteristics with them; helping them identify and implement behaviors for establishing and keeping relationships and friendships; and monitoring their progress by inquiring periodically.

Some students with cognitive disabilities may not have a good sense of personal possessions and boundaries. Consequently, they may take others' belongings; not take turns with others; or go ahead of others in lines. One facet of socially responsible behavior is respecting others' property and rights. Teachers can point out other students' showing such respect; explicitly show intellectually disabled students how to do the same; and give ample positive reinforcement whenever they do. Students with behavior disorders like oppositional defiant disorder will defy/ignore authority and directions. Teachers can establish behavioral contracts with them whereby they gain rewards meaningful to them for complying with clearly defined terms of what to do and not do. Students with ADHD easily act on impulse and become distracted, interfering with following directions. Behavior modification techniques or cognitive-behavioral therapy, sometimes in conjunction with medication, can help. Students also must learn to recognize valuable personal characteristics (e.g., honesty, kindness, or bravery); their personal roles in society; and social etiquette and proper behavior in public.

Independence for students with disabilities

Many students with disabilities have had things done for them that they could not accomplish alone and may have become habituated to passively waiting for others to initiate activities. Educators can help them achieve more independence by first explicitly teaching a student needed skills, giving prompts for each step, and then systematically fading the prompts so the student gradually performs tasks/activities with less and less help, direction, and guidance. Depending on the disability and activity, some students ultimately achieve full independence, while others can do more than before with less assistance. Students also must learn to take responsibility for their behaviors. Teachers/specialists can help students navigate the community by teaching orientation, mobility, street directionality, how to use public transportation, or strategies for coping with getting lost or with timetable changes when traveling. They can also teach them to follow safety procedures. They can counsel them in choosing friends and provide behavioral procedures for choosing clothing and getting to school on time.

Problem-solving skills for students with disabilities

As much as some students with disabilities may want to be completely independent, some disabilities dictate that they will need help with some things at times. A crucial behavior included among problem-solving skills is having the judgment, willingness, and ability to ask for help when they really need it. Educators can help in one on one, small group, or whole class settings by initiating discussions wherein students identify situations they have experienced when they needed help; what they did; what they could have done instead; and discriminate situations where they could have succeeded independently from those where this was impossible. Some students can benefit by learning from the experiences their classmates share. Teachers/specialists can assess and teach student skills for identifying problems, give them practice in predicting the consequences of events/actions, develop various alternatives for responding to problems, and evaluate their relative effectiveness.

They can also work with students individually and in groups on developing their own goals, plans, and solutions to problems.

SWPBS

School-wide positive behavioral support program (SWPBS) is not a practice, intervention, or curriculum per se. It is rather an operating framework for decision-making, toward the goal of assuring access for all students to the most effective possible teaching and behavioral interventions and practices. It guides a school's choice, integration, and application of evidence-based best practices to realize all students' best academic and behavioral outcomes. Six principles guiding SWPBS are: establishing a continuum of behavioral and academic supports and interventions based on science; utilizing real data for problem-solving and decision-making; organizing environments to prevent problem behaviors from occurring or developing; encouraging and teaching pro-social behaviors and skills; accountability and fidelity in implementing evidence-based behavioral practices; and universal screening and continuous monitoring of student performance and progress. Four interrelated elements of SWPBS are: data for making decisions; measurable outcomes, which data evaluate and support; practices backed by evidence they attain from the outcomes; and systems that support implementing the practices with effectiveness and efficiency.

Four integrated parts of SWPBS programs are data, practices, systems, and outcomes. The data educators collect about students' academic and social behaviors support the decisions they make about the academic and behavioral interventions and practices to use. The practices educators choose have science-based evidence of being effective for achieving the educational outcomes they desire. These practices support the desired student behaviors. The systems that educators establish support the most effective and efficient implementation of their chosen practices. These systems support implementation by supporting the behavior of the school personnel. The desired outcomes educators identify are observable and measurable, and the data they collect support these measurements. The students' outcomes in turn support the students' academic achievement and social competence. Well-implemented SWPBS makes learning environments less dangerous, exclusionary, aversive, and reactive, and more preventive, inclusive, engaging, and responsive. Disciplinary and classroom management issues like lateness, attendance, and antisocial behavior are addressed. Student behaviors needing more specialized interventions receive better support. And all students' academic motivation and performance are optimized.

School-wide positive behavioral support programs are typically divided into tiers along a continuum, based on how students respond behaviorally to intervention. In the first tier, all students in the school/system/district are given positive behavioral supports, such as giving positive rewards to reinforce exemplary and acceptable academic and social behaviors, which are implemented by all staff members in all school settings. This universal tier is known as primary prevention. The second tier of secondary prevention is for students whose behaviors do not respond to the behavioral supports given in the first tier, putting them at risk for disciplinary issues. These students are placed in a specialized group, where they receive more intensive behavioral measures. The third tier of tertiary prevention is for students identified as being at high risk of antisocial behaviors resulting in disciplinary problems and possible harm to themselves and/or others. These students receive individualized behavior management plans that are the most specialized and utilize the most intensive interventions.

Communication and emergency situations

An important part of communicating with other people is being able to recognize emergency situations and respond timely and appropriately. This can be difficult for students with intellectual disabilities, behavior disorders, and other conditions. Among those who do not recognize an emergency situation, some will always require supervision, while others can be taught certain basics, such as the smell of smoke; the sight of fire, flooding, or a person needing emergency medical attention; and what to do, like calling 911. Some students with disabilities can recognize emergency situations but may panic. Educators can use explicit, systematic instruction, including task analysis steps and behavioral shaping and chaining, to help them develop strongly entrenched procedures to follow. With enough practice, repetition, and reinforcement, many students with disabilities can implement these series of behaviors instead of panicking. Students with autism spectrum disorders often need explicit instruction in the meanings/purposes of social cues (like facial expressions, vocal intonations, gestures, body language, and verbal expressions) and how to respond appropriately.

Problem-solving procedure to apply to conflict resolution

The teacher introduces the topic to students by explaining that where a conflict exists, a problem exists, and that having a way to think about and try to solve a problem helps. The teacher writes three steps on the board and goes over each step with the students: (1) Define the problem; (2) Brainstorm solutions; and (3) Choose a solution and act upon it. The teacher explains that before solving a problem, people must agree to work out the problem; that for problem-solving to work, they must agree not to call names, yell, or otherwise escalate the conflict. For step (1), the teacher encourages the students to define the problem in a way that does not place blame upon others. For step (2), the teacher encourages the students to think of as many possible solutions as they can. For step (3), the teacher advises the students that they should pick a "win-win" solution wherein all parties benefit and nobody loses.

To help younger and disabled students learn how to resolve conflicts, the teacher can first teach them a three-step problem-solving approach consisting of defining the problem, brainstorming solutions, and choosing and implementing a solution. The teacher then gives students a script for a "fight"/conflict and puppets if appropriate for the students, and then has some students volunteer to act out the conflict script. Then they review the problem-solving approach. Once students agree on one or more solutions, have the volunteer players act out their choice(s). Students who are able may then work in small groups to create and perform their own conflict resolution sketches for the class. The teacher then leads a class discussion, asking the students: (1) Which things in the sketches caused the conflict to escalate; (2) Which things people can say to each other to show they want to stop fighting and solve the problem; and (3) Whether any of the students have experienced similar conflicts in their own lives and how they resolved those conflicts.

ADLs and task analysis

Many of us take activities of daily living for granted. Because we have long ago learned to do them automatically, we do not realize how complex they actually are by involving many different steps. This complexity, however, can baffle special-needs students who have not achieved automaticity. Task analysis provides a solution by separating tasks into smaller, more manageable steps. Educators must also provide support, like going over each step with the student to ensure their understanding; helping with steps the student cannot do independently; answering student questions; and monitoring that they complete all steps correctly and in the right sequence. Daily life skills tasks can easily be connected with general education curriculum. For example, reading care instruction tags on clothing and directions on soap packages when doing laundry and discussing it with others connect with English. Measuring laundry soap, reading washing machine and dryer dials and numbers, sorting and counting clothes, and estimating washing and drying times connect with mathematics. This also applies to cooking, meal preparation, etc.

To function independently in the home or community, special-needs students must learn such ADLs as selecting clothes suitable for the day's weather and activities; doing grocery shopping for the week; performing personal hygiene like toileting, bathing, brushing teeth, etc.; organizing and doing household chores; managing money and paying bills; taking out garbage and retrieving trash/recycling bins; cooking a simple meal; doing laundry; and others. Task analysis breaking a task down into individual steps is effective for special-needs students who otherwise have difficulty remembering all a task's parts and sequence. For example, doing laundry can be broken down into 10–12 steps. Before giving all steps to the student and supervising following them, the educator must follow these steps: Write down the steps, in chronological sequence. Assess what parts of steps the student can already do independently. Assess what steps/partial steps the student can do partly or with some adult assistance. Teach the student the steps that s/he cannot already do. Evaluate whether the instruction was effective for the student's learning.

Steps in task analysis for laundry
(1.) Take the laundry hamper to the laundry room. (2.) Empty the hamper onto the table/floor. (3.) Sort laundry into colors and whites. (4.) Open the washing machine. (5.) Put one sorted pile (or as much of it as will fit easily) into the washer. (6.) Add laundry soap. (7.) Turn on the washer. (8.) Wait until the machine is done. (9.) Open the washer. (10.) Take the laundry out and look to make sure everything is clean. (11.) If not, remove soiled pieces and put them back into the washer for another cycle. (12.) Put laundry in the dryer.* (13.) Choose the right setting for the fabric type. (14.) If needed, set the length of drying time. (15.) Turn the dryer on. *[Alternative: Hang laundry on the clothesline to dry.] (16.) When laundry is dry, remove each piece from the dryer/clothesline. (17.) Fold each piece and put it into the hamper. (18.) Put away the clean laundry in the right closets, drawers, etc.

Picture cards
Many special-needs students encounter difficulty processing information communicated verbally; initiating activities independently; maintaining attentional focus; and completing each step in a multiple-step task. When instructing special-needs students in ADLs, educators find a valuable resource in picture cards because these convey information visually instead of only verbally; they are naturally amenable to task analysis by using one picture card for each step in a task and arranging cards in the correct sequence; and they can be integrated into visual/graphic schedules, functional communication systems, and/or

story strips. "Reminder strips" are short strips of picture cards that help students follow sequential steps when they cannot remember these without visual cues. For example, for hand-washing, a reminder strip placed above a sink can include individual pictures (with word captions) of turning on water, soap, lathering hands, turning off water, and drying hands on a towel, respectively. Many online resources offer printable cards, some designed for students to color themselves, which increases their engagement, enjoyment, and ownership in the learning process.

Adaptive behavior skills

To increase progress toward independent living, two of many important areas are time management and hygiene. While parents commonly wake their children, when they get older teaching them to use an alarm clock/clock-radio frees them from depending on parents. For students with ASDs, parents may need some trial-and-error experimentation with different loudness, sounds (e.g., beeps or buzzes or music, and music types) as many are hypersensitive to sensory stimuli. For those capable, advanced skills include setting the alarm independently and deciding when to set an alarm for by estimating the time they need. Parents/educators can also teach students to use a watch/clock to manage home/school task completion. Students having difficulty with numbers can benefit from graphic visual timers. Students also need to develop hygiene routines for bathing, using deodorant, grooming, and dressing. Many ASD students naturally have rigid behavior, find routines comforting, and are amenable to daily bathing/showering (which is easier long-term than every 2–3 days) and specific instructions, like washing each area four times.

Preparation for independent living

To prepare children with disabilities for more independent living as they grow up, parents and educators can start teaching young children responsibility for their belongings. For example, when young children bring their toys with them in the car or to others' homes, they can be taught a routine to find the toy before leaving, take it to the car, and bring it inside when arriving at home. As they get older, this routine can be transferred to backpacks, school supplies, digital devices, and phones. Adults can also teach young children to employ visual cues for remembering duties. For example, they can keep medications in specific locations as reminders to take them at the specified times. They can use Post-it notes on their backpacks reminding them to pack lunch and/or bring permission slips and completed assignments to school. Adults can begin teaching food preparation and how to make noncooked snacks and sandwiches to young children. As they grow, adults can teach them to follow recipes, safely utilize kitchen tools, and cook.

Adults can help many students with cognitive, behavioral, emotional/social, and mental health disabilities prepare for daily life. For example, for telephone skills, they can first teach young children to answer the telephone, and then take and deliver messages. As they grow, adults can help them progress with skills like calling 411 for phone numbers; calling stores in advance to ask if they have certain products in stock; calling restaurants to order takeout or delivered food; or calling technical support for help with computer issues. Adults can teach young children about walking to nearby neighborhood places; teach middle children about riding bicycles to destinations and taking public transportation when ready; and help adolescents and young adults learn to drive when appropriate. They can teach children as they grow to carry house keys, cell phones with important numbers, and money when leaving home; and personal safety, like judgment about hand-shaking versus hugging/kissing; protecting their personal information online and money in public; and what to do if followed/approached by strangers.

Career awareness

When working with students with disabilities at the elementary school level, career development includes making students aware of workers in the community, and also helping them comprehend individual uniqueness, work's role in life, and fundamental knowledge about various jobs. Teachers can develop programs engaging students in activities involving adult workplaces and familiarize students with the kinds of social interactions they will experience after leaving school. Educators can also teach young students skills related to employment in the classroom, and then reinforce those skills in situations that expose them to workplace experience. Teachers can plan 1 to 3 hour field trips to visit different workplaces in their community. To prepare students, teachers can make them familiar with basic career information. After field trips, teachers can ask students questions like: What are the working environment and conditions? What abilities and skills do the jobs require? Do jobs observed primarily involve things, people, ideas, or information? Where/how can you learn skills for this occupation? Are you interested in this occupation? Why/why not?

To help prepare students with disabilities for futures in the workplace, educators can provide work experience in/around school. They can instruct them in doing laundry for the art room, gymnasium/pool, or lower grades' classrooms. Students can learn to sweep, vacuum, mop, wipe chairs and tables, and refill condiment containers in the cafeteria. Teachers can instruct students, sometimes with assistance from the custodial staff, in janitorial tasks like taking out garbage, dusting, cleaning, floor-waxing/buffing, painting, or refilling soap and paper towel dispensers. They can also enlist groundskeeper staff to help teach students seasonal outdoor tasks like weeding, mulching, mowing grass, and raking leaves. With the cooperation of office staff, teachers can instruct students in clerical tasks like preparing mail, making copies, filing, and data entry. Students can learn to help maintain school buses by vacuuming and washing. They can learn to restock vending machines; collect and count the money and deliver it; recycle materials; or construct and paint scenery and run lights for school plays/assemblies.

School-to-work training

President Clinton signed the School to Work Opportunities Act of 1994 (Public Law 103-239) into law. This law is a joint initiative by the U.S. Department of Education and Department of Labor. In transitions from school to work (STW), students with disabilities may need help with environmental accommodations; job accommodations; assistive technology devices; and additional supports for full participation in STW programs based in schools and/or communities. Key issues affecting success or failure in the workplace are related to social skills, for both nondisabled and disabled workers. In fact, 75 percent of job loss within the nondisabled population is attributed to poor social interactions. Disabled students also need good awareness of their own strengths and weaknesses to succeed at work, and skills for compensating for their deficits and making the most of their talents. Survey research with employers hiring disabled workers indicates that they want employees who are dependable, on time, can follow basic directions, and get along with their coworkers.

Some common STW curriculum subjects include employment-related functional academics; independent living skills; and interpersonal skills, since social skills are critical for nondisabled and disabled workers alike to get and keep jobs. Many opportunities connect school with work so students gain employment experience. Students can get unpaid/paid work experience through internships, structured for practically applying academic knowledge in jobs; job shadowing in one-day workplace visits and observing an employee in a specific job; or adult mentors, who serve as role models by communicating information about workplace norms, giving consistent, caring guidance and support, reviewing progress regularly, and establishing high expectations. Co-op programs combine technical and career classwork with part-time work during school years, with expectations for employers to provide and students to learn defined in training agreements. Community members visit schools on Career Days to share their experiences with interested students. Teachers can learn of academic job preparation through unpaid/paid workplace programs. Additional opportunities include apprenticeships, on-the-job training, field trips, class speakers, school-sponsored enterprises, and health care "clinicals."

Transition planning and Indicator 13

Transition planning helps students with disabilities and their families consider students' lives after high school; identify long-term goals; tailor high school learning for acquiring skills and contacts they will need to meet those goals; and with allocation to local school districts of funding and services supporting transition processes. Students and adults invest in students' future well-being by planning for postsecondary life. The IDEA's Indicator 13 is a provision that students with disabilities age 16 and above must have IEPs including postsecondary transition plans. The U.S. Department of Education's Office of Special Education Programs (OSEP) requires states to develop six-year State Performance Plans, based on about 20 indicators, and submit indicator data in Annual Performance Reports for Indicator 13 by February 2011. The National Secondary Transition Technical Assistance Center (NSTTAC) has developed the I-13 Checklist to aid state data collection. States may use their existing monitoring systems; however, this checklist can be used instead, or to evaluate those systems, or as a supplement, and is approved by the OSEP.

Postsecondary transition planning
The IDEA requires all students with disabilities to have postsecondary transition plans included in their IEPs when they are age 16 and older. When setting goals for students with disabilities to make transitions from school to work, job training and/or higher education, and community living, a few general criteria include that the goals should reflect expectations that are both high and realistic for the student. These goals should also reflect an approach for some kind of forward progress rather than a dead-end situation. When establishing postsecondary goals, the goals and objectives may be of mixed character, reflecting the ability, endurance, and stamina levels of the individual student. The transition plan can and should include external supports as needed. Transition plans can begin with more general goals and incorporate more specific details as the student comes closer to graduation. These goals may change from one school year to the next. Changes can range from minor alterations to major differences, depending on the individual student and situation.

When planning postsecondary transitions for significantly disabled students, adults should consider whether the student is able to express his/her interests. If not, educators should obtain information from parents/caregivers for planning transitions. They should consider the student's special health care needs. They must account for any challenges or needs that keep the student from working outside of home. Transition planners must determine who can provide training and/or education to help the student's transitions. They must determine what the student can already do without others' assistance. And they must also consider what else the student could do if s/he had help from a habilitation training specialist, a job coach, a caregiver, or other service provider(s). Additional ideas for transition planning include connecting students and their families with other students who have similar disabilities and their families; identifying peer mentors for students; supplying the resources the student needs; and inviting others who can make valuable contributions to join the transition planning team.

Vocational assessment and planning: Employment preparation for disabled students contains the same essential components as for nondisabled students: assessing and establishing skills; exposure to career possibilities; and awareness of aptitudes and interests. However, greater and more individualized supports for these components are involved with disabled students. Successful school-to-work transition programs require transdisciplinary, comprehensive vocational assessment to identify student skills and needs by teachers, psychologists, counselors, and representatives from vocational rehabilitation and social services agencies and community mental health/intellectual disabilities departments as well as the students, parents, employers, and business organizations. Assessment should cover academic, daily living, personal, social, occupational, and vocational skills (including performance tests and situational assessments); career maturity; vocational interests; and vocational aptitudes. A number of standardized instruments are available for assessing the latter two. Three major goals for students to learn in school activities for vocational preparation are: understanding themselves, their abilities, interests, and values; understanding the world of work; and learning good decision-making skills. These enable informed, realistic work-related decisions, and are also the main elements of career maturity.

Guidelines and strategies for teachers to observe with cognitively impaired students

It is helpful for teachers to find successful role models in their particular field of study who have disabilities similar to the student's. Teachers can explain to students how the role model succeeded through effort and asking for needed help. Inclusive education provides disabled students with opportunities to learn and socialize with non-disabled peers, affording them a more "normal" life experience and better preparation for community living. Teachers should never evaluate the abilities of a cognitively impaired student based exclusively on their standardized IQ, achievement, or other test scores. Test scores do not take into account experience, social and work abilities, or creativity. Some students have varying strengths in specific areas either not shown by composite test scores or omitted from testing. In addition to offering help when it seems needed, teachers should develop a procedure for each student to ask for help. Encouraging peers to help cognitively impaired classmates is useful to both parties. Teachers should encourage peer socialization as well as academic help.

Teaching and learning strategies that educators should use with cognitively impaired students in general education classrooms

Mnemonics, which include techniques, devices, words, sentences, and pictures, are valuable tools teachers can offer to help both non-disabled and disabled students to remember information. Many non-disabled students (including medical students) have memorized lists or items in a class using sayings or sentences whose initial letters correspond to the lists, whether it is for the planets in the solar system, the lines and spaces on a musical clef, or the names of the cranial nerves. Teachers with cognitively impaired students in their classes should present lessons supported by many concrete objects and materials. They should present information in small steps, always present steps of a task in the correct sequence, and frequently review each step. It is important to deliver immediate feedback to students and do so consistently. Teachers should emphasize student successes more than failures, and reinforce attempts as well as successes. Opportunities to practice skills in real life are priceless. Teachers should also consider alternative learning activities that are more accessible to disabled students but meet the same or at least similar learning objectives.

Tips and strategies that support effective teacher and peer interactions

While teachers' expectations of cognitively impaired students should be realistic, they should still be appropriately high rather than coddling or neglecting them. Teachers should speak to students with cognitive disabilities directly, the same way they address all students. Educators must realize that the way they interact with cognitively impaired students functions as a model for non-disabled peers to interact with these students. This can be especially significant, for example, for helping non-disabled students learn how to communicate with cognitively disabled peers about behaviors that are inappropriate to the classroom. Educational experts also advise that not only do interactions among disabled and non-disabled students happen independently of teacher intervention, but moreover, sometimes the teacher needs to withdraw or "back off" to allow such interactions to occur when the teacher's presence only interferes. Teachers should also observe and note which activities most promote verbal and nonverbal student interactions, and make use of these.

Preparation of cognitively impaired students for adult living

A "free, appropriate public education" (FAPE) is required by the IDEA for all students aged three to 21 years, including the cognitively impaired. Educators can help these students attain both academic and socialization skills in mainstream classrooms by assigning cooperative learning projects, peer tutoring, and paired study ("study buddies") to prepare them better for work and community living. Students who receive special education services should still have access to general education curriculum. Today such students are most often mainstreamed, with teachers providing needed classroom modifications and accommodations. Teachers should emphasize developing functional academic skills with these students—skills used frequently in everyday life, like reading signs, labels, and instructions; counting change; measuring objects, and so on. Students progressing to secondary school should be given increasing emphasis on functional life and career skills. As learning takes longer with these students, they need years to prepare for jobs. Even severely cognitively impaired individuals can learn vocational skills and perform them with supervision, if properly prepared. Being productive contributors to society enhances their self-esteem and equal rights.

Transitions between activities

Many students with cognitive impairments have great difficulty suddenly switching from one activity they are involved in to another. This includes students with severe impairment, as with IQ levels below 35, and with autism spectrum disorders, even for those with normal or high IQs. Abrupt changes without advance notice deprive individuals of environmental control—a likely reason they upset students with neurological differences. Perseveration and deficits in ability to redirect attention likely also contribute. Demanding sudden change triggers problem behaviors in individuals prone to them. For example, in a group home, a 20-year-old student with severe intellectual disability and a history of self-injurious behavior (SIB), tantrums, and property destruction, made progress reported by the houseparents' supervisor: the student was looking at a magazine when the supervisor told her they were going on an outing. Instead of a tantrum, head-banging, or breaking something as previously, the student asked if she could bring her magazine. She created her own transition, her own bridging activities. Providing prior notice and gradual transitions prevent many behavioral incidents.

Teaching functional living skills

While all students with disabilities need to learn life skills to function independently and/or with supervision, the type of disability affects how they learn them. In general, students with only emotional or behavioral disabilities may readily understand the instruction of functional living skills, but might also not perform all of them because of their disabilities. However, students with cognitive impairments are likely to need more assistance understanding functional living skills before they can actually apply them. Situations influence the priority of some skills over others. For example, accessing and navigating public transportation will be critical skills for students living in urban areas, but not for those living in rural communities. Other skills are more universal in that all students will need to learn them. For example, three general areas of life skills are hygiene, including personal care, housekeeping and maintenance, and public behaviors; finances, including handling cash, managing bank accounts, paying bills and taxes, and making household budgets; and social skills, including managing disability's impact on relationships.

Teachers, therapists, and other school personnel can help cognitively impaired students to learn and practice life skills and responsibility through performing and assisting with necessary, useful, common everyday tasks. For example, they can clean chalkboards and erase boards, and they can remove old bulletin board displays and help to put up new ones. They can organize books, pencils, crayons, and other classroom materials. They can hand out tests, worksheets, and finished assignments to other students; pass out class or school newsletters or newspapers; and distribute permission slips, forms, and other materials to be distributed. They can help teachers and/or teaching aides mark off items on checklists for signed permission forms, money for field trips, and food. They can also help teachers, aides, and other students to feed, clean cages, and otherwise care for plants and small animals being kept in the classroom.

To help cognitively impaired students learn everyday functional skills and also promote senses of responsibility, accountability, and competence, teachers may assign them such necessary tasks as delivering, retrieving, and storing audiovisual equipment and materials used in classrooms. In schools that have "AV teams," cognitively impaired students may be appointed to the team and assigned such transport duties, adding senses of belonging and importance to those of responsibility and competence. Similarly, students could be assigned to library duties such as reshelving books and repairing book damage. Teachers may assign regular duties of shutting down and switching off school computers, wiping them off daily, and turning them on each morning. Students can clean PC keyboards using compressed air cans, damp paintbrushes, or hand vacuums with micro attachments. They can return attendance records to classrooms for the next day. They could also help clean up the staffroom or restock vending machines. Some activities transfer to job duties, some to personal life; all generalize to everyday competent, responsible behaviors.

Teachers may assign students with cognitive impairments to assist in the gym with setting up equipment for various physical education activities; with moving and storing equipment, thus keeping the gym's storage room(s) organized; and with setting up furniture and making other preparations for assemblies and other events. In schools having a "cafetorium," they can assist school custodians in cleaning up after meals and before assemblies. They can also help custodians with sweeping, mopping, and buffing school floors; dusting; cleaning windows; and outdoor maintenance tasks like shoveling snow, raking leaves, weeding flowerbeds, helping with lawn-mowing, and so on. They can assist school office personnel in many ways, including putting mail and memos in staff mailboxes; delivering mail and messages from the office to classrooms; delivering messages, forms, and other paperwork from classrooms to the office; helping the staff to make, collate, and count photocopies; and alphabetizing files to support office staff's filing duties. These activities not only build useful life skills; they also valuably boost students' self-esteem, self-confidence, self-efficacy, and social interactions.

One thing that educators should remember is not to assume anything. That is, they should neither take for granted that a cognitively impaired student knows how to perform any basic function, nor that the student does not know how to perform any such function. Individual students vary in both ability and experience and will often surprise their teachers. Teachers should model the skills they want to promote in their students; give direct, explicit instruction in the steps of all tasks, as well as modeling them; give the students plenty of opportunities to attempt the tasks themselves; support students' efforts; and reinforce their attempts and successes. On every new day when a cognitively impaired student performs a task, the teacher should always reinforce it anew, even when the student has performed the same task on previous days. Teachers need understanding, much patience, and great persistence. For some students to succeed in required, everyday personal functions, teachers must provide redundant instruction, much repetition, regular review, and frequent, consistent reinforcement.

Teaching strategies in helping students with cognitive disabilities manage their own finances

Everyone, including those with cognitive impairments, must learn how to handle money in order to live as independently as possible. Any nondisabled person whose numerical skills are not very strong has experienced making errors or having problems balancing a checking account. For students with cognitive impairments, especially in arithmetic and mathematics, this becomes an even greater challenge. Educators may help by teaching everyday financial activities using role-play scenarios involving writing checks and deducting them from balances. They can arrange real-life practice sessions going to the bank to conduct transactions. Another method is to show students how to make weekly plans to calculate their income and expenses, and to subtract the latter from the former. This provides practice for making and managing their own budgets. Another consideration is that some people will take financial advantage of the cognitively impaired. In addition to teaching skills for keeping track of income and expenditures, some students should have highly ethical advocates to protect them from being exploited financially by others.

Behavioral issues in the general area of hygiene that professionals can encounter

Understanding a student's behavior can inform a professional's training and instruction efforts. For example, a young woman with severe intellectual disability needed an IEP goal and daily reminders to apply deodorant when dressing; she did understand the concept of perspiration odor, describing it as "yuck." Her group home supervisor used this understanding to reinforce the daily reminders: "That's right, you smell 'yuck' without deodorant." An intellectually disabled man who grew up "on the street" with nondisabled persons had experience drinking alcohol; placed in a government-funded residential program where alcohol was prohibited, he spent some of his job earnings on large bottles of alcohol-based mouthwash. When staff discovered he was drinking it—not just inappropriate but dangerous—they refunded his money and confiscated the mouthwash. Such situations pose counseling challenges with a client having long experience with drinking, a stubborn personality, and lacking understanding of protective restrictions. While many hygiene behaviors are easily taught because of common-sense bases, it is important to clarify correct product uses, including amounts, frequencies, purposes, and applications.

Cognitively impaired students in general need much repetition, redundancy, and reinforcement to acquire and maintain new personal skills. For example, one student with severe intellectual disability had long since mastered getting dressed daily, yet still needed daily reminders to apply deodorant before dressing. Another student was compliant with oral hygiene instructions, but his fine motor skills were inadequate to brushing and flossing thoroughly enough to prevent decay, requiring substantial support via frequent dental visits. Another student brushed, flossed, and used mouthwash daily, but his seizure medication caused halitosis, which some people—including an instructional staff member—did not understand and complained about until the group home supervisor and behavior specialist explained it. Hygiene also includes learning what public personal behaviors are acceptable and unacceptable. For example, a student thought it amusing to break wind at the dinner table deliberately. When she did not understand why her housemates were "grossed out," the behavior specialist asked how she would feel if someone else did this. She had egocentrically not considered this; the suggestion created a revelation.

Social skills instruction

When students' main need is intellectual disability, some beginning educators might assume they need no instruction in social skills. However, despite the evidence that many intellectually impaired students are quite sociable, there are still some considerations. One is that sociable students might have social skills that are commensurate with their developmental level but appear immature for their chronological age. Educators should help to address this by giving practice in appropriate behaviors for various social interactions and situations through role-play scenarios, giving coaching for behavior in real-life situations, and monitoring social behaviors in school via observation. Another consideration is the impacts a student's cognitive disability can have on his or her social relationships. Others might take advantage of students' cognitive limitations by manipulating them with respect to money, personal possessions, activities, relationships with others, and so forth. Additional factors in the disability's social impact include students' communication skills and/or comfort with explaining their disability to prospective relationship partners and friends to facilitate better understanding and acceptance.

Using existing skills, scheduling, and resources

While students with cognitive impairments are often limited in academic achievement, their intellectual limitations do not necessarily mean they equally lack common sense: some excel in this area. Educators teaching life skills should not treat these as academic skills. They should focus on students' interests and build on their strengths, rather than cognitive abilities; avoid difficult terminology; and use simple vocabulary and concepts. When using role-play and hypothetical situations for instruction and practice, they should propose simple, real-life scenarios demanding common-sense responses. Having structured schedules benefits students with cognitive impairments, as does the plentiful, frequent repetition of practice and real-life activities employing the life skills they are learning. While an intellectually disabled student is likely to experience initial difficulty constructing a schedule, educators can help them. Then once the schedule is made, the student is likely to have no difficulty adhering to it. Schedules define activities, provide procedural directions, and afford a sense of security. For activities students are unable to perform independently, educators should help create a list of resources to contact.

School-wide positive behavioral support (SWPBS) systems

School-wide positive behavioral supports (SWPBS) aim to prevent the occurrence of problem behaviors by optimally arranging the school environment, instead of reacting to them after they occur. As such they are more proactive, less punitive, and safer. Because they promote academic interest and achievement in all students, they are more inclusive of students with disabilities, rather than singling them out for "special" treatment. Yet they also afford better support for cognitively impaired students whose behaviors demand more intensive attention: the SWPBS continuum's primary prevention tier is classroom-wide or school-wide; secondary prevention involves specialized groups of students identified with at-risk behaviors; and the tertiary prevention tier features individualized, specialized, intensive support systems for students with high-risk behaviors. SWPBS practices are evidence-based, that is, proven through research. All students are screened, and student progress is monitored continually. Moreover, SWPBS systems encourage and teach all students, including those with cognitive impairments, pro-social behaviors and skills.

Positive behavioral support (PBS) systems

PBS employs four main elements: (1) Data, on which decisions are based; (2) Outcomes, which are definable, measurable, and evaluated through collecting supporting data; (3) Practices, which have shown through evidence to have the ability to achieve the desired outcomes; and (4) Systems that are effective and efficient in supporting school personnel's implementation of the identified practices. These elements are integrated, as may be seen from the inclusion of each in the others. Associated with these elements are six principles for implementing PBS: (1) Gathering data, and solving problems and making decisions based on the data collected; (2) Developing a continuum of academic and behavioral supports and interventions based on scientific evidence; (3) Implementing evidence-based behavioral practices accurately and accountably; (4) Organizing the environment to prevent problem behaviors from developing and occurring in students; (5) Universally screening students, and continuously monitoring student progress and performance; and (6) Encouraging and teaching pro-social behaviors and skills in all students.

Functional behavior assessment (FBA)

The FBA focuses not on an undesirable behavior itself, but on the motivations behind it. The purpose is to discover the causes of the behavior, and not just to remove or change those causes, but moreover to substitute a more acceptable replacement behavior for the unacceptable response. All behaviors have some purpose: to get something or to avoid it; the FBA identifies this. First the IEP team must operationally define the behavior: exactly what the student does. Then they make this definition more specific, including when, where, with whom, and under what conditions it occurs; and what happens right before it (antecedents), and right after it (consequences). Data are then gathered on the behavior's likely function and analyzed. The team then formulates a hypothesis regarding the behavior's purpose(s). Then they test this hypothesis for accuracy. If the hypothesis is borne out by further evidence that the behavior accomplishes or seeks the hypothesized purpose, a behavior intervention plan is developed to train the student to accomplish that purpose through more desirable behaviors.

Coordinating behavioral interventions among the stakeholders involved in a cognitively impaired student's IEP (individualized educational plan)

When a student with cognitive impairment engages in behaviors that impede learning for himself and/or others or requires disciplinary action, the student's IEP team must conduct a functional behavior analysis to determine the function or purpose of the behavior. They then develop a behavior intervention plan (BIP). This plan not only manipulates the unacceptable behavior's antecedents and consequences to eliminate or reduce triggering and rewarding it; it also identifies and teaches a replacement behavior to substitute, which accomplish the same function or meets the same need as the undesirable behavior in a more desirable way. However, implementing this BIP only in school will not succeed if, for example, the parents are not implementing it at home, and/or even rewarding the undesirable behavior and/or ignoring instances of the more desirable behavior, sabotaging the BIP. Also, if only certain school personnel are following the BIP but others are not, it will be less effective or ineffective. Behavior modification techniques must be consistent for learning to occur. A BIP should include both short-term and long-term plans.

Behavioral intervention plan (BIP)

A BIP should include specifications for how and how often the student's behavioral progress will be evaluated. Any evaluation instruments or methods should be used before implementing the BIP to establish a baseline level of the target behavior. These instruments and methods are repeated at specified time intervals and compared to baseline for decreases in behavior frequency and/or intensity. A BIP is preceded by functional behavior analysis to determine the behavior's function or purpose. The BIP should not only rearrange the environment to eliminate or decrease precipitating antecedent events and rewarding consequences to the problem behavior, but also teach positive replacement behaviors meeting the same need. Therefore, baseline levels of these replacement behaviors should also be established, and reevaluated at specified intervals to measure their increase. The team must investigate sources of BIP ineffectiveness: If not everybody everywhere (school, home, community) is following it, additional outreach and training are indicated. If everyone is, reinforcements more rewarding to the student may be identified and substituted, and/or different replacement behaviors may be identified and taught.

If a student's behavior interferes with learning and/or demands disciplinary measures, to comply with a provision of the federal law IDEA, the student's IEP team must conduct a functional behavior assessment to determine the function of the behavior, and develop a BIP to teach the student more acceptable behaviors that will accomplish that same function. The team must identify and implement supplementary supports addressing the unacceptable behavior to meet IDEA requirements for education in the least restrictive environment. Once they identify the needs the student is meeting through unacceptable behavior, the team must find functionally equivalent, acceptable replacement behaviors to teach to supplant the unacceptable ones. This involves identifying not only socially acceptable behaviors, but also those appealing to the student's individual interests and making use of the student's particular strengths as well as fulfilling the need heretofore met by the unacceptable behaviors. The BIP aims to control, remove, or alter the environmental antecedents triggering the target behavior and the consequences rewarding it, while concurrently rewarding/reinforcing the replacement behavior being taught.

Manifestation determination review (MDR)

In Michigan, if a disabled student is involved in a behavioral incident that would require disciplinary action by general education rules, the student's parents, pertinent IEP team members, and a school district representative meet to conduct the MDR. The MDR is to determine whether or not the incident was due to or significantly related to disability. Detailed incident description includes pre-incident events; precipitating event(s); incident location and time; others involved; and statements by the student and others before, during, and after the incident. Data sources cited include disciplinary records, report cards, student cumulative record, multidisciplinary evaluation team reports, outside agency reports, teacher and parent oral and written statements, current IEP, and interventions used. Data include related behavior patterns; intervention outcomes; parental insights; behavior, attendance, or grades changes; and IEP areas not being implemented. If the MDR team concludes the behavior is related to student disability and/or failed IEP implementation, the student returns to former placement. If not, the student is subject to general education disciplinary measures.

Psychological trauma

Researchers have found the variables affecting relative trauma in individual students' experiences of a crisis include crisis exposure, relationships with crisis victims, crisis reactions, and perceived threat. Exposure includes proximity and duration: Students not near the crisis event and/or briefly exposed to it suffer less trauma, while those nearer and/or exposed longer suffer more trauma. Crises are understandably more traumatic to students having close relationships with victims, and less traumatic to those having no relationship with victims. Students identified with no crisis reactions can manage their initial responses, and arousal by the crisis subsides with time. Those identified as having severe crisis reactions initially respond with panic or dissociation, and arousal does not diminish over time. Students perceiving low threat are less traumatized than those perceiving high threat. Research finds that the cognitive immaturity of young and cognitively impaired children (that is, with mental ages of 2 to 7 years vs. those mentally 8 to 15 years old) can protect them due to their lack of comprehension of a crisis event.

Student reactions to a crisis

Researchers designate personal factors of resiliency vs. vulnerability in responding to crises. External factors include family resource availability: Living with an immediate family member vs. not living with nuclear family; effective, caring parenting vs. ineffective, uncaring parenting; extended family relationships, support, and guidance vs. familial dysfunction (such as violence, mental illness, or substance abuse); caregivers who cope well with trauma vs. caregiver post-traumatic stress disorder or child abuse/neglect. Social resource availability, another external factor, includes close friendships with peers, positive adult role models, and connections with prosocial groups, as opposed to social isolation and no perceived social support; and having vs. not having adequate financial support. Internal factors include mental health vs. mental illness; high vs. low self-esteem; higher IQ and developmental maturity vs. lower developmental levels; good vs. poor emotional self-regulation; active vs. avoidant coping style; history of adaptive coping with crises vs. history of previous traumatization; internal vs. external locus of control (how much an individual attributes events to oneself vs. to external factors); and having religious beliefs vs. having none.

Referral to one-on-one crisis intervention

GCI is not only most cost-effective and efficient, but it also enables crisis intervention teams, during the group process, to identify students who will need additional one-on-one intervention referrals. Identification is based on these factors: (1) The student manifests suicidal ideations and/or plans. (2) The student is unable to control his/her level of arousal or excitation and emotional reactions. (3) The student displays bizarre behavior and/or signs of dissociation. (4) The student engages overly in self-blame, self-punishment, and/or anger introjected against himself/herself. (5) In students who were direct witnesses to the traumatic event, and/or had close relationships with the event's victims, a lack of any emotional reactions. (6) The student was identified or diagnosed with mental illness or emotional or behavioral disturbance before the traumatic event occurred. (7) The student was injured physically during the traumatic event. Any or all of these factors indicate that the group intervention may not be sufficient and the student requires more intensive, individual intervention.

Enhancing comprehension of responsibilities related to friendships, sexuality, family life, and parenting

Students with lower developmental levels are more likely to be cognitively egocentric—that is, they see everything from their own viewpoint without considering others'. However, while considering others' feelings or opinions may not occur to them, many students can understand this concept with instruction. Comprehending the reciprocal nature of friendships, as well as actions, thoughts and feelings, and words that demonstrate this reciprocity, will help students have successful relationships. Students who mature sexually have normal urges but likely lack knowledge and understanding of consequences like pregnancy, STDs, abuse, and violence. Developmentally appropriate group and individual counseling can help, especially with higher-functioning students. Some students with lower developmental levels and/or previous sexual experiences may always require supervision, while others require continued guidance and support. Cognitively impaired individuals with gainful employment may want to start families. Some may not anticipate being overwhelmed by combined work and family demands, although others may handle these with sufficient emotional and social support. Both should receive intensive counseling before attempting life activities with such significant and far-reaching ramifications.

Group crisis intervention (GCI)

GCI's steps are: (1) Introduction: The group leader explains the purpose of GCI — that when something bad happens, it helps to talk about it to understand what happened, how it affected us, how we can help each other cope; identifies leader and support-facilitators; and reviews GCI's steps and rules. (2) Providing facts and dispelling rumors: The team establishes facts, clearing up misunderstandings. Younger or cognitively impaired children especially are more susceptible to distortions of events and their sources because of developmental and experiential limitations. Facilitators should use simplified language and frequent repetition. (3) Sharing stories: Everyone gets a chance to discuss their experiences, alleviating isolated feelings and fostering positive classmate connections. (4) Sharing reactions: Everyone is given the opportunity to discuss trauma reactions, normalizing these and helping students feel more connected to each other. (5) Empowerment: Making plans and taking actions to repair crisis damage or prevent recurrence helps students feel less helpless and reassume control. (6) Closing: Facilitators help students let go of what they lost, put the crisis behind them, and move on with their lives.

Self-care, care for others, health and fitness, and mobility and travel

Some parents have trained their cognitively impaired children well in all these areas; some in certain skills but not others; some have tried but did not know effective techniques; some did not even know what to teach them; and some did not try. Thus some students need to "catch up" on many basic skills through instruction by trained professionals. However, even students with optimal backgrounds need help with life transitions, since cognitively impaired individuals often have difficulty adjusting to major life changes and unfamiliar situations. Long-term, structured training in self-care, health and fitness, and mobility and travel routines promotes developing habits more likely to continue in new circumstances, although training that bridges old to new settings is also needed to ensure transfer. Very young and cognitively impaired children often demonstrate prosocial, altruistic behaviors, which adults should profusely reward to promote recurrence. They should also directly teach these in real-life situations, as well as through role-plays and discussions. It is far easier to focus training only on transferring long-term, already well-learned skills to new situations.

Transitions between teachers, grade levels, schools, or service options

Whenever possible, it is a very good idea for the current or previous teacher to accompany the student in visiting and getting acquainted with the new or future teacher. This helps the cognitively impaired student by establishing positive associations between the two. It also mitigates fear of the unknown. For some with more severe or profound impairments, it may even help them make the mental connection that the new teacher will have the same or similar role and educational relationship to the student as the previous teacher. This technique is also helpful for transitions to new grade levels, since the earlier teacher is then available to help the new teacher explain to the student additional responsibilities and expectations in the higher grade not experienced in previous grades. Both teachers may collaborate with some students to brainstorm activities and procedures that will bridge and build upon attained skills and familiar habits to new, unfamiliar challenges. With students "graduating" to less restrictive service options, educators should explain how greater responsibility and effort are balanced with greater freedom and independence.

Career planning and success with employment

Parents and school personnel familiar with a cognitively impaired student will likely have identified certain areas of interest to the student, as well as areas of ability and achievement. This knowledge is useful in evaluating and discussing with the student any expressed career aspirations. Some students may not have these. Others, particularly those with deficits in communication skills and/or assertiveness, may have interests in certain occupations but have not said so. In such cases, parents, teachers, counselors, and others should ask them and encourage them to express preferences. They should also apply their observations of student behaviors and activity preferences to matching potential jobs. Education should concentrate not just on remediating student deficits, but also on developing student strengths and interests long-term. This serves to better prepare them for employment. Some programs include preparatory job skills training, unpaid internships for workplace experience, and actual on-the-job training. Educators should help motivated students and parents to procure such situations, plus provide support and counseling during their pursuit.

Working in the Professional Environment

History of disabilities and special education

Special education is a relatively new development in human history. Historically, people with disabilities received little or no education and were frequently placed into asylums or hospitals. The ancient Greek and Roman civilizations viewed disability as an evil omen, punishment from the gods. They viewed people as unable to change. Plato and Aristotle recommended euthanizing disabled infants. Cicero cited need for military superiority as reason to rid society of "defectives." The city/state took charge of soldiers disabled by combat. Due to ancient Greek and Roman philosophies, children born with disabilities were often drowned, "dashed against the rocks" as Homer described, thrown off cliffs, left to die on hilltops, chained up, or locked away. And fathers had the right to end a disabled child's life. In historical Christianity, while various physical ailments were treated as ritual impurities in the Old Testament, the New Testament shows Jesus healing the disabled, emphasizing their need for help and the goodness of helping them.

Middle Ages, the Renaissance, and the Enlightenment
In Medieval times (c. 500–1500 CE), society had a rigid caste system with royalty at the top, and no education for the masses. Some people with disabilities were exterminated; others were exploited as clowns, "fools," or servants. Generally, the disabled experienced ridicule for their differences. During the Renaissance (c. 1300–1700), when interest in knowledge was reborn, the Catholic Church made the disabled wards of the state, caring for them in isolation. They received more humane treatment, but initially no education. By the Enlightenment (c. 1650–1800), philosophers like John Locke believed all knowledge was acquired through the senses and all human beings were equal. Enlightenment philosophers believed humanity did not exist without education, increasing potential opportunities. During the Renaissance, in 1578, Spanish explorer Pedro Ponce de León first documented the education of royal deaf children. In 1760 during the Enlightenment, the French Abbé de L'Épée established the first institute for the deaf. In 1829 (the Regency era), Louis Braille invented his tactile reading/writing system for the blind.

Jean-Marc Gaspard Itard
Itard was a French doctor and educator, among the first to propose and prove special teaching methods could help educate children with disabilities. From 1801–1805, Itard used systematic instructional techniques to teach communication and daily living skills to a boy named Victor, discovered in the woods, seemingly without human rearing. Itard's work was made more famous by director/actor François Truffaut in his 1970 film *L'Enfant Sauvage* (*The Wild Child*). Itard's goals were to socialize Victor, improve his awareness of environmental stimuli, expose him to ideas, teach him to communicate, and advance his thinking from concrete/simple to abstract/complex. Some successes included increased regularity and control in Victor's eating, sleeping, and personal hygiene; improved senses of taste and touch; and increased range of interests. Victor learned to sequence objects and utter a few single-syllable words. However, he never developed connected speech or emotional attachments, and longed for his previous life. Some speculate Victor had intellectual disability or autism, which would also explain why he was likely abandoned at an early age.

Édouard Séguin

French doctor Séguin had studied with Jean-Marc Itard, who insisted that children with disabilities could learn via special instruction. In 1848 Séguin came to America, where he developed influential principles for educating intellectually disabled and other special-needs children. In his programs, he emphasized presenting combined physical and intellectual tasks to help disabled children develop self-reliance and independence. He developed the physiological method, consisting of sensory training (particularly tactile) utilizing concrete materials, and also motor training, featuring movement from the simple to the complex, age-appropriate and functional activities, and activities involving both work and play. The major elements that made up the foundation of Séguin's educational philosophy and programs for instructing children with disabilities were: frequently changing activities; task analysis; discrimination between the senses and the intellect; sensory stimulation; physical education; and education with employment as an outcome. One can see from these elements the importance of Séguin's contributions, as these are all still prominent aspects of special education today over 150 years later.

Maria Montessori

Maria Montessori (1870–1952), an Italian doctor and educator, developed an entire philosophy of education with procedures based on its principles. Today there are many Montessori schools worldwide. While the Montessori method is intended for the general education of all children, it has many benefits for children with disabilities and inclusive education. It is based on the way children naturally learn through exploring and experience. Montessori aimed to enable children's optimal exploration and independent learning. To this end, she proposed the concept of the "prepared environment," a learning environment designed to facilitate this learning process. This environment features an uninterrupted continuum of learning experiences. Montessori schools divide classrooms into multiple-age groups: parent and infant for ages 0–3; preschool, ages 3–6; lower elementary, ages 6–9 and upper elementary, ages 9–12; and middle school, ages 12–14. However, this series of classrooms comprise a "flow" experience, wherein the child continuously constructs and builds upon his/her learning throughout the program. Classroom materials each isolate various single qualities/concepts like color, shape, or size.

20th century

In the 1900s, the emphasis regarding disabilities was more biological than psychological or social. Hence many early pioneers of special education were both physicians and educators. Practitioners followed the medical model, and children with disabilities received institutional care. Between the 1900s and 1950s, laws made education compulsory, and educators created schools and classes for children who were blind, deaf, and mentally disabled. Following World War II, the special education system was established, with an organization parallel to the general education system. In the first of four main periods of special-needs education, children with blindness and deafness were most likely to receive instruction, while many children with other disabilities were still excluded from schools. In the second period, children with disabilities were segregated into homogeneous groups and received medical care and rehabilitation. The third period focused on normalizing and integrating the disabled into the community. In the fourth period, laws have mandated educational equality and inclusion rather than segregation in educational services for all children.

Characteristics of special education

Characteristics of "classic" special education include special settings; for example, segregated schools, classes, or resource rooms. Children are considered special, as evidenced by the way they are categorized, which determines their eligibility for special education and related services. "Classic" special education includes special teachers as well; whether they are trained and/or have experience or not, they are designated as special education teachers. Special education also includes therapists and other specialists trained to assess and remediate various conditions that qualify children for special education and related services. Special education traditionally involves a special teacher-student ratio: classes typically contain fewer students than general education classes, and more teachers per student. Another characteristic of special education is special teaching methods and tools; for example, Braille for the blind, sign language for the deaf, or communication boards/books/systems/software for the nonverbal. Special education also includes special goals, such as integration into the social life of the community, and special programs for teaching needed skills not normally needed by other students.

Advantages and disadvantages of segregated settings

In some cases, special schools and classes are still used today; however, in America and many other countries, laws mandate inclusive education for students with disabilities. Before this legislation, segregation was more the norm than the exception, yielding both advantages and disadvantages. Some advantages include: giving students with disabilities more chances of success; fostering cooperation instead of competition; being able to learn physical and social skills in accepting, understanding settings; staff with specialized training, specialized equipment, and specialized services; more opportunities to improve skills needed for greater participation in more inclusive settings; easier student access to individual attention; and more opportunities to meet other students with the same disability. Disadvantages include: developing "disabled" values, attitudes, and behaviors; lowered expectations in students, parents, and educators; resistance to transferring learned skills to regular settings; depriving disabled and nondisabled children of the benefits of interacting; less preparation for future living; greater lifelong expenses; more interactions with adults than with children; and performance standards separate from "normal" standards.

Medical model vs. social model

Historically, early models of special education were based on the medical model of illness. As special education developed, the medical model came to be gradually replaced by the social model. Some key differences in these models are: The medical model viewed the child as defective, whereas the social model values the child as a unique individual. The medical model focused on diagnosing and labeling children by their disabilities; the social model strives to identify children's strengths and needs. The medical model focused on impairment; the social model focuses on identifying obstacles and developing solutions. The medical model dictated segregation and alternative services for the disabled; the social model dictates making necessary resources available to the disabled within inclusive settings. The medical model resulted in being excluded permanently from normal schools and society, or inclusion only if the individual eventually seemed sufficiently "normal" in appearance and behavior; the social model welcomes diversity. The medical model effected no social change; the social model causes society to evolve.

Overrepresentation of certain groups in special education

For the past 30 plus years, court cases and other legal actions have been filed against the special education system over excessive placement of culturally and linguistically diverse students in disability programs. ESL, low-income, African-American, Latino, and Native American students are commonly overrepresented, particularly in programs for LDs, mild intellectual disabilities, and emotional/behavioral disorders. The National Center for Culturally Responsive Educational Systems (NCCREST) advises parents to consult school administrators and/or parent advocates to investigate whether their school has this problem, because researchers disagree about formulae for assessing overrepresentation. However, they also offer one formula for calculating overrepresentation probability: using low-income students as an example, divide their number placed in (for example) LD classes by their total number in the school = percent placed in LD; calculate the same percentage of average income students in LD classes the same way; and divide the low-income percentage by the average income percentage. A result of + 1.0 indicates equal probabilities of special education placement; > 1.0 indicates greater placement probability for lower income students.

Inclusion

Internationally, in 1948, the Universal Declaration of Human Rights addressed rights to inclusive education, as did the UN Convention on the Rights of the Child in 1989. In 1990, the World Declaration for Education for All addressed inclusion. In 1993, the Standard Rules on the Equalization of Opportunities for Persons with Disability established rights of disabled people to equal opportunities in education and employment. In 1994, UNESCO (the United Nations Educational, Scientific, and Cultural Organization) issued the Salamanca Statement and Framework for Action on every child's basic rights to education, stating that educational systems and programs should address children's diversities; special-needs students require adaptations enabling regular school access; and inclusive regular schools most effectively fight and prevent discrimination and make society inclusive. Significant U.S. laws include Section 504 of the 1973 Rehabilitation Act; the Education for all Handicapped Children Act (EHA) (1975/1986); the Americans with Disabilities Act (ADA, 1990); the Individuals with Disabilities Education Act (IDEA, 1997/2004); and the No Child Left Behind (NCLB, 2001) Act.

Recent and current trends related to technology, inclusion, and early intervention

Technological progress has afforded increased opportunities for both students and teachers in special education. Computer software programs enable students with speech and language and visual disabilities to convert text to speech; hearing-impaired students to convert speech to text; and ESL students to read translations in their native languages. Websites offer students more independent schoolwork at their own pace; multimodal presentations for LD students; and the ability for ADHD students to alternate among shorter units and topics. Students with auditory processing difficulties, and teachers needing more instructional materials, can access more graphic/visual stimuli online. The Internet also facilitates student/parent/teacher access to advocates, support groups, and organizations. Trends are increasingly toward inclusion, with more students mainstreamed than ever. Special classes and schools exist when needs require/parents prefer, but the IDEA's LRE requirement moves more students into regular education classes/curricula/schools. Whereas learning disabilities were previously identified and services recommended in upper-elementary grades or later, today screening, assessment, identification, and intervention are advised by early childhood or even earlier.

Behavior management

The Council for Exceptional Children's Code of Ethics states this principle: "Special education professionals participate with other professionals and…parents in an interdisciplinary effort in the management of behavior." No one approach works with all students in all situations. While classroom management interventions may be ideally designed and implemented, not addressing individual children's needs and wants limits their effects. Hence one/several students in a class/setting may need behavior management strategies targeting specific behaviors. Cognitive interventions can affect emotional behaviors and psychomotor interventions can influence cognitive and affective development. Educators, parents, and others frequently ask about changing individual and group student behaviors; whether to punish or ignore behaviors; whether to discuss behaviors with students; and whether interventions are ethical, harmful, or effective. CEC suggests an educator activity like the following. Small groups list target behaviors and individual/group interventions, discussing whether these treat students with dignity, teach new skills, and support/need environmental analysis; whether student responses are clear to everybody, including students; whether educators respond sequentially to target behaviors (e.g., the second time a behavior occurs).

Classroom management and behavior management

According to researchers (e.g., Smith & Rivera, 1995), to establish/maintain classroom order, teachers should develop positive atmospheres and foundations of positive learning environments; use preventive techniques; develop collaboration with parents and other professionals around disciplinary issues; make sure interventions are appropriate to the problems they address; and regularly evaluate student progress. The goal of behavior management strategies is self-discipline, defined as gaining control over one's behavior in varied situations with various groups and individuals. Some ethical concerns include questions like these: Who decides who will manage behavior and whose behavior will be managed? How can others control behavior managers? Which interventions will be used, and who decides on accepted interventions? For what goals/purposes will interventions be implemented? Are/should children be free to make choices? Are student actions observable, measurable, repeated, and congruent with behavioral principles? In schools: Can externals—educators, peers, parents—change student behavior? Who decides which/whose behaviors to change? What interventions are used in classrooms? And who monitors them?

Under its ethical principle regarding behavior management, the Council for Exceptional Children (CEC) includes the following: (1) Professionals must use only behavioral procedures and disciplinary techniques they have been told to use, and that do not compromise individual student dignity or exceptional students' fundamental human rights (e.g., corporal punishment). (2) Professionals must specify clearly in the student's IEP any goals and objectives related to behavior management. (3) Professionals must comply with rules, statutes, and policies of state and local agencies regarding appropriately applying behavioral and disciplinary practices. (4) When they perceive a coworker's behavior as detrimental to special education students, professionals must take sufficient measures for preventing, discouraging, and intervening with those actions. (4) Professionals must avoid

- 99 -

using aversive methods, unless repeated uses of other techniques were ineffective, and then only after consulting with parents and applicable agency officials.

Educators should always explore alternate behavioral interventions before considering any aversive methods. When considering/planning behavioral interventions, educators should first explore any possible injury or side effects these could cause. Before arranging contingencies to apply to student behaviors, educators should discern whether the student understands the contingency. Anyone implementing any behavioral intervention with a student must both have sufficient training in the procedures and feel comfortable applying the intervention. Interventions should be backed by empirical evidence of their effectiveness; be consistent with student programs and parental input; and have written informed parental consent. Behavioral intervention programs must be closely monitored and thoroughly documented. Procedures of legal due process and committee reviews should be followed. Behavioral interventions/programs should comply with the IDEA's Least Restrictive Environment requirement. Interventions should be commensurate with relative seriousness of the behavior; afford student opportunity to succeed; respect individual student worth and dignity; be fair; and address the principle of normalization (disabled students have rights to lives as close to normal as possible).

Legal requirements of school districts and legal rights of parents

Under current federal laws, all public school districts are required to invite parental participation in meetings regarding the evaluation, identification, and placement of their children in special education; notify parents in writing of any intentions to identify/assess/place their child in special education or change their identification/assessment/placement; notify parents in native languages/formats they understand; inform parents of resources available to help them understand written school notifications; and give parents copies of their legal rights and responsibilities and all procedural safeguards. Parents have the right to give written consent for referral, evaluation, re-evaluation, and placement in special education of their children; review all educational records regarding these; have interpreters supplied when they are not native English speakers; contribute input to all assessments, conversations, and decisions, initially and/or subsequently; request independent evaluations not paid by them if they disagree with district evaluation/diagnosis; participate in eligibility determination and placement; receive copies of evaluations, reports, and eligibility determination documents; and receive regular progress reports during their children's special education program placement.

Children's rights during behavior management process

According to the Council for Exceptional Children, children have rights in the areas of normalization, fairness, and respect. The principle of normalization means that a person with a disability has the right to develop a life that is as close as possible to that of normal persons. The principle of fairness includes not only basic fairness, but also the due process of law. Educators must determine whether a specific intervention they choose for modifying a student's behavior is fair to the student as an individual. The principle of respect means the student has the right to be treated as a human being rather than a statistic or an animal. Educators must measure any intervention in light of this principle. For example, physical or psychological punishment, segregation or isolation, medication, shock, restraints, or other punishments usually violate this principle. Ethics encompassing these principles dictate that in behavior management procedures, the means do NOT justify the end unless the principles of normalization, fairness, and respect have been met.

Confidentiality

The National Association of Special Education Teachers (NASET)'s Code of Ethics contains six principles. Principle 5 states: "NASET Members collaborate with parents of children with special needs and community, building trust and respecting confidentiality." Under this principle, subsection 5-E states, "NASET Members respect the private nature of the special knowledge they have about children and their families and use that knowledge only in the students' best interests." (2006/2007, NASET) The Family Educational Rights and Privacy Act (FERPA, 1974, aka Buckley Amendment) is the primary legislation delimiting accessibility and disclosure of student records. Privacy regarding student participation in evaluation, analysis, and surveys is defined by the Grassley Amendment (1994) to the Goals 2000: Educate America Act of 1994. Records of student drug and alcohol treatment kept by any entity receiving federal funding have protection under the Drug Abuse Office and Treatment Act (1976). In addition to these laws, the Individuals with Disabilities Education Act (IDEA, 1997/2004) protects the confidentiality of records for students receiving special education and related services.

Culturally and linguistically diverse students

School's climate and philosophy

A school's principal should advocate strongly for the well-being and interests of culturally and linguistically diverse students receiving special education and related services. Parents and teachers should consider how the principal shows her/his commitment in this respect. A school's curriculum should reflect the viewpoints, contributions, and experiences of diverse linguistic and ethnic groups. Parents should consider whether a school's principal and staff blame diverse students or their families for different educational performance levels, and whether schools pressure diverse families to embrace school values, or work to incorporate cultural and language differences into their instructional programs. It is important to look for ways in which school administrators and staff demonstrate respect for language and cultural differences. Parents will want to consider whether the environment of a given school is orderly and safe for their children. Additionally, a school should demonstrate high expectations and provide sufficient achievable curricular challenges, both supported by evidence, for all of its students.

Approaches to prevent unnecessary referrals to special education

A school should recognize and incorporate cultural and linguistic differences in their practices related to assessment, curriculum planning and design, and instruction. Considering the demographics of American society today, all/most schools should have ESL programs. Classroom instruction and other school functions should include languages other than English. Schools should have support systems in addition to special education, such as tutoring programs, teacher assistance teams, and bilingual education programs. Schools should collaborate with their communities in established programs. They should also support their teachers via professional development offerings that respond to needs expressed by faculty members and continuing collaboration and consultation of teachers with other professionals. Educators should build upon students' existing knowledge and use interactive discourse to promote both fundamental and higher order student skills for reading, math, and writing. Schools should systematically and continually evaluate student progress and the quality of their programs. Decision-making should include all relevant stakeholders. School educators should include cooperative learning methods and thematic instructional techniques in their teaching.

Assessment

The assessment stage is when professionals collect data used to determine or rule out disability; therefore, parents and cultural diversity experts should be included in the assessment team. Assessment plans should always include multiple instruments and settings to be comprehensive and reflect multiple perspectives and approaches. How student difficulties are addressed and what consequences result across various settings should also be considered. Suspected disabilities in ELLs should be assessed in a student's dominant language. Educators should gather data on student proficiency and educational achievement in both his/her first language and English. Assessment teams must obtain parental perceptions, beliefs, values, and expectations about children's learning/behavioral challenges. Schools should avoid interpreters and test translations. However, if these are unavoidable, they should document interpreter skills; ensure multiple formal and informal assessments and information sources; use peers from normative groups; and, if tests are invalidated, seek performance patterns rather than absolute scores. With behavioral referrals, educators should consider obtaining more information to corroborate interpretations of projective instruments, which can be subjective.

Eligibility determination and placement

Parents of culturally and linguistically diverse backgrounds should become involved in all stages of the special education process if their children are referred. In addition to being included on referral and assessment teams, parents as well as cultural diversity experts should be included in decision-making for eligibility determination and placement. This team should consider whether a student's difficulties are caused by a possible disability, cultural/social differences, or both. Immigration, switching schools, and school absences should be considered. Evidence of different sources of student difficulty should be provided. If a student is identified with a disability, parents should determine whether the school has specific plans for reviewing the student's circumstances in the future, determining whether the student might be reclassified. If a student is determined eligible for special education, parents should know whether team members work for placement in the least restrictive environment and seek proof/evidence of such efforts. They should find out if students with the same disability type and age are placed in similar programs and why..

Special education referral process

Because diverse students are frequently overrepresented in special education referrals, their parents should be included on referral teams, as well as persons with expertise regarding cultural diversity. Educators should review these factors before recommending comprehensive evaluations: the school and classroom climate; all attempts at pre-referral intervention and their results; any temporary problems in the classroom, home, and/or community; educator effort in building on students' cultural experiences and knowledge and their strengths; and observations by parents when possible, and by qualified others with knowledge of cultural differences, of the student's current classroom—particularly if the referral is for behavior management, as these problems can be influenced by teacher behavior management approaches. In addition, it is only appropriate to refer ESL/ELL students if: students have good communication skills in their native languages but are behind peers in English, and instructional adaptations have been implemented; students are academically proficient in English, receive effective reading instruction, and still demonstrate significant reading problems; and/or effective ESL or bilingual instruction do not improve academic English-language skills.

Collaboration between special educators and general educators

As all teachers have various strengths and needs, special educators should share these. General educators are likely less familiar with specialized resources for matching practices to student skill levels when these are far beneath grade level; special educators are likely less acquainted with the richness of grade-level projects and activities. Both types of teachers can pool their knowledge of proactive/preventive and disciplinary techniques, and two pairs of eyes can better prevent misbehavior and identify desirable behavior to reinforce. General educators have training in using and instructing students with many kinds of software; special educators contribute working familiarity with assistive technology. For routine planning, special and general educators can help each other develop simple student routines. While structure and content often easily combine in general education, special-needs students must learn how assignment directions are structured before addressing assignment contents. Teachers can use tracing/matching routines to plan independent student activities. Praise motivates teachers as well as students: collaborating special and general educators should regularly praise each other's successes verbally.

When collaborating, teachers must schedule *at least* one weekly planning session, even if it must be after school. Co-teachers will fail through unmet expectations and lack of communication without such planning. As in any relationship, co-teachers do not know everything about one another. They must share their ideas and experiences, not only to succeed in teaching their students, but to understand their own teaching and learning processes and to experience job satisfaction. Teacher collaboration processes will undergo changes, just as students discover new concepts over time through their teachers and their instructional methods. While these changes mean that co-teachers and students alike will encounter surprises and adjustments, they also mean that teachers will develop better ways of meeting student needs. Collaboration also affords teachers new perspectives. They can take advantage of these by making focused observations and asking reflective questions whenever not directly occupied in instructional delivery. Taking brief but specific notes helps co-teachers discuss observations later, troubleshoot/problem-solve, fine-tune instruction, and communicate student successes.

Regardless of which co-teacher is leading a lesson/activity at the time, both should be actively interacting with students, which includes physical movement: one's viewpoint is narrowed when sitting at one's desk/in a classroom corner, whereas moving about enables a global view. Co-teachers should determine shared organizational goals and periodically review these. During the school year, considering organization is often sacrificed under time pressures; however, small enhancements in organization can have major influences. Co-teachers can examine their total classroom environment for smooth flow of activities and how well students stay organized. Special educators can contribute techniques to establish regular external structures for students with deficits in executive functioning who do not generate such structure internally. They can help general education teachers with monitoring students and supporting their organizational needs through simple structures incorporating task analysis for following step-by-step routines, visual cues, and instruction in self-monitoring routines. Co-teachers should reflect on their entire process, analyze it, and respond. They can experiment with co-teaching methods they could not use individually.

<u>Curriculum and data collection</u>

Many special educators, such as special education resource teachers, often teach students in multiple grades. To support their students' various educational needs, the special education teacher must know the general education curriculum. When this teacher works with multiple grade levels, s/he has to know multiple different curricula. This teacher must also collaborate with all students' general classroom teachers to ensure s/he supports what they teach. This entails both making time and being organized to speak with each teacher individually. Special education teachers must also provide data for each student, to document instruction that implements the student's IEP and document their reports of student success or difficulty in each area. They must monitor data collection, analyze data, and adjust instruction accordingly. They need the cooperation of general education teachers in collecting data when they are not in the general classrooms with students. While parents/others may volunteer to help collect data, special education confidentiality laws can prohibit volunteers without permission from the parents of every student in class.

Communicating and collaborating with community agencies

When special education students have already had interactions with some government departments like the juvenile justice system, the mental health system, or the department of social services, those agencies may initiate contact with schools/teachers. In other cases, educators may need to contact them. Community agencies dedicated to children with disabilities and all those working with/for them serve as liaisons/links to public and private schools and government departments, local officials, and legislators. Some community agencies offer services like direct representation; educators can invite them to IEP meetings and due process mediations and hearings on behalf of disabled students and their families to ensure effective advocacy, information, and support. Teachers can help get parents training on their rights and special education services from community agencies. Community agencies can provide professional educators and families with consultations on technical assistance for students with disabilities. If parents and school districts disagree, educators can enlist mediation services from some community agencies to prevent escalation into court cases.

Working with other professionals, teaching aides, assistants, and paraprofessionals

When educational research investigates high turnover rates among special educators, some researchers have thought the voluminous paperwork in special education was responsible, only to hear from some special education teachers that they attribute turnover more to being appreciated less than general education teachers. Special education teachers often must coordinate their schedules with art teachers, music teachers, physical education teachers, and 10–20 other teachers, and also show consideration to physical therapists, occupational therapists, and speech-language pathologists, as well as accounting for lunch and recess when making resource schedules. Even minor changes in general education teachers' schedules can alter the special education teacher's whole day or week. Most special education teachers are enormously grateful to their aides, assistants, and paraprofessionals; however, the reality is they must also devote significantly more time and effort to train them and create daily schedules for them. A teacher's aide differing in opinion from the teacher's, especially if the aide is older/more experienced than the teacher, presents an additional challenge to teamwork, for which the teacher is responsible.

Standards for credentials and employment of special education professionals

Some of the Council for Exceptional Children practice standards for special education professionals in credentials and employment include: represent oneself accurately, legally, and ethically regarding their expertise and knowledge to prospective employers; assure that those representing themselves and/or practicing as special education administrators, teachers, and related service providers have the qualifications of professional credentials; operate within their limits of professional skills and knowledge, and appropriately seek consultation and/or support from sources outside themselves as necessary; comply with contractual terms of employment; comply with policies and contracts of local education agencies for notifying them when terminating their positions; advocate for supportive and suitable educational conditions, and for staffing resources sufficient to keep absences of support staff or substitute teachers from causing special education services to be denied; and get professional help for personal problems affecting work performance.

In addition to nine others, the CEC (Council for Exceptional Children) identifies standards for special education professionals that include: documenting and reporting objectively any deficits in resources, and offering solutions for these to their supervisors/administrators; evaluating employment applicants and grievances objectively, without discrimination; utilizing established procedures to resolve professional workplace problems; expecting their responsibilities to be conveyed to coworkers, and assuring their understanding and respect of those responsibilities; requesting clear written statements of their employment conditions, duties, and responsibilities; participating actively in planning, management, and evaluation of special education programs and general education programs, and in associated policy development; expecting sufficient support and supervision for special education professionals, and for programs delivered by qualified professionals in special education; and expecting there to be clearly defined chains of accountability and responsibility regarding the supervision and administration of professionals in special education.

Professional development

Special education professionals cannot allow their training, knowledge, and expertise to remain at the same level throughout their working lives as when they received their degrees and certification and began working. They must continually update, improve, and expand their skills, both to remain current in this dynamic, changing profession and to grow as educators. Special education professionals acquire and apply knowledge about developmental levels and readiness for various instructional interventions. They learn about research evidence-based instructional strategies, and then apply these for teaching fundamental skills in literacy and numeracy to students with special needs. They know how to individualize their instruction for each student, and they continue to learn new strategies and techniques to improve this individualization process. They assess student progress on an ongoing basis and refine their assessment techniques to increase their accuracy and applications to adjustments and modifications in their instructional approaches. They make use of data and continually inform themselves of newer data from emergent research to apply to their problem-solving endeavors. They prepare students to become independent.

In the area of professional development, the Council for Exceptional Children (CEC) has standards that include: systematically keeping individualized plans for their own professional development, designing these to increase their own skills, knowledge, and cultural competence to sustain high competency levels; keeping current in their knowledge of laws, policies, and procedures related to their practices; systematically and objectively evaluating themselves, their coworkers, and their programs and services to enhance their professional performance continually; advocating for effective, schoolwide professional development and individual professional development plans being provided by their employing agencies; participating in supervised, systematic field experiences for special education professional candidates as a part of their educator preparation degree and certification programs; and functioning as mentors for other special educators in whichever times, places, and circumstances that their doing so is appropriate.

A number of organizations offer professional development courses. For example, the National Association of Special Education Teachers (NASET) has many classes. Professionals can learn more about modifications for alternative assessments; the annual and triennial review processes; assistive technologies for students with disabilities; ADHD, anxiety disorders, autism, pervasive developmental disorders, bipolar disorder, depression, Down syndrome, eating disorders, emotional disturbances, epilepsy, LDs, intellectual disabilities, orthopedic impairments, multiple disabilities, PTSD, Rett syndrome, schizophrenia, speech-language disorders, spina bifida, Tourette syndrome, traumatic brain injuries, blindness and visual impairments, deafness and hearing impairments, and deaf-blindness; auditory processing disorders; developmental and psychological disorders in special education; criteria for eligibility determination for special education services related to each disability; educational implications of some disorders; factors influencing curriculum for special-needs students; identification of high-risk students in classrooms; developing, writing, implementing, reviewing, and modifying IEPs; medications; services related to special education; team transitional planning; and helping students cope with disasters and violence.

Self-assessments

Many school districts and systems have created self-assessment rubrics or instruments for special educators. These instruments generally list specific standards for an array of required skills and knowledge, including operational definitions that describe what knowledge, skills, and behaviors the special educator should demonstrate. These descriptions are accompanied by incremental rating scales. The educator reads each competency and checks a box corresponding to whether s/he thinks s/he, for example, models it, adjusts upon reflecting, and is a resource for others (the highest score); or works independently to apply the competency across settings and self-initiates planning (the second highest); applies the competency with support and shows emerging self-initiation of planning (the middle score); understands and tries to apply the competency, and uses resources for improving his/her teaching (the second lowest); or is aware of the competency but has no experience in and/or does not demonstrate it (the lowest score). Another example states competence areas for self-rating as highly effective, effective, minimally effective, or ineffective.

Strategies to reflect on effectiveness of work

Research finds viewing video recordings of their teaching practices in combination with collaborative professional development courses and activities helps teachers enhance and change their practices. In one pilot study (Osipova, et al, 2011) teachers viewed many video recordings of themselves teaching throughout the school year. They self-reflected, noting what they did effectively, generating suggestions for future teaching, and rating their instruction. The researchers found this process altered teachers' initial self-reflections overestimating their practices to more critical self-examinations. It changed teachers' self-reflection comments, vague at first, to more specific descriptions. Teachers particularly realized they attended to certain students and not others. Because not all teachers apply what they learn in professional development to their classroom practices, researchers find guided/coached critical self-reflection instrumental for changing teacher beliefs about learning and teaching, which are frequently unspoken and even unconscious. Teachers are more likely to change their practices once they change their beliefs, and also when they view themselves as learners. Video self-reflection affords self-analyses with multiple foci, and also repeated self-analyses of teaching practices.

Milestones in the history of special education in the United States

Following World War II, parents began organizing advocacy groups for disabled children. The American Association on Mental Deficiency first convened in 1947. Starting early in the 1950s, the Civil Rights movement's emphasis on equal rights for all people contributed to more parent groups like the Muscular Dystrophy Association, United Cerebral Palsy Association, and John F. Kennedy's Panel on Mental Retardation. Local and state access to schools for disabled children increased in the 1960s. However, by 1970 U.S. schools still enrolled only 20% of disabled children. Many state laws excluded blind, deaf, and cognitively impaired children. The Education for All Handicapped Children Act (EHA/PL 94-142, 1975) provided federal funds for special education, guaranteeing disabled children a free, appropriate public education in the least restrictive environment. State-level parent training and information centers were added to the provisions in 1983, and infant early-intervention programs and preschool educational services in 1986. A 1990 reauthorization renamed the law the Individuals with Disabilities Education Act (IDEA), with succeeding reauthorizations and expansions since.

Legal issues and standards in the education of students with cognitive impairments

When a student has difficulty in school due to cognitive problems, typically schools will first implement classroom interventions to facilitate the student's learning process. If these fail, they then refer the student for special education assessment. Federal laws dictate parents have the right to due process; that is, if they disagree with the school's assessment results, identification of their child's disability, and/or educational placement decisions, they are entitled to dispute these; to participate in mediation procedures; and if these fail, to a due process court hearing where an administrative law judge adjudicates decisions regarding assessment, identification, and/or placement. Parents should know their child's identification or diagnosis with disability, even one included in the categories listed under the IDEA Section 504 of the Rehabilitation Act, does not necessarily confer eligibility for special education services. The disability must additionally affect the student's school performance or functioning. Federal law also protects the confidentiality of disabled students' records, which cannot be made public except by court order, or shared with others (with certain exceptions) without written, informed parental consent.

Contemporary trends in special education for the cognitively impaired

Historically, many cognitively impaired children received no interventions or special services until school attendance, when it became apparent their school readiness was delayed or that they learned more slowly or could not perform at age/grade level. More recently, research has shown the significant benefits of early intervention with infants and toddlers in homes and communities. Providing cognitive stimulation earlier often accelerates the development of children with deficits, optimizing growth and school adaptation. Whereas historically these children were segregated for separate educational treatment, the IDEA's mandate of free, appropriate public education in the least restrictive environment possible drove the trend toward inclusion. Disabled students have increasingly been mainstreamed into regular schools and classes, with educators adopting classroom modifications, accommodations, and individualized instruction to enable participation in learning. Humanistic psychologist Carl Rogers' "person-centered therapy," as well as the IDEA, influenced individualized educational planning overall in addition to required IEPs. The Internet has afforded parents more access to early intervention information and community resources. PCs and software enable students to transcend cognitive, neurological, vision, hearing, speech, physical, emotional, and behavioral deficits to learn, communicate, and work.

ESEA and NCLB federal laws regarding students with disabilities

Public pressure beginning in the 1950s motivated the federal government to address the educational needs of economically disadvantaged and disabled children. President Lyndon Johnson passed the Elementary and Secondary Education Act (ESEA) in 1965 to remedy inequities for low-income, minority, bilingual, and disabled students. Amendments to ESEA in 1966 specifically benefited disabled students: (1) Congress founded the National Advisory Council and Bureau of Education of the Handicapped; and (2) Title VI authorized creating and funding educational programs for disabled students, including state grants to schools and institutions serving this population. ESEA has been estimated to have tripled federal spending on K-12 students. When ESEA was enacted, Southern Democrats feared federal involvement in segregated locations, while Republicans feared total or excessive federal authority in education. No Child Left Behind (NCLB, 2001) used ESEA as its foundation and requires schools and educators to be accountable to the federal government for educational outcomes with disadvantaged students. Neither law was written expressly for disabled students, yet both had huge impacts on opportunities, resources, and programs in special education.

No Child Left Behind Act (NCLB)

One significant benefit of NCLB is affording greater flexibility to local and state educators in how they use federal funds. Another is requiring "highly qualified" teachers. Stressing early literacy for young children is an additional boon. Sanctions, including other schools and busing, imposed on schools failing to meet yearly progress standards afford parents more school choices, but these are also viewed as costly and punitive to schools. NLCB requires annual standardized or alternative assessments, reasonable classroom accommodations, and special education teacher qualifications. Criticisms of NLCB include unrealistic standards; difficulty in implementation; underfunding relative to requirements; rigid assessments and guidelines; "all-or-nothing" lack of differentiation between individual subgroups and subjects failed within some schools vs. all subgroups and subjects failed in others; neglecting multiple forms of academic evaluation; focusing on mathematics and reading to the detriment of other subjects; overlooking individual students' annual progress in favor of passing a test; wasting money and resources on sanctions, not teaching; and states' potentially constructing easier standardized tests in response to pressure for yearly progress.

Family Educational Rights and Privacy Act (FERPA)

All schools receiving federal funding under U.S. Department of Education programs are subject to FERPA. Parents of minor child students, and students aged 18 years or attending post-secondary schools, have the right to review the school's records on the student, and to request schools' corrections of records they find misleading or inaccurate. If schools refuse, parents and students have the right to a formal hearing. If schools still refuse following the hearing, parents and students have the right to add a statement to the records regarding the information they dispute. FERPA requires written consent from parents or postsecondary (or age 18 and above) students to disclose records. Exceptions include school officials with valid educational motives, other schools when students transfer, evaluating or auditing officials, financial aid personnel, groups conducting research on behalf of or for a school, accreditation organizations, by court order or subpoena, health and safety emergency officials, and local or state juvenile justice system authorities. Schools may disclose student directory information without consent, but with sufficient advance notice to allow students and parents to request nondisclosure. Schools must notify parents and students of their FERPA rights yearly.

Michigan Professional Educator's Code of Ethics

Adopted by the Michigan State Board of Education (2003), this code articulates the ethical standards in job performance expected of professional educators. Its principles are: (1) Service toward common good: The main goal of professional educators is supporting all learners' growth and development, to the end of developing and sustaining an informed citizenry in our democratic society, (2) Mutual respect: Every individual's intrinsic value and dignity are respected by professional educators, (3) Equity: Professional educators advocate for every individual's equal access to educational opportunities, (4) Diversity: By valuing and honoring individual differences and supporting all individuals' strengths, professional educators advance cross-cultural awareness and assure that the world's diversity and realities are reflected in education, and (5) Truth and honesty: Professional educators demonstrate trustworthy behaviors and professional and personal integrity; follow current state laws, national and state guidelines for student assessment, and socially acceptable practices; and apply solid professional judgment.

Section 504 of the Rehabilitation Act

Section 504 of the Rehabilitation Act of 1973 is a civil rights law prohibiting discrimination against disabling conditions by federally supported programs or activities. Unlike the IDEA, Section 504 does not require additional federal funds for disabled students, but it does require schools to offer reasonable accommodations for them; and if the Office of Civil Rights finds an area of noncompliance with Section 504, a school can lose federal funding. Fewer regulations and procedural criteria in Section 504 than in the IDEA allow more flexibility, but they also allow schools to provide students less monitoring and support. The IDEA is confined to ages 3 through 21 years and focuses more on public education; Section

504 is life-long and thus protects the rights of disabled individuals in education, plus employment and public access to transportation, buildings, and other public facilities. Both laws address identification, eligibility, education, and due process; however, their specific criteria differ. For example, the IDEA requires school districts to evaluate all in-district children suspected of disabilities, while Section 504 does not.

Council for Exceptional Children (CEC)'s Code of Ethics for Educators of Persons with Exceptionalities

Adopted by its Delegate Assembly in 1983 and published in its Policy Manual in 1993, CEC's Code of Ethics for special educators specifies that special education professionals: (1) Have commitment to promoting optimal potential in exceptional individuals for education and quality of life, (2) Further and sustain high levels of expertise and ethics in professional practice, (3) Participate in professional endeavors benefiting exceptional students, their families, and/or other colleagues, students, or research participants, (4) Practice their professions exercising objective, professional judgment, (5) Work to further their skills and knowledge relative to the education of students with exceptionalities, (6) Operate within the policies and standards of the special education profession, (7) Work to observe, and when indicated, better the laws, policies, and regulations controlling how special education and related services are delivered and how their profession is practiced, and (8) Refuse to participate in or condone illegal or unethical actions, or to violate the professional standards adopted by the CEC's Delegate Assembly.

Lifelong professional development for special educators

Special educators should join professional organizations designated for their profession. Students still in school for teacher preparation may often join these organizations prior to graduation or certification. Such organizations confer access to attending workshops and conferences, important for updating their knowledge as the field changes and advances; for supplementing basic preparation courses with additional learning they did not have time for during formal degree or certification programs; and for studying certain areas in greater depth, to address issues in their specific student populations and their own pedagogical interests. Organizations offer discounts on publications, courses, and continuing education credits. They additionally provide educators with the opportunity for direction and contact information for local resources, including mentors. Professional organizations' websites allow convenient access to journals, books, and other publications to keep educators informed of new research studies' findings; and laws, issues, trends, and practices in their field. For teachers embroiled in everyday teaching challenges, this helps them find solutions and look beyond immediate details and problems to the deeper level of philosophies and principles. Organizations also afford interaction, sharing, and support among members.

Practice Test

Practice Questions

1. According to Jean Piaget, the earliest stage of human cognitive development is:
   a. Preoperational
   b. Concrete Operations
   c. Sensorimotor
   d. Formal Operations

2. In Sigmund Freud's developmental theory, the anal stage occurs approximately between the ages of:
   a. Birth and 18 months
   b. 18 months and 3.5 years
   c. 3.5 years and 6 years
   d. 6 years and puberty

3. The stage in Erik Erikson's theory of psychosocial development most associated with adolescence is:
   a. Autonomy vs. shame and doubt
   b. Intimacy vs. isolation
   c. Industry vs. inferiority
   d. Identity vs. role confusion

4. Which of the following is true if your 20-month-old child is speaking in two-word phrases?
   a. Your child's language development is normal.
   b. Your child's language development is delayed.
   c. Your child's language development is advanced.
   d. Your child's language development is unclassifiable.

5. What percentage of babies can walk by their first birthday?
   a. 90
   b. 50
   c. 100
   d. 33.3

6. Most toddlers are able to hop or jump with both feet off the floor by or around the age of...
   a. Two years
   b. One year
   c. Three years
   d. Four years

7. Which of the following did Lev Vygotsky's social development theory say about cultural tools like speech and writing that humans develop?
    a. Children develop these tools to serve necessary social functions
    b. Children develop these tools to communicate their needs and wants
    c. Children develop higher thinking skills by internalizing these tools
    d. Children accomplish all of these results by developing these tools

8. According to Lev Vygotsky's theory of social development, the zone of proximal development is...
    a. The distance between a student's ability to do a task and a more knowledgeable other's ability to do the same task
    b. The distance between a student's ability to do a task with adult/peer help and his/her ability to do the same task alone
    c. The distance between a student's inability to do a task and the same student's later ability to perform the same task
    d. The distance between a student's ability to do a task without instruction and his/her ability to do it after instruction

9. Which of the following is a stage that someone cannot become fixated in, according to Sigmund Freud's theory of psychosexual development?
    a. Genital
    b. Latency
    c. Phallic
    d. Oral

10. Which of the following stages is typically associated with the oldest ages in Erik Erikson's theory of psychosocial development?
    a. Generativity vs. stagnation
    b. Trust vs. mistrust
    c. Ego integrity vs. despair
    d. Intimacy vs. isolation

11. Which of the following statements is true regarding individuals with autism spectrum disorders?
    a. Some people having autism spectrum disorders have intellectual disabilities and some do not
    b. Every individual with an autism spectrum disorder has some degree of intellectual disabilities
    c. Individuals having autism spectrum disorders do not typically also have intellectual disabilities
    d. Individuals having autism spectrum disorders have a specialized form of intellectual disabilities

12. Which of the following is most likely to be a symptom in a person with an autistic disorder?
    a. Impairment in their social skills and interactions
    b. Deficits in communication skills and behaviors
    c. Restrictions in their interests and activities
    d. All of the above are symptoms of autistic disorders

13. Which of the following statements is most accurate regarding learning in individuals with intellectual disabilities?
    a. People with intellectual disabilities learn in very different ways than people with normal IQs do
    b. People with intellectual disabilities learn the same way that other people do, but at slower rates
    c. People with intellectual disabilities learn the same way as others, but only to a certain degree
    d. People with intellectual disabilities learn things as well as others, but cannot retain their learning

14. About what percentage of babies are born with Down syndrome to mothers under the age of 35?
    a. 30 percent
    b. 50 percent
    c. 80 percent
    d. 20 percent

15. Genetically, individuals with Down syndrome have:
    a. A missing chromosome
    b. Two broken chromosomes
    c. Malformed chromosomes
    d. An extra chromosome

16. Which of the following medical disorders is not commonly associated with Down syndrome?
    a. Hypothyroidism
    b. Hyperthyroidism
    c. Heart disease
    d. Vision disorders

17. What percentages of children with Down syndrome have significant hearing loss, at least unilaterally?
    a. 66 to 89 percent
    b. 34 to 57 percent
    c. 22 to 45 percent
    d. 42 to 65 percent

18. Between five and 13 percent of children with Down syndrome have seizure disorders. This range is:
    a. Five times more often than the general population
    b. Ten times more often than the general population
    c. About the same as the rate in the general population
    d. Three times more often than the general population

19. Mothers of infants with Down syndrome usually find breast or bottle feeding them takes longer. This is primarily not due to:
    a. Tongue protrusion
    b. Hypotonic muscles
    c. Low mental ability

d. Small oral cavities

20. Early in life, children with Down syndrome are _____ to develop leukemia.
    a. Equally likely as other children
    b. Less likely than other children
    c. Twice as likely as other children
    d. 10-15 times more likely than other children

21. Tommy is a second-grader referred to the speech-language pathologist for delayed language development. He has a seizure disorder controlled by pharmacotherapy. In therapy sessions, his attention wanders, he sometimes responds slowly, and he appears markedly sleepy. The most likely explanation for these observations is:
    a. Intellectual disabilities
    b. Medication effects
    c. An autistic disorder
    d. A behavior disorder

22. The current consensus is that an individual's intelligence is best measured by:
    a. Scores on tests of intellectual ability only
    b. Evaluations of adaptive behaviors only
    c. Both intellectual and adaptive functions
    d. Neither intellectual nor adaptive ability

23. Which of the following is not an assessment type on MI-Access, a Michigan state alternative assessment for students with disabilities?
    a. Assessment for students with profound cognitive impairment
    b. Assessment for students with moderate cognitive impairment
    c. Assessment for students with mild cognitive impairment
    d. Assessment for students with severe cognitive impairment

24. Which of the following is a type of assessment recommended for English Language Learners (ELLs)?
    a. Teacher observations
    b. Portfolio assessment
    c. Performance assessment
    d. All the above

25. A task analysis involves:
    a. Analyzing a task that a student has completed to find patterns in types of errors
    b. Analyzing a task to identify potential problems for some students
    c. Breaking a task down into smaller, separate steps to achieve one at a time
    d. Correlating task difficulty with a student's level to ensure appropriateness

26. The Vineland Adaptive Behavior Scales are among the most popular tests of adaptive behavior in the United States. Which of the following is not one of the other most widely used adaptive behavior tests in the country?
    a. Scales of Independent Behavior-Revised (SIB-R)
    b. The AAIDD Adaptive Behavior Scales (ABS)
    c. Inventory for Client and Agency Planning (ICAP)
    d. All of the above are the most widely used AB scales

27. The Scales of Independent Behavior-Revised (SIB-R) tests gross and fine motor skills. Which of the following does it not assess?
    a. Personal living skills
    b. Community living skills
    c. Social and communication skills
    d. All of the above are assessed by the SIB-R

28. Which of the following is not included on the maladaptive behavior scale of the Scales of Independent Behavior-Revised (SIB-R)?
    a. Internalized
    b. Externalized
    c. Antisocial
    d. Asocial

29. The Support score on the Scales of Independent Behavior-Revised (SIB-R) and the Service score on the Inventory for Client and Agent Planning (ICAP) are both:
    a. Combinations of the adaptive and maladaptive behavior scores
    b. Derived from certain components of the adaptive behavior scales
    c. Derived from certain components of the maladaptive behavior scales
    d. Obtained from a scale separate from the adaptive and maladaptive scales

30. Which of the following is true regarding the of Scales of Independent Behavior-Revised (SIB-R), the standard form of the Vineland Adaptive Behavior Scales, the American Association on Intellectual and Developmental Disabilities (AAIDD) Adaptive Behavior Scales (ABS), and the Inventory for Client and Agency Planning (ICAP)?
    a. They all give comparison scores for students with/without disabilities
    b. They all supply intercorrelations among their own different subscales
    c. They all give discriminating analyses for school placement and intellectual disabilities level
    d. All of the above are incorporated components in their analytical content

31. Which of the following tests is not an alternative or developmental instrument for assessing intelligence?
    a. Hawaii Early Learning Profile (HELP)
    b. Miller Assessment for Preschoolers (MAP)
    c. Learning Accomplishment Profile-Revised (LAP-R)
    d. Bayley Scales of Infant Development, 2nd ed. (BSID-II)

32. Which of the following is not a test to assess intelligence in students who do not use verbal communication (i.e., speech, writing)?
    a. The Merrill-Palmer Scale
    b. Raven's Progressive Matrices
    c. Leiter International Performance Scale-Revised
    d. All of the above are nonverbal tests

33. For which students would a nonverbal intelligence measure be appropriate?
    a. Deaf students
    b. Autistic students
    c. Students with INTELLECTUAL DISABILITIES

d. All the above

34. Which of the following CAMS (compensations, accommodations, modifications, strategies) for students with cognitive impairment is not designed to maintain student concentration?
    a. Reducing clutter in the student's work environment
    b. Making daily to-do lists and checking off items done
    c. Increasing natural lighting or full-spectrum lighting
    d. Permitting earphones with music or white noise

35. Which of the following CAMS (compensations, accommodations, modifications, strategies) for students with cognitive impairment is not designed to manage memory problems?
    a. Supplying students with flow charts and other pictorial diagrams
    b. Permitting students to make audio/video recordings of lectures
    c. Giving instructions to students in both oral and written versions
    d. Providing environmental cues to help locate materials/supplies

36. Which of the following would not be included under the Present Levels section of an Individual Education Plan (IEP)?
    a. Results of standardized tests
    b. Teacher/parent observations
    c. Student strengths and needs
    d. Need for assistive technology

37. Under which section of a student's IEP (Individual Education Plan) would an ESL or ELL student's English proficiency be included?
    a. Present Levels
    b. Transition Services
    c. Special Considerations
    d. Procedural Safeguards

38. According to the IDEA 2004 law, when do students become involved in their own transition planning as a part of their IEP (Individual Education Plan)?
    a. When the student reaches the age of 14
    b. When the student reaches the age of 16
    c. The ages vary by the individual student
    d. Students are never involved at any age

39. Which of the following is the poorest example of an IEP goal?
    a. "John will stay in his seat during classroom seatwork periods."
    b. "John will raise his hand to get the teacher's attention in class."
    c. "John will keep his hands to himself while in the classroom."
    d. "John will improve his behavior while he is attending school."

40. What are the words represented by the acronym SMART relative to ideal IEP goals?
    a. Specific, Measurable, Achievable, Relevant, Time-Limited
    b. Specialized, Modifiable, Accurate, Rationalized, Temporary
    c. Socializing, Memorable, Accountable, Real, Task-Oriented
    d. Scholastic, Mentally challenging, Active, Rotating, Truthful

41. Which of the following strategies would apply both to working effectively with your staff and to managing your students' stressors and feelings?
    a. Giving written instructions for activities/tasks
    b. Writing clear expectations for responsibilities
    c. Giving praise and other positive reinforcement
    d. Writing down short-term and long-term goals

42. Which of the following is not a strategy for helping cognitively impaired students stay organized and meet deadlines?
    a. Using personal data devices and wrist watches or timers
    b. Reorganizing tasks for only the most important and basic goals
    c. Breaking assignments down into smaller increments/steps
    d. Assigning mentors/coaches to guide students with goals

43. Which of the following is the best strategy for helping cognitively impaired students manage frustration and stress?
    a. Let students make phone calls during the school day to doctors/other support sources
    b. Let students take breaks during the school day to use stress management techniques
    c. Refer students experiencing stress to student assistance and/or counseling programs
    d. All of the above are effective strategies for helping students manage frustration and stress

44. How is sensitivity training for peers and school staff likely to affect cognitively impaired students' management of stress and frustration?
    a. It is likely to help cognitively impaired students
    b. It is likely to help the staff, but not the students
    c. It is likely to help the students, but not the staff
    d. It is likely to be of no help to any of the parties involved

45. Which of the following teacher responses is least likely to help cognitively impaired students manage changes?
    a. Scheduling regular meetings with students to review progress and talk about school concerns
    b. Instructing such students that they must accept that change is a normal part of everyday life
    c. Acknowledging that changes in the school setting and/or staff are difficult for these students
    d. Ensuring students can communicate openly with new and old staff for smoother transitions

46. Which of the following is least likely to support the stamina of a cognitively impaired student during the school day?
    a. Having the student take breaks more often
    b. Permitting the student to take longer breaks
    c. Planning uninterrupted student working time
    d. Allowing flexibility in scheduling student time

47. Which of the following teacher strategies can best address both cognitively impaired students' frustration/stress and their limited stamina?
    a. Assigning class work that the students can do at their own pace
    b. Affording students the option of working from home part-time
    c. Allowing students longer times for learning new responsibilities
    d. Permitting students time off from school to receive counseling

48. Which of the following is generally more conducive to preventing exhaustion in cognitively impaired students?
    a. Occasions to participate in cooperative/collaborative learning activities
    b. Being assigned to complete individual learning activities that are timed
    c. None of the above are conducive to preventing exhaustion
    d. Both (a) and (b) are equally conducive to preventing exhaustion

49. Which of the following is essential to teachers' establishing rapport with their students?
    a. Being able to stay calm
    b. Having a positive attitude
    c. Initially setting boundaries
    d. All of the above are essential

50. Which of the following is true regarding teachers' monitoring their relationship with their students in class?
    a. When a teacher has good rapport with students, they will never get bored
    b. Observing students' body language is not a reliable way to assess interest
    c. Teachers with good student rapport can more easily revive flagging energy
    d. None of the above is true regarding teacher-student relationships

51. Once a teacher has established rapport with his/her students, which of the following is not true about maintaining that rapport?
    a. The teacher's motivation inspires the students' motivation
    b. Student engagement with content does not affect behavior
    c. The teacher's past issues with a student must not be retained
    d. The teacher's fairness and flexibility will foster students' respect

52. Which of the following is least likely recommended by educators for teachers to develop rapport with students?
    a. The teacher should get to the classroom early before the class begins
    b. The teacher can write "Welcome" and the students' names on the board
    c. The teacher should avoid informal chatting with students before class
    d. The teacher could greet each student when he or she arrives for class

53. Which of the following would be the most effective way for a teacher to prepare a nonverbal autistic student to use a computer for communication?
  a. The teacher models using the computer and then observes the student as s/he imitates the teacher's model
  b. The teacher has the student practice the typing and mousing actions needed before actually using the computer
  c. The teacher repeats instructions several times, speaking slowly and clearly, inviting questions from the student
  d. The teacher gives the student printed instructions and a computer and lets him/her work with it independently

54. Which of the following is most accurate about cultural diversity in families of students with cognitive impairments?
  a. Families from other cultures are still likely to place priority on teachers' recommendations
  b. Families in the cultural minority experience more stress due to their children's disabilities
  c. Culturally sensitive teachers promote better attitudes toward disability in diverse families
  d. A family's view and position toward disability is greatly affected by its cultural background

55. Anthony, who just turned 16, has mild cognitive impairment, with a short attention span and trouble generalizing learned material to new situations. He is meeting with his teacher prior to an IEP meeting for transition planning. His teacher wants to prepare him to self-advocate. Which of the following would be the most appropriate way to do this?
  a. Relating his current intellectual and adaptive functioning status to potential job choices
  b. Showing him examples of other students' transition plans and their participation in them
  c. Helping him name his post-graduation interests and relating them to jobs and living choices
  d. Explaining government regulations and their impact on his choices following high school

56. Which of the following students is most likely to need help with developing the social skills of starting and participating in conversation and cooperating with others for school and job success?
  a. A student with an autistic disorder
  b. A student with Down syndrome
  c. A student with seizure disorder
  d. A student with cerebral palsy

57. Which student is least likely to need help with staying on task to perform school or job activities?
  a. A student with moderate intellectual disabilities
  b. A student with an autism spectrum disorder
  c. A student with attention deficit/hyperactivity disorder
  d. All of the above would need equal help

58. Which of the following would enhance the communication skills of a student with verbal deficits?
a. A picture board/book that represents various needs, wants, and emotions
b. A chart with a photo/drawing representing each step in a set of directions
c. Separating printed text into cards containing smaller, illustrated portions
d. All of the above would enhance a verbally challenged student's communication

59. Eleni is a mainstreamed deaf student who uses American Sign Language (ASL). Which of the following actions is most appropriate to facilitate her communication with peers, faculty, and staff at school?
a. Teach Eleni speech reading so she can communicate with the hearing
b. Transfer Eleni to a school for the Deaf where everybody is using ASL
c. Teach Eleni's teacher, classmates and school staff some use of ASL
d. Teach Eleni Total Communication, which uses both ASL and speech

60. Which of the following is not a strategy that would help improve self-control in a student with attention deficit hyperactivity disorder (ADHD)?
a. Providing the student with schedules/routines in advance
b. Explaining the consequences for misbehaving beforehand
c. Plan specific goals and give rewards for achieving those goals
d. If the student argues, counter him/her with a better argument

61. Which of the following would promote more behavioral self-management in students with ADHD?
a. Finding an activity that the student is interested in/enjoys and encouraging it
b. Setting a very short time limit for desired behavior and gradually increasing it
c. Teaching the student to channel excess energy into meeting classroom goals
d. All of the above would promote better student behavioral control/management

62. Diego's family belongs to a culture that values collectivism and cooperation. They have come to America, where the culture values individualism and competition. Which of the following strategies would make Diego's education in the United States more familiar to his cultural background?
a. Assigning him to participate in a collaborative learning exercise
b. Assigning him to one of two teams trying to win a class contest
c. Assigning him to do an individual project and present it in class
d. Assigning him to supervise a class group to promote leadership

63. Patrick is a young man with mild cognitive impairment and mild autistic symptoms who has expressed a desire to learn to count money. He is not interested in the numerical process or the denominations of bills and coins; his main motivation is to pay for items in a store without having to go shopping with his mother. Which of the following would be the most helpful strategy for his visiting therapist to use?
a. Sit with him and teach the value of each bill and coin using real money
b. Go to the store together and show him at the cash register how to pay
c. Practice by playing the cashier, then go to the store and shadow him
d. Suggest that he go to the store independently and try his best to pay

64. If a cognitively impaired student has generally acquired a good amount of academic knowledge but has gaps or areas with missing information, the best teaching strategy is:
    a. To teach only the rudiments of the areas of missing information
    b. To teach missing information for mastery in the acquisition phase
    c. To teach the basics in acquisition and work toward mastery later
    d. To enhance existing knowledge rather than teaching new things

65. Which of the following is the best example of integrating academic skills into everyday routines for cognitively impaired students?
    a. Having a student write down a daily schedule or to-do list
    b. Having a student complete a set of math exercises in class
    c. Having a student read a book chapter and give an oral report
    d. Having a student practice preparing and serving a meal

66. Stan has mild cognitive impairment and is approaching graduation. He is being considered for a warehouse job. The managers agree he is capable of performing the work, but with the reservation that he will need additional initial instruction. Which of the following is the best arrangement his teacher can make to support Stan's transition?
    a. Ask the vocational rehabilitation counselor to accompany him at first
    b. Ask other employees to help Stan until he can work independently
    c. Ask a job coach to train Stan initially and gradually fade this support
    d. Ask Stan's supervisor to make time for 1:1 training at the beginning

67. You are teaching various functional living skills to your cognitively impaired class in a school environment. Which of the following would not facilitate their transferring this learning to the life situations where they need to use them?
    a. Teaching your students very general cases
    b. Giving them a broad variety of examples
    c. Offering them a wide range of settings
    d. Teaching specific cases for generalizing

68. Stephanie has moderate cognitive impairment and has learned a number of functional living skills, but is inconsistent in applying them. Which of the following should her teacher do to improve her consistency?
    a. Make ongoing progress assessments and adjust teaching accordingly
    b. Have Stephanie do the same task in exactly the same way repeatedly
    c. Take advantage of the inconsistency by assigning a diversity of tasks
    d. Focus only on the tasks that Stephanie can perform more consistently

69. Rico's behavior is characterized by impulsivity, and he does not seem to learn well from the consequences of his actions, even when they are rather punishing. Which of the following would be the most effective approach to behavior management for him?
    a. Explain the consequences of his behaviors in advance
    b. Focus positive behavioral support on antecedents
    c. Alter the consequences for undesirable behaviors
    d. Use only positive reinforcement, nothing negative

70. Which of the following types of intervention has generally been found most successful with students with poor self-regulation, disinhibited behavior, and aggression?
    a. Attribution training
    b. Metacognitive tools
    c. Cognitive-behavioral
    d. Antecedent-based

71. Which of the following is not one of the goals of conducting a functional behavior assessment?
    a. To determine the purpose(s) of an individual's problem behavior(s)
    b. To develop a plan to change variables that perpetuate the behavior
    c. To identify measures that will suppress and eradicate the behavior
    d. To teach suitable replacement behaviors via positive interventions

72. Which of the following is not a component of a functional behavior assessment?
    a. Defining what things comprise a targeted problem behavior
    b. Planning for, collecting, and analyzing data on the behavior
    c. Developing, implementing, and monitoring intervention plans
    d. All of the above are parts of a functional behavior assessment

73. When you are interviewing other teachers and/or parents to get information for a functional behavior analysis, you should ask certain questions, such as, "Who is there when the behavior occurs?" Which of the following choices is a poor example of other questions you should ask?
    a. "What happens right before and right after the behavior occurs?"
    b. "How is the student feeling when s/he engages in the behavior?"
    c. "When and where does this behavior occur?"
    d. "When and where does this behavior not occur?"

74. With regard to behavioral observation and assessment, what does the A-B-C form denote?
    a. Antecedent-Behavior-Consequence
    b. Alphabetized ordering of behaviors
    c. A student's knowledge of the alphabet
    d. Alternative Behavior Consequences

75. Which of the following is the best example of defining a student's problematic behavior?
    a. "Rebecca's behavior in the classroom is disruptive"
    b. "Rebecca's behavior interferes with class lessons"
    c. "Rebecca is out of her seat and yelling during class"
    d. "Rebecca's behavior is distracting to classmates"

76. Caitlin, 15, has severe cognitive impairment and can do work tasks sorting items. Her main work obstacle is that she frequently does not put down favorite objects that she likes to hold in her hands. One tactic her instructor uses is to give positive reinforcement in the form of verbal praise whenever Caitlin lets go of favorite objects to do her work. Which of the following is not another technique that could help?
   a. Reward Caitlin for working faster with time off work to hold her favorite objects
   b. Give Caitlin a smaller number of items to sort, such as one third of the usual number
   c. Teach Caitlin to raise her hand to ask for a break from work when she needs it
   d. All of the above are techniques the instructor could use to enhance Caitlin's working

77. In general, which of the following are the main functions of any kinds of problem behaviors?
   a. To get or obtain something
   b. To get away from something
   c. Both (a) and (b)
   d. Neither (a) nor (b)

78. Carly has mild cognitive impairment and was taught in a self-contained classroom for elementary school. She is progressing to a junior high school where she will have to go from one classroom to another for each period. Her sense of direction is impaired and she is not used to this routine, so she has difficulty getting to classes on time. Which of the following would be the best strategy to help her transition?
   a. Having an orientation and mobility trainer accompany her for the first few weeks
   b. Giving her a simple, clear map/floor plan of the school with color-coded rooms and routes
   c. Assigning a school "buddy system" whereby other students take turns helping her
   d. Explaining the situation to Carly's teachers and asking them to excuse her lateness

79. Eugene has a cognitive impairment and is nearing high school graduation. He has a good idea of what areas/fields he has both ability and interest in, but he is not sure what kind(s) of job(s) within those fields would be a good match for him. Which of the following represents the best order in which to use the strategies indicated?
   a. Paid on-the-job training, application to a school-to-work program, career counseling services, student internship
   b. Application to a school-to-work program, paid on-the-job training, student internship, career counseling services
   c. Student internship, career counseling services, application to a school-to-work program, paid on-the-job training
   d. Career counseling services, application to a school-to-work program, student internship, paid on-the-job training

80. Audrey is a high school teacher who will be getting three new mainstreamed deaf or hard of hearing students this year. These students can all read and write Standard English, but they primarily use American Sign Language (ASL) to communicate. Audrey wants to take a course in ASL, but realizes that this will not help her immediately. In the meantime, which of the following websites will help her learn a number of signs that she can use for basic communication with her deaf students?
    a. Michigan State University's "American Sign Language Browser"
    b. "Literary Resources for Teaching Deaf Children" at about.com
    c. "Strategies for Teaching Students with Hearing Impairments"
    d. All of the above would be equally helpful for Audrey's goal

81. When parents have concerns about their cognitively impaired children, on which of the following topics can a teacher provide them with tips and resources?
    a. Opportunities for conversations with their children
    b. Ways to teach their children how to control anxiety
    c. Techniques to teach their children to keep a journal
    d. All of the above are appropriate topics with tips and resources

82. Parent-teacher conferences may be requested by parents, teachers, school psychologists, social workers, or counselors for various reasons. Of these, who is most responsible for the relationship between the parents and the school?
    a. The parents are most responsible
    b. The teacher is most responsible
    c. Other school professionals are most responsible
    d. All of the above are equally responsible

83. Which of the following is not a good strategy for creating an atmosphere that encourages parents to participate in their child's IEP meetings?
    a. The members of the school's IEP team sit facing the parents and student across the table
    b. The teacher tells parents before the meeting what it will cover and how they can take part
    c. All IEP meetings begin with first parents, then teachers, identifying the student's strengths
    d. School team members show respect for student and family when discussing student needs

84. According to family systems theory, which of the following is not accurate?
    a. School settings and school-family relations are affected by family dysfunction
    b. Systems practitioners often get schools involved with family-based problems
    c. A student's problem behaviors in school have their origins within the student
    d. Systems practitioners often get families involved with school-based problems

85. Lia and Poe work with students having cognitive impairments and physical disabilities. They plan a field trip for a small group of students. The school has a limited number of wheelchair vans, and while public buses stop on campus frequently, the buses with wheelchair lifts stop there less often, and only at certain times. Lia and Poe have submitted a requisition in advance for a van. However, when one van breaks down, a team that made a prior requisition gets the last one. With their first plan ruined, which of the following is the best alternative?

    a. They tell the students they will have to reschedule their field trip for another day
    b. As a backup plan, they got the schedule of lift bus stops on campus and take one
    c. They report to their supervisor that they were denied a van despite a requisition
    d. All of the above would be equally acceptable alternatives for this team to take

86. Which of the following is not an example of integrating and applying therapy services into the daily routines of cognitively impaired students?

    a. Having a student receiving speech-language therapy for delayed language development use a word-a-day calendar at home to increase her vocabulary
    b. Having a student receiving physical therapy gradually increase the time he spends standing rather than sitting while getting dressed in the mornings
    c. Having a student receiving occupational therapy for fine motor skills apply learned OT techniques to brushing her teeth and setting the table
    d. All of the above demonstrate adequate ways of integrating and applying therapy services into the daily routines of cognitively impaired students

87. Which of the following is the least likely location for a community service program for preschoolers administered by a county school district?

    a. A psychological counseling clinic
    b. A Head Start or other preschool
    c. A special education therapy group
    d. A community child care center

88. Which of the following is the least likely school employee needed to collaborate with the special education teacher in planning a comprehensive educational program for a cognitively impaired first grade student?

    a. The classroom teacher
    b. Therapists (OT/PT/SLP)
    c. A vocational instructor
    d. The school social worker

89. Andrew has a cognitive impairment and also uses a wheelchair. His chair will not fit through the doorways of many rooms in his new school. As a special education teacher, who might you consult with about this?

    a. The principal of the school
    b. The school facilities manager
    c. The occupational therapist
    d. With any and/or all of the above

90. A special education teacher who instructs a class of multiply handicapped students within a regular public school will most likely consider which of the following an advantage?
  a. Peers and resources for the students
  b. Inclusion and integration of students
  c. Peers and resources for the teacher
  d. All of the above are advantages in this case

91. What began the history of special education in the United States?
  a. Grassroots advocacy groups formed by parents of exceptional children
  b. Grassroots advocacy groups formed by teachers and educators
  c. New legislation passed by the government at the federal level
  d. New legislation passed by the governments at the state levels

92. Which of the following organizations for special needs children was not formed in the 1950s?
  a. The Muscular Dystrophy Association
  b. The United Cerebral Palsy Association
  c. John F. Kennedy's Panel on Mental Retardation
  d. All of the above organizations were formed in the 1950s

93. Which of the following American Presidents established the President's Committee on Intellectual disabilities?
  a. John F. Kennedy
  b. Lyndon B. Johnson
  c. Richard M. Nixon
  d. George H. W. Bush

94. Which of the following is not a correct statement about the Family Educational Rights and Privacy Act (FERPA)?
  a. When passed in 1974, FERPA prohibited schools with federal funding from disclosing personal information from student records without consent
  b. As it was amended in 2009, FERPA now allows schools with federal funding to disclose personal information from student records without consent
  c. As it was amended in 2009, FERPA now allows schools with Federal funding to disclose student information without consent if needed to protect health/safety
  d. One of three areas of the 2009 amendments to FERPA was prompted by a major 2007 incident involving murders at a technical and state university

95. Which of the following is least accurate regarding reasons for educational inclusion of cognitively impaired students?
  a. The majority of students are found to learn better in inclusive settings
  b. Educational inclusion supports development of students' self-esteem
  c. Inclusion teaches all students what equal rights and equal value mean
  d. Federal law mandates that all students must have inclusive educations

96. The National Association of Special Education Teachers (NASET) states that the term "high-quality professional development" for teachers refers to the definition of professional development found in Title IX, Section 9101(34) of:
    a. ESEA
    b. IDEA
    c. ADA
    d. ADEA

97. Which of the following is not one of the ethical principles found in the Michigan Professional Educator's Code of Ethics?
    a. Having respect for every individual's intrinsic value and dignity
    b. Promoting equal access to educational opportunities for all
    c. Sustaining expectations that challenge exceptional learners
    d. Supporting cross-cultural awareness and recognizing diversity

98. Which code of ethics includes a principle that specifically prohibits doing or allowing anything that harms people with special needs?
    a. The Michigan Professional Educator's Code of Ethics
    b. The Council for Exceptional Children's Code of Ethics
    c. Both (a) and (b)
    d. None of the above

99. Special educators who participate in professional organizations and activities are likely to benefit most from this participation by:
    a. Advancing their careers in terms of their pay grades and job titles
    b. Learning more of the history and philosophy of special education
    c. Obtaining information from their fellow educators by networking
    d. Upholding the highest standards regarding professional practices

100. Which of the following is the best way for a parent to advocate for a child with cognitive impairment?
    a. Joining (an) organized advocacy group(s)
    b. Mounting individual efforts for advocacy
    c. Engaging a professional special advocate
    d. It depends on the individual and situation

Answers and Explanations

1. C: Piaget termed the earliest stage of cognitive development Sensorimotor (c), which is characteristic of infants. They are learning about the input they receive from the environment through their senses, and about their motor activities and what impacts they have on the environment. The Preoperational (a) stage follows the Sensorimotor stage and is typical of toddlers/early childhood. The stage of Concrete Operations (b) is typical of middle childhood, and the stage of Formal Operations (d) characteristically emerges just before or during adolescence.

2. B: The Anal stage corresponds to the approximate ages between 18 months and 3.5 years (b). This is the period of toilet training, when Freud theorized that the child's focus of erotic attention is the anal area as bowel control is learned. From birth to about 18 months (a) is the Oral period, when the baby is nursing and erotic focus is thus on the mouth area. Ages 3.5 to 6 years (c) corresponds to Freud's phallic stage, when the child discovers his or her genitals and focuses on them. Freud termed the time from around 6 years old to puberty (d) as the Latency stage, when sexual and aggressive urges are submerged while the child focuses outward on school activities and social relationships.

3. D: In Erikson's theory, the stage of identity vs. role confusion (d) is when adolescents are developing their personal identity and sense of self. Erikson's stage of autonomy vs. shame and doubt (a) corresponds to early childhood (around 2-3 years of age) when children are developing feelings of control and independence. Erikson's stage of intimacy vs. isolation (b) is associated with young adulthood, when people form intimate relationships with others. His stage of industry vs. inferiority (c) typically occurs during the school years before adolescence, around 6-11 years of age, when children learn to accomplish new academic and social tasks.

4. A: Your child's language development would be perfectly normal (a) if s/he is speaking in two-word sentences, which is considered typical between the approximate ages of 18 and 24 months. Your child's language development would not be delayed (b) in this example; using only two-word utterances could classify a child's language development as delayed at the age of 36 months, when a child should normally be using multiple-word utterances and grammatical features. Your child's language development would not be advanced (c) in this example; a child who uses two-word utterances before the ages of 9-18 months would be considered advanced in language acquisition. It is not true that the child's language development is unclassifiable (d), as there are age norms for each developmental stage.

5. B: About 50 percent (b) of babies can walk by their first birthday. 90 percent (a) of those that cannot walk by the age of one year can typically walk by the age of 15 months. It follows that not all babies, or 100 percent (c), can walk by their first birthday. Because about half of all babies can walk by the age of one year, the figure of 33.3% (d) is incorrect.

6. C: Most toddlers can hop or jump with both feet off the floor by around the age of three years old (c). Most toddlers cannot do this at the age of two years (a), but they can walk up and down stairs holding onto a railing or someone's hand. These activities are both examples of gross motor skills. About half of babies can walk by the time they are one year

- 128 -

old (b), but those who can walk by this age have not developed the gross motor coordination to hop up and down with both feet. Four years old (d) would be a later age than is normal for a child to be able to do this.

7. D: Vygotsky believed that children accomplish all of these results by developing these tools (d). He stated that children initially develop such cultural tools as speech and writing only as a way to accomplish basic social functions that they need (a); in other words, at first they only develop such tools as language to communicate what they need or want (b) to others. Vygotsky further posited in his theory that as they grow older and come to internalize such cultural tools, and that internalization enables children to develop higher, more abstract thinking skills (c).

8. B: Vygotsky defined the Zone of Proximal Development (ZPD) as the distance between a student's ability to perform a task guided by an adult or collaborating with a peer and the student's ability to perform that task independently (b). Vygotsky identified this zone as the area wherein learning takes place. The adult or peer who helps the student is the More Knowledgeable Other (MKO); the ZPD is not the distance between the student's ability and the MKO's ability to do a task (a), nor is it the distance between a student's inability and later ability to perform a task (c). It also does not represent the distance between a student's ability to do the task without instruction and his/her ability to do it after being instructed (d).

9. A: According to Freud's theory, a person cannot be fixated in the Genital (a) stage, because this was his final stage of psychosexual development after puberty. Freud considered a well-adjusted adult to be in this stage for the rest of his/her life, but fixation involves earlier developmental stages which were not resolved successfully. Thus a person could be fixated in the Latency (b) stage, wherein sexual urges and aggression are not expressed; in the Phallic (c) stage, wherein the individual is as preoccupied with his/her genitals as the child who is just discovering them; or in the Oral (d) stage typical of nursing babies, wherein an older child or adult engages in excessive oral activities.

10. C: Erikson identified the stage of ego integrity vs. despair (c) as typical of adults in old age, when they review their lives and feel either satisfaction and peace, or regret and bitterness at how they have lived. Erikson's stage of generativity vs. stagnation (a) corresponds to middle adulthood, when people either feel a sense of accomplishment by creating a legacy for posterity, or feel superficially connected to society for not having done this. Trust vs. mistrust (b) is the stage Erikson assigned to infants, who learn either to trust in the environment when their early needs are sufficiently and consistently met, or to mistrust the world when their needs are inadequately or inconsistently met. The stage Erikson called intimacy vs. isolation (d) is associated with young adulthood, when people either succeed at forming intimate relationships, or they fail and become isolated.

11. A: The only true statement is that some people with autism spectrum disorders have intellectual disabilities and some do not (a). About 50 percent of persons diagnosed with some form of autistic disorder are also diagnosed with intellectual disabilities, while the other half has normal IQ scores; of these, many are highly intelligent. Therefore it is not true that every person with an autistic disorder has some degree of intellectual disabilities (b). It is, however, not true either that individuals with autism do not typically also have intellectual disabilities (c), as both diagnoses are found in about half of those with autism. Autism is also not a specialized form of intellectual disabilities (d). It does have specific

symptoms, and both autism and intellectual disabilities result from neurological deficits, but the autism spectrum constitutes a separate class of disability from that of INTELLECTUAL DISABILITIES.

12. D: All of the answers provided are symptoms of autistic disorders (d). One of the core domains of dysfunction in autism is social (a): Autistic individuals typically have difficulty interpreting others' social cues and interacting socially, and frequently never develop normal social skills. Another core domain is communication (b): Among those with autistic disorders, some do not develop functional speech, and some speak excessively and have difficulty with interacting in conversations. Even with adequate verbal development, most autistics have trouble using and understanding nonverbal, pragmatic communication functions, such as eye contact, voice modulation, facial expression, and body language. They tend to take speech and action literally and not understand figurative usages. Another feature of autism is restricted interests and activities (c): Autistic people tend to focus exclusively on one or a few things.

13. B: The most accurate statement is that people with intellectual disabilities typically learn by the same process as others, but at slower rates (b). Therefore, age norms for those with normal IQs do not apply for developmental or educational milestones. It is thus not accurate to say that people with intellectual disabilities learn in very different ways than others (a), or that people with intellectual disabilities can only learn up to a certain amount (c). Depending on individual differences and the kind of instruction, a person with intellectual disabilities may be able to learn a great many things, albeit more slowly than others. It is also incorrect to state that people with intellectual disabilities cannot retain what they learn (d). Although many intellectually disabled individuals require more repetition to learn something, once that learning is solidified, many people with intellectual disabilities will never forget what they have learned, even more so than others.

14. C: About 80 percent (c) of babies with Down syndrome are born to mothers under age 35. In spite of the fact that both the risk and the prevalence of Down syndrome increase with maternal age, the majority of cases are still not those with older mothers. Thus many more than 20 percent (d), 30 percent (a), or even 50 percent (b) of Down syndrome babies are born to mothers below the age of 35.

15. D: Genetically, individuals with Down syndrome have an extra chromosome (d) for a total of 47 instead of the normal 46. This is known as Trisomy 21; of 23 pairs of chromosomes, pair number 21 has an extra third copy in every cell. Down syndrome is not caused by a missing chromosome (a), two broken chromosomes (b), or by malformed chromosomes (c).

16. B: Hyperthyroidism (b), or an overactive thyroid gland, is not commonly associated with Down syndrome; however hypothyroidism (a), or an underactive thyroid gland, is slightly more prevalent in the Down syndrome population. Congenital heart disease (c) affects about half of all Down syndrome children. Vision disorders (d) are also associated with Down syndrome in early life, and about three percent of Down syndrome babies have congenital cataracts.

17. A: A significant hearing loss, defined as a loss of more than 15 to 20 dB (decibels) in at least one ear, is diagnosed in 66 to 89 percent of children with Down syndrome (a). Hearing testing is important due to this very high incidence of hearing losses in this population. The

ranges of 34-57 percent (b), 22-45 percent (c), and 42-65 percent (d) are all understatements of the prevalence of hearing loss found in children with Down syndrome.

18. B: Although the 5-13 percent incidence of seizure disorders in children with Down syndrome is not as high as that of other medical conditions associated with Down syndrome, it is still ten times more frequent than in the general population (d). Therefore, the prevalence of seizure disorders among the Down syndrome population is not five times more than in the general population (a), but double that. This is far more than three times as frequent (d), and is definitely not about the same as the rate of seizure disorders in the general population (c).

19. C: Nursing Down syndrome infants takes longer, but this is not due to lower mental abilities (c) in the babies. Down syndrome can cause anything ranging from profound intellectual disabilities to normal IQs, but suckling is a brain stem reflex, not a higher cerebral function. The main factors causing nursing to be slower in Down syndrome infants are their tongue protrusion (a), their typical hypotonia causing a weak sucking action (b), and the fact that their oral cavities are smaller than normal (d).

20. D: Children with Down syndrome are actually 10 to 15 times more likely than others to develop leukemia (a blood or bone marrow cancer which can be fatal) early in life (d). Therefore, they are not equally likely as other children (a) to develop leukemia, not less likely than other children (b) to develop leukemia, and far more than twice as likely as other children (c) to develop leukemia.

21. B: The most likely explanation for Tommy's behaviors is side effects of his seizure medication (b). Many such drugs cause excessive daytime sleepiness, which leads to inattention and interference with cognitive processing. The question does not indicate any diagnosis or symptoms of intellectual disabilities (a), only a medicated seizure disorder. Autistic disorders (c) were also not indicated because slow responses and sleepiness are not signs of autism. Individuals with autism may be socially withdrawn, but they are more often intensely focused (even if on something other than the therapy session) than displaying wandering attention. In a second-grader, a behavior disorder (d) would likely have more symptoms of acting out, aggression, impulsivity, defiance, lack of empathy, etc., as well as inattention (depending on the specific disorder), but not sleepiness and slow reactions.

22. C: Currently, experts agree that intelligence is best assessed by measuring both intellectual ability with standardized IQ scales and adaptive skills that enable one to perform daily life activities and function in society (c). Historically, only intelligence test scores (a) were used to measure intelligence. While adaptive behaviors are very important, especially in individuals with cognitive impairment as they may be able to perform a great many adaptive functions, these should not be used alone (b) because IQ measures give important information relative to vocabulary, numerical ability, memory, comprehension, processing speed, etc., which can help determine appropriate educational placement and planning. As a result, measuring neither intellectual nor adaptive ability (d) is necessarily incorrect.

23. A: As of 2005, MI-Access did not include an assessment for students with "profound" cognitive impairment (a). MI-Access does include Interim Phase 2 BRIGANCE, a commercial test tailored for Michigan students demonstrating mild cognitive impairment (c); Supported

Independence, an assessment for students functioning at the moderate level of cognitive impairment (b); and Participation, an assessment designed for students who demonstrate severe cognitive impairment (d).

24. D: All of the answers provided are recommended (d) for assessment of ELL students. This is because educators recommend varying the assessment strategies used with ELLs. Experts at the Northwest Regional Educational Laboratory as well as many others, name observations (a), portfolios (b), and performance assessments (c) as examples of ways to vary assessment strategies when testing students who are learning English as a second language.

25. C: A task analysis involves breaking a task down into smaller, separate steps to achieve one at a time (c). Many cognitively impaired students (among others) may be unable to learn a complex task with many steps, but if they learn one step at a time, the teacher can teach each successive step, and then teach the first two steps connected, then the first three, etc. Behaviorism calls this chaining when each step is new learning, and shaping when previously learned behaviors are connected. Task analysis does not refer to analyzing a completed task for error patterns (a), does not mean analyzing a task to identify problem areas for certain students (b), and is not defined as correlating task difficulty with student level (d).

26. A: All of the answers provided represent the most widely used AB scales (d). The Scales of Independent Behavior-Revised (SIB-R) (a), which measures overall independence based on a combination of adaptive and maladaptive behaviors, is designed for ages three months to 80 years and up, and includes short forms for children and the blind. The AAIDD (American Association on Intellectual and Developmental Disabilities) Adaptive Behavior Scales (ABS) (b) has a form for schools and another for residential and community settings, and both forms assess an individual's way of managing his/her environment's natural and social exigencies. The Inventory for Client and Agency Planning (ICAP) (c) measures adaptive and maladaptive behaviors using items from the SIB-R, plus demographics, diagnoses, required and received support services, and social and leisure activities.

27. D: The Scales of Independent Behavior-Revised (SIB-R) assesses skills in all of the answers provided (d). It has sections to evaluate personal living skills (a), community living skills (b), and social and communication skills (c). It also incorporates a scale for assessing maladaptive behaviors.

28. C: The maladaptive behavior scale in the Scales of Independent Behavior-Revised (SIB-R) does not include "Antisocial" behavior (c). It is divided into Internalized behaviors (a), which include hurting oneself, displaying repetitive behaviors, and being withdrawn or inattentive; Externalized behaviors (b), which include hurting others, destroying property, and being disruptive; and Asocial behaviors (d), which include being socially offensive and uncooperative.

29. A: The Support score on the Scales of Independent Behavior-Revised (SIB-R) and the Service score on the Inventory for Client and Agent Planning (ICAP) are both combinations of each test's respective adaptive and maladaptive behavior scores (a). They are not derived only from components of the adaptive (b) or maladaptive behavior scales (c), nor are they obtained from a separate scale from the adaptive and maladaptive behavior scales in their respective tests (d).

30. B: The only true statement is that these tests all supply intercorrelations among their own different subscales (b) to show relationships among their individual test components. It is not true that they all give comparison scores between students with and without disabilities (a). Only the SIB-R and the ICAP provide this information for age-matched populations. None of the four tests give discriminant analyses to aid with school placements and determining level of intellectual disabilities (c); again, only the SIB-R and the ICAP supply these. Therefore, it is not true that these tests all incorporate all of these components (d).

31. D: The Bayley Scales of Infant Development, 2nd ed. (BSID-II) is not an alternative or developmental instrument for assessing intelligence (d), it is a standardized test for assessing intellectual functioning. The Hawaii Early Learning Profile (HELP) (a), the Miller Assessment for Preschoolers (MAP) (b), and the Learning Accomplishment Profile-Revised (LAP-R) (c), however, are all alternative or development instruments for assessing intelligence in children who cannot be tested using the usual standardized instruments due to various disabilities or impairments.

32. D: All of the listed answers are nonverbal tests of intelligence (d). The Merrill-Palmer Scale (a) is for assessing intellectual functioning in children from 18 months to four years old. Raven's Progressive Matrices (b) have three levels: one that is colored for mentally and physically handicapped students, one that is standard for students aged 6-16 and 17+ years, and one that is advanced for students aged 12-16 and 17+ years. The Leiter International Performance Scale-Revised (c) is for children aged 2 to 18 years.

33. D: A nonverbal intelligence test would be appropriate for all of the students listed (d). Deaf students (a), especially those deaf from birth and those who only use sign language, are at a disadvantage when taking many standardized IQ tests based on written and spoken language. Autistic students (b) frequently have deficits in verbal skills which prevent them from demonstrating their intellectual competence. Students with intellectual disabilities (c) also often have verbal deficits. Some students with autism and/or intellectual disabilities are completely nonverbal.

34. B: Making daily to-do lists and checking off items as they are done (b) is not designed to maintain student concentration; it is a CAMS (compensation, accommodation, modification, strategy) designed to help students stay organized and meet deadlines. Examples of CAMS for maintaining concentration include helping students reduce clutter in their work environment (a); increasing the natural light or providing full-spectrum lighting (c); and letting students wear earphones with calming music, white noise, or environmental sounds (d). These CAMS facilitate focused attention and eliminate distractions.

35. A: Supplying students with flow charts and other pictorial diagrams (a) is a CAMS designed to help them manage deficits in problem-solving skills, as they provide visual representations of the steps to follow in solving a problem. Permitting students to record lectures (b) is an example of CAMS to help students manage memory deficits if they cannot retain the information they hear. Giving students instructions in both spoken and written forms (c) is another example of CAMS for students who have trouble remembering, as it reinforces information through redundancy while also delivering the information in two different modalities, aural and visual. Giving students environmental cues to help them

locate materials or supplies (d) is also designed to assist students who cannot simply remember where things are on their own.

36. D: A student's specific need for assistive technology (d) would not be included under the Present Levels section of the IEP, but in the Special Considerations section of the IEP. Results of standardized tests (a) the student has taken, observations of the student by teachers and parents (b), and the student's educational strengths and needs (c) would all be included in the Present Levels section of the IEP. Note: Each of the student's needs identified in this section must be addressed either in the Educational Goals and Objectives section or in the Specially Designed Instruction under the section for Related Services, Accommodations, Modifications, or Supplementary Aids and Services.

37. C: If a student is learning English as a Second Language (ESL) or is termed an English Language Learner (ELL), then that student's English proficiency level would be included under the Special Considerations section of the student's IEP (c). This section also covers physical, communicative, and behavioral challenges that interfere with education. The IEP's Present Levels (a) section covers findings from formal tests, informal observations, and strengths and needs. The Transition Services (b) section of the IEP covers plans to help students move from school to college or employment. The Procedural Safeguards (d) Notice is state-specific and describes the special education process and the rights of children and parents.

38. B: According to IDEA (Individuals with Disabilities Education Act) 2004, students become involved in their own transition planning, which is included in their IEPs, when they reach the age of 16 (b). At this age, students are also expected to sign their IEPs. The 1994 IDEA mandated beginning transition planning when the student reached the age of 14 (a), but this was changed in the newer version of the law. Educators, parents, and students are still encouraged to begin transition planning when the student is 14, as it can take several years with some students, but it is not legally required until the student is 16. It is not true that the ages vary by individual student (c) because IDEA is a federal law specifying a uniform age, nor is it true that students are never involved at any age (d) because they must be included to identify their preferences and choices.

39. D: The poorest example of an IEP (Individual Education Plan) goal is stating that "John will improve his behavior" (d) because it is too general, broad, and vague to be implemented or measured. Stating that he will stay in his seat during classroom seatwork (a), that he will raise his hand to get the teacher's attention (b), or that he will keep his hands to himself in class (c) are all better IEP examples because they specify the actual behavior targeted by the goal. Note: Complete IEP goals would specify not only what the student will do and when he will do it, but also how he will do it, within what time frame, and the criterion for success (e.g., for how many consecutive times, periods, or classes; with what percentage of correct responses; how frequently, etc.).

40. A: Many educators use the acronym SMART as a mnemonic device to help them remember the important attributes of the ideal IEP goal: Specific, Measurable, Achievable, Relevant, and Time-Limited (a). They should be Specific, specifying exactly what the student is to do. They should involve behaviors that are Measurable, meaning that they can be quantified objectively in some way. They should be Achievable, not beyond the student's capacity to attain. They should be Relevant by involving a behavior or accomplishment that is pertinent to the individual student's educational needs and abilities and that furthers the

student's success. They should be Time-Limited, specifying a realistic yet manageable length of time when the student should be able to achieve them. Answers (b), (c), and (d) are invented terms that do not correctly expand the SMART acronym for IEP goals.

41. C: Giving praise and other positive reinforcement (c) applies both to working effectively with your staff and to managing your students' stressors and feelings. Both staff and students need acknowledgment for their efforts and positive reinforcement to continue desirable behaviors. Giving written instructions for activities or tasks (a), writing clear expectations for responsibilities (b), and writing down short-term and long-term goals (d) are all examples of strategies for working effectively with your staff. Although these things could also be applied to working effectively with your students, they are not effective at managing student emotions and stress.

42. B: Reorganizing tasks for only the most important basic goals (b) is not a strategy for helping cognitively impaired students stay organized and meet deadlines, it is a strategy for helping them sustain their attention and avoid distraction. Using personal data devices and wrist watches or timers (a) is a strategy to help students keep track of class times, appointments, due dates for assignments, etc., so they can be on time and meet deadlines. Breaking assignments down into smaller increments or steps (c) is a strategy to help students to stay organized when completing them and avoid the confusion they might have over longer, more complex tasks, which contributes to a disorganized approach. Assigning mentors or coaches to guide students daily and help them identify goals (d) is another way to help students approach schoolwork in a more organized fashion.

43. D: All of the choices are effective strategies for helping students manage frustration and stress (d). Letting them phone doctors or other sources of support (a) helps students address needs that teachers, other staff, or peers cannot meet, and can relieve frustration. For students who have learned stress management techniques, allowing them to take breaks during the day (b) to apply these can mitigate high levels of negative emotions and stress so that they can return to class more able to participate in their education. And for students who are struggling with managing their inner feelings and outer environmental stressors, referring them to a counseling and/or student assistance program (c) is appropriate, as they may require more support than is available in the school setting.

44. A: Arranging sensitivity training for peers and staff is likely to help cognitively impaired students (a). When peers and school staff are more aware of how the cognitively impaired students are affected emotionally by the daily challenges of school, they can relate to them with more empathy, understanding, and patience. They will also learn techniques for encouraging cognitively impaired students and not adding to their stress. It is not true that sensitivity training will help school staff but not students (b) because the training teaches staff ways to help students. It is also not true that sensitivity training will not help staff (c) because the staff's addressing of students' issues more appropriately will result in better attitudes, behavior, and learning by the students, which makes the staff's jobs easier and more rewarding. Finally, it is untrue that sensitivity training will not help anybody involved (d): it is actually recommended as an effective strategy by educators, including special education needs consultants.

45. B: The least likely response to help cognitively impaired students manage change is instructing them that they must accept that change is normal (b). Many students with cognitive deficits have much greater difficulty adjusting to changes than others. Teachers

- 135 -

should accept this fact (c) and work with it, because trying to make the students accept the fact that change is normal will not help them deal with it. Teachers can help them by scheduling regular meetings to discuss their progress and concerns with school (a). Because many cognitively impaired students need activities or objects that provide a more gradual transition from one thing to another rather than an abrupt change, teachers can also help by ensuring that students have communication with previous teachers and new ones (d).

46. C: Planning uninterrupted student working time (c) is least likely to support the student's stamina. Many students with physical and/or cognitive challenges have diminished endurance. Arranging work time with no interruptions is an effective strategy for limiting distractions and helping the student sustain attention and focus, but not for sustaining stamina. Some things that can help with endurance are giving the student more frequent breaks (a) for rest, allowing longer breaks (b) to recover from the strain of concentrating on schoolwork, and permitting flexible scheduling (d) to respond more appropriately to their individual needs.

47. D: Permitting time off for counseling (d) is the best strategy of the listed choices for addressing both frustration/stress and limited stamina in cognitively impaired students. Special education consultants recommend time off for counseling to help students sustain their energy as it provides support, relieves draining stress, and is a break from school activities. Assigning work that students can do at their own pace (a) is primarily a strategy to help maintain their strength, though it might also secondarily relieve stress for some. Letting students work from home part-time (b) likewise might secondarily relieve some stress, but it primarily lessens the energy drain of going to and being at school. Allowing more time to learn new duties or activities (c) similarly might have a secondary benefit of preventing or relieving stress, but more importantly is less taxing on the student's endurance.

48. A: Participating in cooperative/collaborative learning activities (a) is generally more conducive to preventing exhaustion in cognitively impaired students who frequently have lower endurance than others and/or lose stamina more quickly. Assigning individual activities that are timed (b) is more likely to tire these students than to assign them work that they are able to self-pace according to their energy. Therefore, answer (c), neither one of these, and answer (d), both of these, are incorrect.

49. D: All of the choices provided are essential (d) for a teacher to establish a rapport with students. Teachers must be able to stay calm (a) for students to trust them. Teachers who display a positive attitude (b) will encourage the same in their students. A new teacher or a teacher with a new class must initially set boundaries (c) for students to establish their leadership and let students know what is and is not acceptable. Teachers must also set boundaries while still showing respect for all students, rather than using the boundaries to distance themselves from students.

50. C: Teachers who have established good rapport with their classes can more easily revive students' flagging energy when they get tired or bored (c). This is likely at times even when the teacher and class have a good relationship, so it is not true that good rapport means students will never get bored (a). It is also not true that observing students' body language is not a reliable way to assess their interest (b). Teachers who pay attention to students' body language will be able to tell when the students are losing interest or energy. The option that none of the choices listed are true (d) is incorrect.

51. B: It is not true in maintaining established rapport that student engagement with content does not affect behavior (b). Students who are interested and involved in class subject matter are less likely to display problem behaviors than those who are not. It is true that the teacher's motivation inspires the students' motivation (a): enthusiasm is contagious, so if a teacher shows interest and excitement for the subject, his/her enthusiasm is communicated to the students, and they are more likely to become enthusiastic about it themselves. It is true that a teacher's past issues with a student must not be retained (c): a teacher who holds a grudge or relates to a student based on previous conflicts will undermine rapport, not only with that student but with the whole class. It is also true that a teacher's being fair and flexible is conducive to students' respect for the teacher (d).

52. C: Educators have suggested some things teachers can do to develop rapport with their students. They are least likely to recommend that the teacher avoid informally chatting with students before class starts (c) because chatting with them before class is a suggestion for promoting rapport. Educators also suggest that the teacher get to the classroom early (a), write "Welcome" on the board and write the students' names around it (b), and greet each student as he or she arrives for class (d).

53. A: The most effective technique would be to model the necessary actions for the student so s/he has an example to follow (a), and then observe to see that s/he is able to reproduce the modeled actions successfully. Having the student practice the actions first (b) is not as effective as letting him/her try them on the actual computer, whether s/he can type or not, because practicing isolated actions is not as relatable to the reality. Giving and repeating instructions and inviting questions (c) is also not as effective as seeing the actual activity modeled and then learning by doing. Letting the student work independently (d) does not give the student an example of how to do it first.

54. D: The most accurate statement is that a family's view and position toward disability are strongly affected by the family's cultural background (d). It is not true that families from other cultures will prioritize teachers' recommendations (a); they are more likely to do what their culture dictates. Families in the cultural minority do not necessarily experience more stress due to their children's disabilities (b) than the majority. A culturally sensitive teacher can promote better family attitudes toward that teacher and even toward the school, but not necessarily toward the child's disability (d), though cultural sensitivity will certainly facilitate teacher-student and teacher-family interactions.

55. C: The most appropriate method for Anthony's teacher would be to help him name his interests and then show him what kinds of jobs and living situations would mesh well with those interests after he graduates (c). Relating his current functioning to possible job choices (a) would not be as effective because it would not take into account his interests. Showing him examples of other students' transition plans and participation (b) would also be less effective because he may not have much in common with those students and their plans may not be relevant to him personally, and also because his difficulty with generalizing learned material to new situations would interfere with his ability to apply the others' examples to his life. Finally, explaining government regulations (d) would not be effective because, although laws concerning students with cognitive impairments provide them with certain rights, they should not have any impact on their occupational or living interests or choices.

56. A: A student with an autistic disorder (a) is most likely to need help developing social skills of starting and participating in conversations and working cooperatively with others. Autism is characterized by deficits in recognizing and understanding others' social cues and interacting socially with others. Some autistic students will show no interest in conversation, some may hold monologues but not know how to converse, some may have echolalia, and some may be nonverbal. Students with autism also tend to engage in solitary activities and have difficulty working cooperatively with others. A student with Down syndrome (b) is less likely to need help developing these skills as most Down syndrome individuals tend to be either socially normal or more friendly than others. A student with seizure disorder (c) is more likely to experience cognitive and motor impacts than social ones from seizures and/or anti-seizure medication. A student with cerebral palsy (d) has motor and mobility challenges rather than social ones.

57. B: A student with an autism spectrum disorder (b) is the least likely of the choices provided to need help staying on task if the school or job activity is one that interests him/her. Intense, focused, exclusive, and sustained attention to one activity is a prominent characteristic of individuals with autism. A student with moderate intellectual disabilities (a) is more likely than an autistic student to be more interested in social interaction and be distracted from work tasks by socializing. A student with attention deficit/hyperactivity disorder (ADHD) is more likely to go off task due to the limited ability to focus attention and the impulsivity associated with this disorder. And because answer (b) is less likely to go off a preferred task, answer (d), any of the choices, is incorrect.

58. D: All of the choices listed would enhance a verbally challenged student's communication skills (d). A picture board or book/notebook with pictures illustrating needs, wants, and emotions (a) would allow the student to point to the appropriate picture to express what s/he needs, wants, or feels to others. A chart that pictorially shows each step in a set of directions (b) would enable a verbally challenged student to both follow and give directions more easily. And breaking a mass of printed text—which can be overwhelming for a student with limited ability to read and comprehend it—into separate cards with smaller amounts of information and visual illustrations (c) to supplement the words would facilitate the student's access to the material.

59. C: The most appropriate action would be to teach Eleni's teacher, classmates, and any able and willing school staff some use of ASL (c). While this might involve more effort, the other options may violate the IDEA law and/or her family's wishes. Teaching Eleni speechreading (a) could be objectionable to her parents if the whole family only uses sign language. Many people in the Deaf community reject speech as part of their Deaf identity and confine their communication exclusively to ASL. Transferring Eleni to a school for the Deaf where everybody signs (b) would make it much easier for her to communicate, but IDEA's Least Restrictive Environment (LRE) provision mandates students' placement in the environment with the fewest restrictions where they can still learn. If Eleni and/or her parents desired her to attend a school for the Deaf, then she would likely already be there. Teaching Eleni Total Communication (d), like teaching her speechreading, could be something that she and/or her parents do not want.

60. B: Stress/pressure can trigger sudden stimulation in students with ADHD, making them readily lose self-control. Teachers can avoid stressful situations by maintaining calmness and not arguing with students, so countering the student with a better argument (d) is not a

- 138 -

strategy to improve self-control. ADHD students can also feel frustration and stress when presented with unscheduled activities, so teachers' planning schedules in advance (a), having students make a matching schedule, and having teachers' aides help them follow it will reduce stress and enhance students' ability to control their feelings and behavior. It will also help self-control to inform students of the consequences of misbehaving ahead of time (b). Knowing these consequences allows them to consider the outcome first rather than acting on their impulses. Planning specific goals for ADHD students (d) helps them focus on what is expected of them, and rewarding their achievement of goals is positive reinforcement, which increases their likelihood of repeating goal achievement.

61. D: All of the choices listed would promote better student behavioral control/management (d). Finding an activity that the student likes (a) and encouraging the student to engage in it can allow the student to excel and enhance self-esteem, self-efficacy, and self-control. Setting a very short time limit, like five minutes, for a student to demonstrate a desired behavior and increasing the time little by little (b) as the student begins to display the desired behavior for longer durations allows them to extend their ability for self-control and positive behaviors gradually, which is more realistic than expecting a big improvement all at once. Because ADHD students have excessive energy, teachers can show them how to direct that energy toward fulfilling expectations in the classroom (c).

62. A: Assigning Diego to a collaborative learning project (a) would be most in tune with his cultural background. Collectivist cultures champion working for the good of the group and cooperating with others rather than competing with them, and cooperative learning is an accepted and useful technique in America (cf. Dr. Robert Slavin). Assigning Diego to one of two teams in a class contest (b) emphasizes competition, another very American value, but one that goes against Diego's culture, which frowns on competing. An individual project echoes the American emphasis on individualism, and presenting in class (c) would make Diego the center of attention. He is likely to be uncomfortable with these values, which clash with his cultural background. Making him a group's supervisor (d) is also not the best initial strategy because he is likely to be more comfortable helping others and being a member of a group rather than its leader. In time, if Diego shows aptitude or interest in leadership, he can then be given activities and roles to promote it.

63. C: The most helpful strategy would be to practice with Patrick first (c), with the therapist playing the role of cashier and Patrick playing the role of the paying customer while using real money. Once he shows some ability to differentiate bill and coin denominations with a low error rate, the therapist can shadow him at the store, staying a discreet distance away and observing him. Sitting and teaching money values (a) is too academic: Patrick shows a lack of interest in this aspect of money and it is not related enough to the reality of shopping. Going together and showing him how to pay at the register (b) would also be embarrassing for Patrick because he is already uncomfortable about shopping with his mother. This could also cause difficulty for the cashier, and delay and irritate other customers in line, resulting in more embarrassment for Patrick and an unsuccessful overall experience, which would erode his confidence in future transactions. Suggesting that he just try it on his own (d) would be ineffective: Because he has expressed a desire to learn how to pay, he does not feel confident to do it independently yet. If he did not feel intimidated, he would already have tried this. With no prior guidance or preparation, he is also likely to feel humiliated by an unsuccessful attempt.

64. B: The best strategy is to teach missing information for mastery during the acquisition phase (b). Researchers have found that teaching toward mastery in the initial phase enhances learning. Teaching only rudimentary forms of missing information (a) would be less effective, as the student would not achieve mastery during acquisition. Teaching the basics during acquisition and working toward mastery in later phases (c) is less effective because students who achieve early mastery have better learning outcomes. Teaching to enhance existing knowledge rather than new things (d) would not remedy a gap in the student's knowledge base.

65. A: Having a student write down a daily schedule or to-do list (a) is an example of integrating the academic skill of writing into the daily routine of things s/he must do in school or at home. Having a student complete math exercises (b) is not integrating academic skills into everyday activities, but simply an academic activity in itself. Having a student read a book chapter and give an oral report on it (c) is also an academic activity that is not integrated into everyday routines. Having a student practice preparing and serving a meal (d) is good training in daily living skills, but does not integrate any academic information into everyday routines.

66. C: The teacher should arrange for a job coach to train Stan in his job duties at the beginning and gradually withdraw this support (c) as Stan learns to do the work independently. Job coaching such as this is not the role of the vocational rehabilitation counselor (a). Asking other employees to help Stan (b) impinges on their time and work production. This is unfair, especially if training is not in their job description. It would not only interfere with their productivity but could also create resentment. Similarly, asking Stan's supervisor to give him 1:1 training at the beginning (d) is making an unrealistic demand on the supervisor's time. Also, the supervisor doing something s/he does not normally do for other employees could be regarded as unfair and promote resentment.

67. D: Teaching specific cases (d) does not facilitate generalization across instances and settings. Teaching very general cases (a) is more effective in promoting the students' generalization of their learning. Giving them a broad variety of examples (b) also helps them to generalize their knowledge across various situations. Similarly, offering a wide range of settings (c) in teaching will help the students to apply what they have learned in different environments.

68. A: The teacher should make ongoing assessments of Stephanie's progress and adjust his/her teaching accordingly (a). Research shows that modifying teaching methods based on continuing assessment promotes learning in cognitively impaired students. Having Stephanie perform the same task over and over in exactly the same way (b) will not necessarily work: because her inconsistent performance is a result of her cognitive impairment, consistent performance cannot simply be forced. This approach is also likely to frustrate the student. Assigning diverse tasks (c) would also not take advantage of Stephanie's inconsistent application of learned skills. She is likely to perform any or all of them inconsistently. Focusing only on the tasks she can do more consistently (d) would limit her repertoire of usable skills and would not improve her overall consistent application of skills. Also, there might not be any tasks she does more consistently than others.

69. B: Research on students with developmental disabilities finds that providing positive behavior support with a general focus on antecedents (b), or what happens before the

behavior rather than after it, is effective for those with poor impulse control who do not learn well from the consequences of their behaviors. While explaining consequences in advance (a) can help impulsive students improve self-control, those who do not learn well from those consequences will not benefit as much as they do from antecedent-focused approaches. Likewise, simply changing the consequences (c) is also unlikely to help someone who does not respond well to consequences. Positive reinforcement is more powerful overall than punishment (d) and positive behavior support is advocated, but with disruptive behaviors, restricting intervention to only positive reinforcement for desirable behaviors may not be sufficient. Shifting the focus to antecedents can prevent many undesirable behaviors by replacing antecedents that stimulate undesirable behaviors with those evoking desirable ones.

70. C: Researchers have found that cognitive-behavioral (c) therapies were the most successful for addressing student problems with poor self-regulation, disinhibition, and aggression. Attribution training (a) has been found successful for increasing self-awareness in students with learning problems by helping them learn the parts they play in their own learning. Metacognitive tools (b) and strategies are effective for helping students with and without disabilities to learn new and difficult academic material, improve their organizational skills, and remedy deficits in strategic behaviors. Antecedent-based (d) interventions, especially those incorporated into positive behavior support programs, help students with histories of failure, defiant or impulsive behavior, impairments in working memory, and problems with initiating tasks.

71. C: It is not a goal of conducting a functional behavior assessment to identify measures that will suppress and eradicate the behavior (c). Maladaptive behaviors will not go away without something to take their place that fulfills the same need with more appropriate actions. The functional behavior assessment helps educators/therapists determine the purpose(s) of an individual's problem behavior(s) (a). Knowing what the individual needs to accomplish via the behavior helps teachers/therapists find more suitable behaviors that will achieve the same results, which can be done via positive interventions (d). Another goal of functional behavior assessment is to develop a plan for altering the factors that perpetuate the individual's engaging in a behavior (b). While the behavior is emitted for a purpose, other environmental variables can also promote its maintenance.

72. D: All of the choices listed are parts of a functional behavior assessment (d). A functional behavior assessment includes multiple components. First, you must define what things comprise the problem behavior (a) that you want to change. Then, you must devise a plan for gathering data on the target behavior, collect it, and then analyze the data collected (b) to see what it shows about the behavior's antecedents, consequences, frequency, duration, locations, times, occasions, people involved, etc. Based on your analysis of the data, you then form a hypothesis about the behavior. Guided by this hypothesis, you then develop a behavior intervention plan, implement the plan, and monitor whether and how the plan is affecting the target behavior (c).

73. B: A poor example is "How is the student feeling when s/he engages in the behavior?" (b) Behavioral interventions only address observable, measurable behaviors, not inner feelings. You might ask how the student appears to feel, e.g., angry, frustrated, etc. Although it may help to know the student's behavior is a response to frustration, for example, it will not help your intervention. However, discovering what actual antecedent events or situations lead to the frustration will help (a), because those are things that you can modify.

Sometimes a student's frustration is inevitable, but the student's behavioral response to that frustration is not. In some cases you can reduce or eliminate frustration, such as by shortening waiting time or length or difficulty of tasks. In others, you cannot, such as when the student's frustration is a result of his/her cognitive impairment. But sometimes the student's behavior in response to the emotion can be changed. Other factors associated with the behavior can be identified and then modified, including when and where the behavior occurs (c) and when and where it does not occur (d).

74. A: The A-B-C form denotes Antecedent-Behavior-Consequence (a). This refers to what occurs immediately before the target behavior (antecedents), the target behavior that then occurs, and what occurs immediately after the target behavior (consequences). Answers (b), (c), and (d) are invented choices that do not correspond to the meaning of the A-B-C form for analyzing an individual's actions according to the principles of behaviorism.

75. C: The best example of a behavioral definition is "Rebecca is out of her seat and yelling during class" (c). This specifies what she is doing. Saying her behavior is "disruptive" (a) is too vague because many behaviors are disruptive. Saying Rebecca's behavior interferes with class lessons (b) is the same as saying it is disruptive because it does not specify what she does. In the same vein, describing her behavior as distracting to classmates (d) may be accurate, but again does not state what she is doing. Saying that Rebecca is out of her seat and yelling is the only description of observable behaviors that can be measured (e.g. how many times, when, for how long, under what circumstances, etc.). To specify further, you could include that she is out of seat during seatwork activities (as opposed to when all students are up gathering supplies), yelling during silent reading time (as opposed to during recess or during a class game), etc.

76. D: All of the choices listed are good techniques that the instructor can use to enhance Caitlin's work progress (d). Because her favorite objects are reinforcing to her, offering her time off of work with them as a reward is positive reinforcement that can motivate her to work faster to gain the reward (a). Giving Caitlin a third of the number of items to sort that the instructor would usually give (b) will require a shorter duration of attending to work and allow her to accomplish it more quickly. This is a modification of the activity. Teaching Caitlin to raise her hand to ask for a break from work (c) is a replacement behavior for holding her favorite objects during work activities, which she can then do during her break instead.

77. C: Both of the first two choices (c) are essentially the primary functions of any problem behaviors: to get something (a), such as attention, stimulation (as with self-stimulating behaviors), control, power, etc; or to get away from something (b), like avoiding or escaping from a situation, place, person, activity, or emotion that is undesirable to the individual. If you analyze a number of problem behaviors for their specific functions or purposes, you will find that you can make a generalization with each that involves either getting something, getting away from something, or both. Therefore answer (d), neither of these, is incorrect.

78. B: The best of the choices listed is giving Carly an easy-to-read map or floor plan of the school, with rooms for her classes highlighted and routes to take shown in colors (b). This gives her guidance but also allows independence. Having an orientation and mobility trainer accompany her for the first few weeks (a) in full view of other students could be stigmatizing and embarrassing for Carly. Also, a trainer's availability 1:1 for that duration is

questionable. However, a trainer could walk through the routes with her after/before class hours when fewer people are around on several days as a supplement to the map/floor plan for additional support. A buddy system (c) could also embarrass Carly. However, if some students volunteered when invited, this method could be useful and also help form friendships; the disadvantages are that Carly would not start out as autonomously, and it could be logistically problematic. Asking teachers to excuse lateness (d) would not help Carly find rooms more efficiently and she would still miss part of class.

79. D: The best sequence of strategies in the choices listed is (d). First, Eugene should receive career counseling services. The counselor can help him identify specific jobs that best match his self-identified abilities and interests, and then narrow the possibilities down to a manageable number. Once he knows more specifically what jobs he wants to pursue, he should apply to school-to-work programs in appropriate fields. If he is accepted into one of these programs, he can then become a student intern, which will give him exposure to a company culture and allow him to observe company policies and procedures and the duties of various jobs. This will give him a better idea of which jobs he may prefer to pursue. If paid on-the-job training is available at some companies, then his internship experience will make him more prepared for this final step toward employment. Answers (a), (b), and (c) all represent the wrong order in which to take these steps. For example, work experience should not precede career counseling when the student is not sure what job(s) he wants to seek.

80. A: Michigan State University's "American Sign Language Browser" (a) is the best choice for Audrey's particular goal. This site allows her to select specific words from alphabetical lists and view videos of an interpreter making the ASL sign for that word, along with a brief printed explanation of how the sign expresses the concept. "Literary Resources for Teaching Deaf Children" at about.com (b) cannot help Audrey with her goal because her new students can already read and write and they are mainstreamed in a public high school; also, this site only lists and links to resources, and does not actually teach signs. "Strategies for Teaching Students with Hearing Impairments" (c) by Ed Keller is a comprehensive list of tips and techniques very valuable for teachers unfamiliar with deaf/hard of hearing students to facilitate the most effective instructional practices, but it does not teach signs. Therefore, answer (d), any of these, is incorrect.

81. D: All of the choices listed are appropriate (d). Many parents want to know more about how their cognitively impaired children are feeling about life, school, and their exceptionalities, but may not know how to approach this. There are tips online for places, times, and situations that provide opportunities for talking with one's children (e.g., about.com) (a). There are websites and books that help parents learn how to help their children manage their anxieties (b); e.g., Freeing Your Child from Anxiety by Tamar E. Chansky, Ph.D. (2004) and The Pressured Child by Michael Thompson, Ph.D. with Teresa Barker (2004). Keeping a journal (c) can be a great help to exceptional children because it helps them express emotions, practice writing skills, and experience a daily discipline. Jill Schoenberg's Journal Buddies (2007) books come in girls' and boys' versions; there is a journalbuddies.com website, and many other online and printed resources to help parents teach their children and journal together.

82. B: The individual most responsible for the relationship between the parents and the school is the teacher (b). Researchers have found that the interaction between parents and teachers is crucial to both communication with and guidance of students' parents. While

parents may often request meetings to discuss concerns about their child's educational progress because they are angry or unhappy with the school, to report changes in their child's behavior they have observed at home, or to get information or support, the main responsibility for the parent-school relationship is not theirs (a) but the teacher's. The school psychologist, social worker, counselor or other professional (c) is not most responsible for this relationship either. Therefore, to say that all of the people are equally responsible (d) is also incorrect.

83. A: Having the school's IEP team members sit facing the parents and student across the table (a) is not a good strategy to encourage parent participation because it can convey an adversarial relationship. One or more of the IEP team members should sit next to the parents and the student to reinforce the sense that they are all collaborating in planning the student's education. A good strategy is for the teacher to tell parents before the meeting begins what it will cover and how they can participate (b) in the discussion and planning. This can alleviate parental anxiety and fear of the unknown, and make parents feel more prepared for the meeting so they are more willing to contribute. It is a good practice to begin IEP meetings by having the parents identify their child's strengths, followed by teachers doing the same (c). This begins the meeting on a positive note and emphasizes assets rather than liabilities. The student's needs can be discussed later in the meeting; when they are, the school team members must always show respect for the student and family (d).

84. C: It is not a belief of family systems theory that a student's problem behaviors in school originate from the student (c). Rather, family systems theory holds that the causes and perpetuation of such problems originate in the contexts of the student's relationships. However, family systems theory does find that school settings and relations between schools and families are affected by dysfunctional behaviors within the family (a). Because this theoretical approach views problems as both contextual and reciprocal, systems practitioners commonly get schools involved with family-based problems (b) and families involved with school-based problems (d).

85. B: The best alternative of the choices listed is to have a schedule of lift bus stops on campus as a backup plan (b). Because they had the schedule of the lift buses' less frequent stops on their campus, Lia and Poe were able to get the students to the campus bus stop at the right time and use handicapped-accessible public transportation instead. Telling the students that they will have to reschedule (a) could be an option if there were no other alternatives, but is likely to disappoint the students and cause other scheduling problems for that day. Reporting to their supervisor (c) is not likely to accomplish anything, least of all resolving this or future similar issues. Therefore, expecting any of the provided answers to work effectively (d) is incorrect.

86. D: All of the choices listed (d) are examples of integrating and applying therapy services into daily routines for cognitively impaired students. The student receiving speech-language therapy (a) should not only work on her language development with the therapist in sessions, but should also incorporate methods in her daily life to improve her language skills. One way to do this would be to have her use a word-a-day calendar at home to learn a new vocabulary word every day. The student working with a physical therapist (b) on gross motor skills can apply his therapy to his daily life by following directions to increase standing time by a few minutes daily or weekly while dressing. The student receiving

occupational therapy for fine motor skills (c) can apply techniques she has learned from the therapist and practice her dexterity while brushing her teeth and setting the table.

87. A: A psychological counseling clinic (a), where psychological services are offered such as individual, group, marital, and family counseling and/or substance abuse counseling using outpatient or inpatient services or both, is the least likely location for delivering community services for preschoolers in a school district's program. For example, the Lenawee Intermediate School District in southeastern Michigan has a community service program for young children aged birth to five years in Lenawee County, a rural area. They deliver services at Head Start sites and other preschools (b), at special education therapy groups (c) for toddlers, and at community child care centers (d). This program also makes home visits to deliver individual services to preschool children.

88. C: Although a vocational instructor (c) will be very important to educational planning for most cognitively impaired high school students, vocational planning is rather premature for a first grader. The school employees best suited for collaborating with the special education teacher in planning a comprehensive educational program for the cognitively impaired first grade student are the classroom, or general education, teacher (a); therapists such as an occupational therapist, a physical therapist, and/or a speech-language pathologist (b) (depending on the individual student's needs); and the school social worker (d), who can work with emotional, social, family, and financial needs and community services and resources.

89. D: As special education teacher, you might consult with any and/or all of the personnel listed (d). For example, the school's principal (a) and facilities manager (b) can help, if funds are available, to widen some of the school's room doors. The occupational therapist (c) may be able to identify a different type of chair that would accommodate Andrew's needs while having a narrower profile. Additionally, the social worker could help if Andrew's parents cannot afford another wheelchair by seeking and procuring funds, or locating and contacting organizations that provide adaptive equipment for the disabled.

90. B: A special education teacher with a multiply handicapped class will most likely find the inclusion and integration of the students into the mainstream as an advantage (b). There are likely to be fewer peers and resources for the students (a) in the situation, so this would not be an advantage. This scenario would afford fewer peers and resources for the teacher (c) as well, so this is not an advantage. Therefore, to say all of the choices listed are advantages (d) is incorrect.

91. A: In America, grassroots advocacy groups formed by parents (a) began the history of special education. Following World War II, the American Association on Mental Deficiency formed, holding its first convention in 1947. Soon, a number of other advocacy groups were created in the 1950s. These early groups were not formed by teachers and educators (b), but by parents. New legislation passed by the federal government (c) was stimulated by, and followed, the formation of these advocacy groups: Congress passed Public Law 94-142, the Education for all Handicapped Children Act, in 1975, and it went into effect in 1977. (It was renamed IDEA in 1990.) New legislation was not passed by state governments (d) because the federal law provides for federal funding of special education and supports the states in protecting the rights and meeting the needs of exceptional children and their families.

92. C: John F. Kennedy formed his Panel on Intellectual disabilities (c) in 1961 and its first meeting was held in 1962, stimulating Congress to create new programs for those with cognitive impairments. The Muscular Dystrophy Association (a) and the United Cerebral Palsy Association were organizations founded by parents stimulated by the Civil Rights Movement during the 1950s. As Kennedy's Panel was established in the early 1960s, to say that all of the answers provided were formed in the 1950s (d) is incorrect.

93. B: President Lyndon B. Johnson (b) established the President's Committee on Intellectual disabilities in 1966 by signing Executive Order 11280. President John F. Kennedy (a) formed the Panel on Intellectual disabilities five years earlier. President Richard M. Nixon (c) signed Executive Order 11776, focusing on deinstitutionalization, prevention, family and community services, and stronger human and legal rights for individuals with cognitive impairments. President George H. W. Bush (d) signed the Americans with Disabilities Act (ADA) in 1990, a landmark law setting standards for equal opportunities in jobs, communications, transportation, and public facilities for people with disabilities.

94. B: The incorrect statement is (b): As amended in 2009, FERPA does not always allow schools with federal funding from the Department of Education to disclose personal student information without consent. Rather, it allows schools to do this only if it is necessary to protect the health and/or safety (c) of the student and/or others. When passed in 1974, FERPA uniformly prohibited the disclosure by schools with federal funding of personal information from student records without consent (a). Amendments to FERPA in 2009 covered three areas, one being school safety. Amendments in this category were prompted by a notorious incident in 2007 at Virginia Polytechnic Institute and State University (d), aka Virginia Tech, wherein a student with a record of mental health issues murdered 32 students and faculty members. Because the student's school records had information on his behavioral health, many people believed disclosing this information could have facilitated intervention to avert his actions. As a result, FERPA was amended to provide for such circumstances.

95. D: The least accurate statement is that federal law mandates that all students must have inclusive educations (d). Federal law does not mandate this, but what it does mandate is that all students must have the opportunity for the most inclusive education in the least restrictive environment (LRE) that still allows them to acquire a free and appropriate public education (FAPE). Some students may be unable to obtain such an education in an inclusive setting, which is why other educational options exist. Research has found that most students, however, do learn better in inclusive educational settings (a). Educators point out that inclusion is more supportive to cultivating students' self-esteem (b) than segregation, and that being singled out or deemed different has had negative impacts on many students' sense of self-worth. Special educators also note that all students can learn directly what equal rights and equal value mean (c) by being in inclusive settings: They can develop awareness, sensitivity, and tolerance for individual differences in such settings, learn that everybody has abilities and disabilities, and should work together.

96. A: Criteria for special education teachers' professional development are found in Title IX, Section 9101(34) of ESEA (a), the Elementary and Secondary Education Act of 1965. ESEA was reauthorized in 2001 as the No Child Left Behind Act, which is its current title. IDEA (b) is the Individuals with Disabilities Education Act, passed in 1975 as Public Law 94-142 and called the Education for All Handicapped Children Act. It was amended in 1997 to

its current title, and amended again in 2004, retaining the same title. IDEA protects the rights of disabled students and provides that all states receiving federal funds must ensure that their teachers have sufficient preparation in training, but does not have a Title IX about professional development. ADA (c) is the Americans with Disabilities Act, which provides equal opportunities for persons with disabilities but does not address teachers' professional development. ADEA (d) stands for the Age Discrimination in Employment Act of 1967, which addresses age-based job discrimination, not special education teacher development.

97. C: Sustaining expectations that challenge exceptional learners (c) is not one of the ethical principles of the Michigan Professional Educator's Code of Ethics. It is one of the ethical principles found in the Council for Exceptional Children (CEC)'s Code of Ethics: "Maintaining challenging expectations for individuals with exceptionalities to develop the highest possible learning outcomes and quality of life potential..." Respecting every individual's intrinsic value and integrity (a) is one of the principles of the Michigan Professional Educator's Code of Ethics: Principle #2, "Mutual Respect," states, "Professional educators respect the inherent dignity and worth of every individual." Promoting equal access to educational opportunities for all (b) is also part of the Michigan code: Principle #3, "Equity," states, "Professional educators advocate the practice of equity. The professional educator advocates for equal access to educational opportunities for each individual." Supporting cross-cultural awareness and recognizing diversity (d) is addressed in the Michigan code's Principle #4, "Diversity," which states, "Professional educators promote cross-cultural awareness by honoring and valuing individual differences and supporting the strengths of all individuals to ensure that instruction reflects the realities and diversity of the world."

98. B: The Council for Exceptional Children's (CEC) Code of Ethics (b) states that professional special educators are "committed to upholding... the following principles" and lists 12 principles (adopted in 2010), the eighth of which is "Neither engaging in nor tolerating any practice that harms individuals with exceptionalities." The Michigan Professional Educator's Code of Ethics (a) does not include this specification in its five ethical principles, which are entitled Service toward Common Good, Mutual Respect, Equity, Diversity, and Truth and Honesty. Therefore, both of the choices listed (c), and neither of the choices listed (d), are both incorrect.

99. D: Participating in professional organizations and activities will most benefit special educators by upholding the highest standards regarding professional practices (d). The purpose of such organizations and activities is not to advance educators' careers in pay and title (a); those are based more on outstanding job performance, knowledge, initiative, dedication, and other factors rather than just on professional membership and activities. It is not to learn more of the history and philosophy of special education (b), which should have been covered in the academic portion of the professional's teaching preparation. And it is not to obtain information from fellow educators by networking (c), which is certainly an opportunity afforded by professional organizations and activities, but is not their main purpose—the knowledge and ideas gleaned from networking are the means to the end of upholding high professional standards rather than an end in itself.

100. D: The best way for a parent to advocate for a child with cognitive impairment depends on the individual and the situation (d). Advocacy groups (a) are especially effective when a parent wants support from other parents, when new laws addressing disabilities are pending, or when a current law is being broken. They also afford individual empowerment

for some parents. Other parents may dislike the politics or organization of groups, not have time or energy for them, or find that internal power struggles in some groups distract from meeting children's special needs. Judy Winter, board member of United Cerebral Palsy Michigan and parent of a child with cerebral palsy, finds individual advocacy (b) can include teaching a child to use technology or to read, asking a business for better access, helping someone with special needs find housing, or spending time with one's exceptional child. All of these options improve quality of life, which she states is the true definition of advocacy. There are no professional special advocates (c) whose work is confined to this role: parents, teachers, administrators, therapists, social workers, counselors, and others involved with exceptional children may all advocate for them.

Secret Key #1 - Time is Your Greatest Enemy

Pace Yourself

Wear a watch. At the beginning of the test, check the time (or start a chronometer on your watch to count the minutes), and check the time after every few questions to make sure you are "on schedule."

If you are forced to speed up, do it efficiently. Usually one or more answer choices can be eliminated without too much difficulty. Above all, don't panic. Don't speed up and just begin guessing at random choices. By pacing yourself, and continually monitoring your progress against your watch, you will always know exactly how far ahead or behind you are with your available time. If you find that you are one minute behind on the test, don't skip one question without spending any time on it, just to catch back up. Take 15 fewer seconds on the next four questions, and after four questions you'll have caught back up. Once you catch back up, you can continue working each problem at your normal pace.

Furthermore, don't dwell on the problems that you were rushed on. If a problem was taking up too much time and you made a hurried guess, it must be difficult. The difficult questions are the ones you are most likely to miss anyway, so it isn't a big loss. It is better to end with more time than you need than to run out of time.

Lastly, sometimes it is beneficial to slow down if you are constantly getting ahead of time. You are always more likely to catch a careless mistake by working more slowly than quickly, and among very high-scoring test takers (those who are likely to have lots of time left over), careless errors affect the score more than mastery of material.

Secret Key #2 - Guessing is not Guesswork

You probably know that guessing is a good idea. Unlike other standardized tests, there is no penalty for getting a wrong answer. Even if you have no idea about a question, you still have a 20-25% chance of getting it right.

Most test takers do not understand the impact that proper guessing can have on their score. Unless you score extremely high, guessing will significantly contribute to your final score.

Monkeys Take the Test

What most test takers don't realize is that to insure that 20-25% chance, you have to guess randomly. If you put 20 monkeys in a room to take this test, assuming they answered once per question and behaved themselves, on average they would get 20-25% of the questions correct. Put 20 test takers in the room, and the average will be much lower among guessed questions. Why?

1. The test writers intentionally write deceptive answer choices that "look" right. A test taker has no idea about a question, so he picks the "best looking" answer, which is often wrong. The monkey has no idea what looks good and what doesn't, so it will consistently be right about 20-25% of the time.
2. Test takers will eliminate answer choices from the guessing pool based on a hunch or intuition. Simple but correct answers often get excluded, leaving a 0% chance of being correct. The monkey has no clue, and often gets lucky with the best choice.

This is why the process of elimination endorsed by most test courses is flawed and detrimental to your performance. Test takers don't guess; they make an ignorant stab in the dark that is usually worse than random.

$5 Challenge

Let me introduce one of the most valuable ideas of this course—the $5 challenge:

You only mark your "best guess" if you are willing to bet $5 on it.
You only eliminate choices from guessing if you are willing to bet $5 on it.

Why $5? Five dollars is an amount of money that is small yet not insignificant, and can really add up fast (20 questions could cost you $100). Likewise, each answer choice on one question of the test will have a small impact on your overall score, but it can really add up to a lot of points in the end.

The process of elimination IS valuable. The following shows your chance of guessing it right:

If you eliminate wrong answer choices until only this many remain:	Chance of getting it correct:
1	100%
2	50%
3	33%

However, if you accidentally eliminate the right answer or go on a hunch for an incorrect answer, your chances drop dramatically—to 0%. By guessing among all the answer choices, you are GUARANTEED to have a shot at the right answer.

That's why the $5 test is so valuable. If you give up the advantage and safety of a pure guess, it had better be worth the risk.

What we still haven't covered is how to be sure that whatever guess you make is truly random. Here's the easiest way:

Always pick the first answer choice among those remaining.

Such a technique means that you have decided, **before you see a single test question**, exactly how you are going to guess, and since the order of choices tells you nothing about which one is correct, this guessing technique is perfectly random.

This section is not meant to scare you away from making educated guesses or eliminating choices; you just need to define when a choice is worth eliminating. The $5 test, along with a pre-defined random guessing strategy, is the best way to make sure you reap all of the benefits of guessing.

Secret Key #3 - Practice Smarter, Not Harder

Many test takers delay the test preparation process because they dread the awful amounts of practice time they think necessary to succeed on the test. We have refined an effective method that will take you only a fraction of the time.

There are a number of "obstacles" in the path to success. Among these are answering questions, finishing in time, and mastering test-taking strategies. All must be executed on the day of the test at peak performance, or your score will suffer. The test is a mental marathon that has a large impact on your future.

Just like a marathon runner, it is important to work your way up to the full challenge. So first you just worry about questions, and then time, and finally strategy:

Success Strategy

1. Find a good source for practice tests.
2. If you are willing to make a larger time investment, consider using more than one study guide. Often the different approaches of multiple authors will help you "get" difficult concepts.
3. Take a practice test with no time constraints, with all study helps, "open book." Take your time with questions and focus on applying strategies.
4. Take a practice test with time constraints, with all guides, "open book."
5. Take a final practice test without open material and with time limits.

If you have time to take more practice tests, just repeat step 5. By gradually exposing yourself to the full rigors of the test environment, you will condition your mind to the stress of test day and maximize your success.

Secret Key #4 - Prepare, Don't Procrastinate

Let me state an obvious fact: if you take the test three times, you will probably get three different scores. This is due to the way you feel on test day, the level of preparedness you have, and the version of the test you see. Despite the test writers' claims to the contrary, some versions of the test WILL be easier for you than others.

Since your future depends so much on your score, you should maximize your chances of success. In order to maximize the likelihood of success, you've got to prepare in advance. This means taking practice tests and spending time learning the information and test taking strategies you will need to succeed.

Never go take the actual test as a "practice" test, expecting that you can just take it again if you need to. Take all the practice tests you can on your own, but when you go to take the official test, be prepared, be focused, and do your best the first time!

Secret Key #5 - Test Yourself

Everyone knows that time is money. There is no need to spend too much of your time or too little of your time preparing for the test. You should only spend as much of your precious time preparing as is necessary for you to get the score you need.

Once you have taken a practice test under real conditions of time constraints, then you will know if you are ready for the test or not.

If you have scored extremely high the first time that you take the practice test, then there is not much point in spending countless hours studying. You are already there.

Benchmark your abilities by retaking practice tests and seeing how much you have improved. Once you consistently score high enough to guarantee success, then you are ready.

If you have scored well below where you need, then knuckle down and begin studying in earnest. Check your improvement regularly through the use of practice tests under real conditions. Above all, don't worry, panic, or give up. The key is perseverance!

Then, when you go to take the test, remain confident and remember how well you did on the practice tests. If you can score high enough on a practice test, then you can do the same on the real thing.

General Strategies

The most important thing you can do is to ignore your fears and jump into the test immediately. Do not be overwhelmed by any strange-sounding terms. You have to jump into the test like jumping into a pool—all at once is the easiest way.

Make Predictions

As you read and understand the question, try to guess what the answer will be. Remember that several of the answer choices are wrong, and once you begin reading them, your mind will immediately become cluttered with answer choices designed to throw you off. Your mind is typically the most focused immediately after you have read the question and digested its contents. If you can, try to predict what the correct answer will be. You may be surprised at what you can predict.

Quickly scan the choices and see if your prediction is in the listed answer choices. If it is, then you can be quite confident that you have the right answer. It still won't hurt to check the other answer choices, but most of the time, you've got it!

Answer the Question

It may seem obvious to only pick answer choices that answer the question, but the test writers can create some excellent answer choices that are wrong. Don't pick an answer just because it sounds right, or you believe it to be true. It MUST answer the question. Once you've made your selection, always go back and check it against the question and make sure that you didn't misread the question and that the answer choice does answer the question posed.

Benchmark

After you read the first answer choice, decide if you think it sounds correct or not. If it doesn't, move on to the next answer choice. If it does, mentally mark that answer choice. This doesn't mean that you've definitely selected it as your answer choice, it just means that it's the best you've seen thus far. Go ahead and read the next choice. If the next choice is worse than the one you've already selected, keep going to the next answer choice. If the next choice is better than the choice you've already selected, mentally mark the new answer choice as your best guess.

The first answer choice that you select becomes your standard. Every other answer choice must be benchmarked against that standard. That choice is correct until proven otherwise by another answer choice beating it out. Once you've decided that no other answer choice seems as good, do one final check to ensure that your answer choice answers the question posed.

Valid Information

Don't discount any of the information provided in the question. Every piece of information may be necessary to determine the correct answer. None of the information in the question is there to throw you off (while the answer choices will certainly have information to throw you off). If two seemingly unrelated topics are discussed, don't ignore either. You can be confident there is a relationship, or it wouldn't be included in the question, and you are probably going to have to determine what is that relationship to find the answer.

Avoid "Fact Traps"

Don't get distracted by a choice that is factually true. Your search is for the answer that answers the question. Stay focused and don't fall for an answer that is true but irrelevant. Always go back to the question and make sure you're choosing an answer that actually answers the question and is not just a true statement. An answer can be factually correct, but it MUST answer the question asked. Additionally, two answers can both be seemingly correct, so be sure to read all of the answer choices, and make sure that you get the one that BEST answers the question.

Milk the Question

Some of the questions may throw you completely off. They might deal with a subject you have not been exposed to, or one that you haven't reviewed in years. While your lack of

- 153 -

knowledge about the subject will be a hindrance, the question itself can give you many clues that will help you find the correct answer. Read the question carefully and look for clues. Watch particularly for adjectives and nouns describing difficult terms or words that you don't recognize. Regardless of whether you completely understand a word or not, replacing it with a synonym, either provided or one you more familiar with, may help you to understand what the questions are asking. Rather than wracking your mind about specific detailed information concerning a difficult term or word, try to use mental substitutes that are easier to understand.

The Trap of Familiarity

Don't just choose a word because you recognize it. On difficult questions, you may not recognize a number of words in the answer choices. The test writers don't put "make-believe" words on the test, so don't think that just because you only recognize all the words in one answer choice that that answer choice must be correct. If you only recognize words in one answer choice, then focus on that one. Is it correct? Try your best to determine if it is correct. If it is, that's great. If not, eliminate it. Each word and answer choice you eliminate increases your chances of getting the question correct, even if you then have to guess among the unfamiliar choices.

Eliminate Answers

Eliminate choices as soon as you realize they are wrong. But be careful! Make sure you consider all of the possible answer choices. Just because one appears right, doesn't mean that the next one won't be even better! The test writers will usually put more than one good answer choice for every question, so read all of them. Don't worry if you are stuck between two that seem right. By getting down to just two remaining possible choices, your odds are now 50/50. Rather than wasting too much time, play the odds. You are guessing, but guessing wisely because you've been able to knock out some of the answer choices that you know are wrong. If you are eliminating choices and realize that the last answer choice you are left with is also obviously wrong, don't panic. Start over and consider each choice again. There may easily be something that you missed the first time and will realize on the second pass.

Tough Questions

If you are stumped on a problem or it appears too hard or too difficult, don't waste time. Move on! Remember though, if you can quickly check for obviously incorrect answer choices, your chances of guessing correctly are greatly improved. Before you completely give up, at least try to knock out a couple of possible answers. Eliminate what you can and then guess at the remaining answer choices before moving on.

Brainstorm

If you get stuck on a difficult question, spend a few seconds quickly brainstorming. Run through the complete list of possible answer choices. Look at each choice and ask yourself, "Could this answer the question satisfactorily?" Go through each answer choice and consider it independently of the others. By systematically going through all possibilities, you may find something that you would otherwise overlook. Remember though that when you get stuck, it's important to try to keep moving.

Read Carefully

Understand the problem. Read the question and answer choices carefully. Don't miss the question because you misread the terms. You have plenty of time to read each question thoroughly and make sure you understand what is being asked. Yet a happy medium must be attained, so don't waste too much time. You must read carefully, but efficiently.

Face Value

When in doubt, use common sense. Always accept the situation in the problem at face value. Don't read too much into it. These problems will not require you to make huge leaps of logic. The test writers aren't trying to throw you off with a cheap trick. If you have to go beyond creativity and make a leap of logic in order to have an answer choice answer the question, then you should look at the other answer choices. Don't overcomplicate the problem by creating theoretical relationships or explanations that will warp time or space. These are normal problems rooted in reality. It's just that the applicable relationship or explanation may not be readily apparent and you have to figure things out. Use your common sense to interpret anything that isn't clear.

Prefixes

If you're having trouble with a word in the question or answer choices, try dissecting it. Take advantage of every clue that the word might include. Prefixes and suffixes can be a huge help. Usually they allow you to determine a basic meaning. Pre- means before, post- means after, pro - is positive, de- is negative. From these prefixes and suffixes, you can get an idea of the general meaning of the word and try to put it into context. Beware though of any traps. Just because con- is the opposite of pro-, doesn't necessarily mean congress is the opposite of progress!

Hedge Phrases

Watch out for critical hedge phrases, led off with words such as "likely," "may," "can," "sometimes," "often," "almost," "mostly," "usually," "generally," "rarely," and "sometimes." Question writers insert these hedge phrases to cover every possibility. Often an answer choice will be wrong simply because it leaves no room for exception. Unless the situation calls for them, avoid answer choices that have definitive words like "exactly," and "always."

Switchback Words

Stay alert for "switchbacks." These are the words and phrases frequently used to alert you to shifts in thought. The most common switchback word is "but." Others include "although," "however," "nevertheless," "on the other hand," "even though," "while," "in spite of," "despite," and "regardless of."

New Information

Correct answer choices will rarely have completely new information included. Answer choices typically are straightforward reflections of the material asked about and will directly relate to the question. If a new piece of information is included in an answer choice that doesn't even seem to relate to the topic being asked about, then that answer choice is likely incorrect. All of the information needed to answer the question is usually provided for you in the question. You should not have to make guesses that are unsupported or choose answer choices that require unknown information that cannot be reasoned from what is given.

Time Management

On technical questions, don't get lost on the technical terms. Don't spend too much time on any one question. If you don't know what a term means, then odds are you aren't going to get much further since you don't have a dictionary. You should be able to immediately recognize whether or not you know a term. If you don't, work with the other clues that you have—the other answer choices and terms provided—but don't waste too much time trying to figure out a difficult term that you don't know.

Contextual Clues

Look for contextual clues. An answer can be right but not the correct answer. The contextual clues will help you find the answer that is most right and is correct. Understand the context in which a phrase or statement is made. This will help you make important distinctions.

Don't Panic

Panicking will not answer any questions for you; therefore, it isn't helpful. When you first see the question, if your mind goes blank, take a deep breath. Force yourself to mechanically go through the steps of solving the problem using the strategies you've learned.

Pace Yourself

Don't get clock fever. It's easy to be overwhelmed when you're looking at a page full of questions, your mind is full of random thoughts and feeling confused, and the clock is ticking down faster than you would like. Calm down and maintain the pace that you have set for yourself. As long as you are on track by monitoring your pace, you are guaranteed to have enough time for yourself. When you get to the last few minutes of the test, it may seem like you won't have enough time left, but if you only have as many questions as you should have left at that point, then you're right on track!

Answer Selection

The best way to pick an answer choice is to eliminate all of those that are wrong, until only one is left and confirm that is the correct answer. Sometimes though, an answer choice may immediately look right. Be careful! Take a second to make sure that the other choices are not equally obvious. Don't make a hasty mistake. There are only two times that you should stop before checking other answers. First is when you are positive that the answer choice you have selected is correct. Second is when time is almost out and you have to make a quick guess!

Check Your Work

Since you will probably not know every term listed and the answer to every question, it is important that you get credit for the ones that you do know. Don't miss any questions through careless mistakes. If at all possible, try to take a second to look back over your answer selection and make sure you've selected the correct answer choice and haven't made a costly careless mistake (such as marking an answer choice that you didn't mean to mark). The time it takes for this quick double check should more than pay for itself in caught mistakes.

Beware of Directly Quoted Answers

Sometimes an answer choice will repeat word for word a portion of the question or reference section. However, beware of such exact duplication. It may be a trap! More than likely, the correct choice will paraphrase or summarize a point, rather than being exactly the same wording.

Slang

Scientific sounding answers are better than slang ones. An answer choice that begins "To compare the outcomes..." is much more likely to be correct than one that begins "Because some people insisted..."

Extreme Statements

Avoid wild answers that throw out highly controversial ideas that are proclaimed as established fact. An answer choice that states the "process should used in certain situations, if..." is much more likely to be correct than one that states the "process should be discontinued completely." The first is a calm rational statement and doesn't even make a definitive, uncompromising stance, using a hedge word "if" to provide wiggle room, whereas the second choice is a radical idea and far more extreme.

Answer Choice Families

When you have two or more answer choices that are direct opposites or parallels, one of them is usually the correct answer. For instance, if one answer choice states "x increases" and another answer choice states "x decreases" or "y increases," then those two or three answer choices are very similar in construction and fall into the same family of answer choices. A family of answer choices consists of two or three answer choices, very similar in construction, but often with directly opposite meanings. Usually the correct answer choice will be in that family of answer choices. The "odd man out" or answer choice that doesn't seem to fit the parallel construction of the other answer choices is more likely to be incorrect.

Special Report: How to Overcome Test Anxiety

The very nature of tests caters to some level of anxiety, nervousness, or tension, just as we feel for any important event that occurs in our lives. A little bit of anxiety or nervousness can be a good thing. It helps us with motivation, and makes achievement just that much sweeter. However, too much anxiety can be a problem, especially if it hinders our ability to function and perform.

"Test anxiety," is the term that refers to the emotional reactions that some test-takers experience when faced with a test or exam. Having a fear of testing and exams is based upon a rational fear, since the test-taker's performance can shape the course of an academic career. Nevertheless, experiencing excessive fear of examinations will only interfere with the test-taker's ability to perform and chance to be successful.

There are a large variety of causes that can contribute to the development and sensation of test anxiety. These include, but are not limited to, lack of preparation and worrying about issues surrounding the test.

Lack of Preparation

Lack of preparation can be identified by the following behaviors or situations:

Not scheduling enough time to study, and therefore cramming the night before the test or exam
Managing time poorly, to create the sensation that there is not enough time to do everything
Failing to organize the text information in advance, so that the study material consists of the entire text and not simply the pertinent information
Poor overall studying habits

Worrying, on the other hand, can be related to both the test taker, or many other factors around him/her that will be affected by the results of the test. These include worrying about:

Previous performances on similar exams, or exams in general
How friends and other students are achieving
The negative consequences that will result from a poor grade or failure

There are three primary elements to test anxiety. Physical components, which involve the same typical bodily reactions as those to acute anxiety (to be discussed below). Emotional factors have to do with fear or panic. Mental or cognitive issues concerning attention spans and memory abilities.

Physical Signals

There are many different symptoms of test anxiety, and these are not limited to mental and emotional strain. Frequently there are a range of physical signals that will let a test taker know that he/she is suffering from test anxiety. These bodily changes can include the following:

Perspiring
Sweaty palms
Wet, trembling hands
Nausea
Dry mouth
A knot in the stomach
Headache
Faintness
Muscle tension
Aching shoulders, back and neck
Rapid heart beat
Feeling too hot/cold

To recognize the sensation of test anxiety, a test-taker should monitor him/herself for the following sensations:

The physical distress symptoms as listed above
Emotional sensitivity, expressing emotional feelings such as the need to cry or laugh too much, or a sensation of anger or helplessness
A decreased ability to think, causing the test-taker to blank out or have racing thoughts that are hard to organize or control.

Though most students will feel some level of anxiety when faced with a test or exam, the majority can cope with that anxiety and maintain it at a manageable level. However, those who cannot are faced with a very real and very serious condition, which can and should be controlled for the immeasurable benefit of this sufferer.

Naturally, these sensations lead to negative results for the testing experience. The most common effects of test anxiety have to do with nervousness and mental blocking.

Nervousness

Nervousness can appear in several different levels:

The test-taker's difficulty, or even inability to read and understand the questions on the test
The difficulty or inability to organize thoughts to a coherent form
The difficulty or inability to recall key words and concepts relating to the testing questions (especially essays)
The receipt of poor grades on a test, though the test material was well known by the test taker

Conversely, a person may also experience mental blocking, which involves:

Blanking out on test questions
Only remembering the correct answers to the questions when the test has already finished.

Fortunately for test anxiety sufferers, beating these feelings, to a large degree, has to do with proper preparation. When a test taker has a feeling of preparedness, then anxiety will be dramatically lessened.

The first step to resolving anxiety issues is to distinguish which of the two types of anxiety are being suffered. If the anxiety is a direct result of a lack of preparation, this should be considered a normal reaction, and the anxiety level (as opposed to the test results) shouldn't be anything to worry about. However, if, when adequately prepared, the test-taker still panics, blanks out, or seems to overreact, this is not a fully rational reaction. While this can be considered normal too, there are many ways to combat and overcome these effects.

Remember that anxiety cannot be entirely eliminated, however, there are ways to minimize it, to make the anxiety easier to manage. Preparation is one of the best ways to minimize test anxiety. Therefore the following techniques are wise in order to best fight off any anxiety that may want to build.

To begin with, try to avoid cramming before a test, whenever it is possible. By trying to memorize an entire term's worth of information in one day, you'll be shocking your system, and not giving yourself a very good chance to absorb the information. This is an easy path to anxiety, so for those who suffer from test anxiety, cramming should not even be considered an option.

Instead of cramming, work throughout the semester to combine all of the material which is presented throughout the semester, and work on it gradually as the course goes by, making sure to master the main concepts first, leaving minor details for a week or so before the test.

To study for the upcoming exam, be sure to pose questions that may be on the examination, to gauge the ability to answer them by integrating the ideas from your texts, notes and lectures, as well as any supplementary readings.

If it is truly impossible to cover all of the information that was covered in that particular term, concentrate on the most important portions, that can be covered very well. Learn these concepts as best as possible, so that when the test comes, a goal can be made to use these concepts as presentations of your knowledge.

In addition to study habits, changes in attitude are critical to beating a struggle with test anxiety. In fact, an improvement of the perspective over the entire test-taking experience can actually help a test taker to enjoy studying and therefore improve the overall experience. Be certain not to overemphasize the significance of the grade - know that the result of the test is neither a reflection of self worth, nor is it a measure of intelligence; one grade will not predict a person's future success.

To improve an overall testing outlook, the following steps should be tried:

Keeping in mind that the most reasonable expectation for taking a test is to expect to try to demonstrate as much of what you know as you possibly can.
Reminding ourselves that a test is only one test; this is not the only one, and there will be others.
The thought of thinking of oneself in an irrational, all-or-nothing term should be avoided at all costs.
A reward should be designated for after the test, so there's something to look forward to. Whether it be going to a movie, going out to eat, or simply visiting friends, schedule it in advance, and do it no matter what result is expected on the exam.

Test-takers should also keep in mind that the basics are some of the most important things, even beyond anti-anxiety techniques and studying. Never neglect the basic social, emotional and biological needs, in order to try to absorb information. In order to best achieve, these three factors must be held as just as important as the studying itself.

Study Steps

Remember the following important steps for studying:

Maintain healthy nutrition and exercise habits. Continue both your recreational activities and social pass times. These both contribute to your physical and emotional well being.
Be certain to get a good amount of sleep, especially the night before the test, because when you're overtired you are not able to perform to the best of your best ability.
Keep the studying pace to a moderate level by taking breaks when they are needed, and varying the work whenever possible, to keep the mind fresh instead of getting bored. When enough studying has been done that all the material that can be learned has been learned, and the test taker is prepared for the test, stop studying and do something relaxing such as listening to music, watching a movie, or taking a warm bubble bath.

There are also many other techniques to minimize the uneasiness or apprehension that is experienced along with test anxiety before, during, or even after the examination. In fact, there are a great deal of things that can be done to stop anxiety from interfering with lifestyle and performance. Again, remember that anxiety will not be eliminated entirely, and it shouldn't be. Otherwise that "up" feeling for exams would not exist, and most of us depend on that sensation to perform better than usual. However, this anxiety has to be at a level that is manageable.

Of course, as we have just discussed, being prepared for the exam is half the battle right away. Attending all classes, finding out what knowledge will be expected on the exam, and knowing the exam schedules are easy steps to lowering anxiety. Keeping up with work will remove the need to cram, and efficient study habits will eliminate wasted time. Studying should be done in an ideal location for concentration, so that it is simple to become interested in the material and give it complete attention. A method such as SQ3R (Survey, Question, Read, Recite, Review) is a wonderful key to follow to make sure that the study habits are as effective as possible, especially in the case of learning from a textbook. Flashcards are great techniques for memorization. Learning to take good notes will mean that notes will be full of useful information, so that less sifting will need to be done to seek out what is pertinent for studying. Reviewing notes after class and then again on occasion will keep the information fresh in the mind. From notes that have been taken summary sheets and outlines can be made for simpler reviewing.

A study group can also be a very motivational and helpful place to study, as there will be a sharing of ideas, all of the minds can work together, to make sure that everyone understands, and the studying will be made more interesting because it will be a social occasion.

Basically, though, as long as the test-taker remains organized and self confident, with efficient study habits, less time will need to be spent studying, and higher grades will be achieved.

To become self confident, there are many useful steps. The first of these is "self talk." It has been shown through extensive research, that self-talk for students who suffer from test anxiety, should be well monitored, in order to make sure that it contributes to self confidence as opposed to sinking the student. Frequently the self talk of test-anxious students is negative or self-defeating, thinking that everyone else is smarter and faster, that they always mess up, and that if they don't do well, they'll fail the entire course. It is important to decreasing anxiety that awareness is made of self talk. Try writing any negative self thoughts and then disputing them with a positive statement instead. Begin self-encouragement as though it was a friend speaking. Repeat positive statements to help reprogram the mind to believing in successes instead of failures.

Helpful Techniques

Other extremely helpful techniques include:

Self-visualization of doing well and reaching goals
While aiming for an "A" level of understanding, don't try to "overprotect" by setting your expectations lower. This will only convince the mind to stop studying in order to meet the lower expectations.
Don't make comparisons with the results or habits of other students. These are individual factors, and different things work for different people, causing different results.
Strive to become an expert in learning what works well, and what can be done in order to improve. Consider collecting this data in a journal.
Create rewards for after studying instead of doing things before studying that will only turn into avoidance behaviors.
Make a practice of relaxing - by using methods such as progressive relaxation, self-hypnosis, guided imagery, etc - in order to make relaxation an automatic sensation.
Work on creating a state of relaxed concentration so that concentrating will take on the focus of the mind, so that none will be wasted on worrying.
Take good care of the physical self by eating well and getting enough sleep.
Plan in time for exercise and stick to this plan.

Beyond these techniques, there are other methods to be used before, during and after the test that will help the test-taker perform well in addition to overcoming anxiety.

Before the exam comes the academic preparation. This involves establishing a study schedule and beginning at least one week before the actual date of the test. By doing this, the anxiety of not having enough time to study for the test will be automatically eliminated. Moreover, this will make the studying a much more effective experience, ensuring that the learning will be an easier process. This relieves much undue pressure on the test-taker.

Summary sheets, note cards, and flash cards with the main concepts and examples of these main concepts should be prepared in advance of the actual studying time. A topic should never be eliminated from this process. By omitting a topic because it isn't expected to be on the test is only setting up the test-taker for anxiety should it actually appear on the exam. Utilize the course syllabus for laying out the topics that should be studied. Carefully go over the notes that were made in class, paying special attention to any of the issues that the professor took special care to emphasize while lecturing in class. In the textbooks, use the chapter review, or if possible, the chapter tests, to begin your review.

It may even be possible to ask the instructor what information will be covered on the exam, or what the format of the exam will be (for example, multiple choice, essay, free form, true-false). Additionally, see if it is possible to find out how many questions will be on the test. If a review sheet or sample test has been offered by the professor, make good use of it, above anything else, for the preparation for the test. Another great resource for getting to know the examination is reviewing tests from previous semesters. Use these tests to review, and aim to achieve a 100% score on each of the possible topics. With a few exceptions, the goal that you set for yourself is the highest one that you will reach.

Take all of the questions that were assigned as homework, and rework them to any other possible course material. The more problems reworked, the more skill and confidence will form as a result. When forming the solution to a problem, write out each of the steps. Don't simply do head work. By doing as many steps on paper as possible, much clarification and therefore confidence will be formed. Do this with as many homework problems as possible, before checking the answers. By checking the answer after each problem, a reinforcement will exist, that will not be on the exam. Study situations should be as exam-like as possible, to prime the test-taker's system for the experience. By waiting to check the answers at the end, a psychological advantage will be formed, to decrease the stress factor.

Another fantastic reason for not cramming is the avoidance of confusion in concepts, especially when it comes to mathematics. 8-10 hours of study will become one hundred percent more effective if it is spread out over a week or at least several days, instead of doing it all in one sitting. Recognize that the human brain requires time in order to assimilate new material, so frequent breaks and a span of study time over several days will be much more beneficial.

Additionally, don't study right up until the point of the exam. Studying should stop a minimum of one hour before the exam begins. This allows the brain to rest and put things in their proper order. This will also provide the time to become as relaxed as possible when going into the examination room. The test-taker will also have time to eat well and eat sensibly. Know that the brain needs food as much as the rest of the body. With enough food and enough sleep, as well as a relaxed attitude, the body and the mind are primed for success.

Avoid any anxious classmates who are talking about the exam. These students only spread anxiety, and are not worth sharing the anxious sentimentalities.

Before the test also involves creating a positive attitude, so mental preparation should also be a point of concentration. There are many keys to creating a positive attitude. Should fears become rushing in, make a visualization of taking the exam, doing well, and seeing an A written on the paper. Write out a list of affirmations that will bring a feeling of confidence, such as "I am doing well in my English class," "I studied well and know my material," "I enjoy this class." Even if the affirmations aren't believed at first, it sends a positive message to the subconscious which will result in an alteration of the overall belief system, which is the system that creates reality.

If a sensation of panic begins, work with the fear and imagine the very worst! Work through the entire scenario of not passing the test, failing the entire course, and dropping out of school, followed by not getting a job, and pushing a shopping cart through the dark alley where you'll live. This will place things into perspective! Then, practice deep breathing and create a visualization of the opposite situation - achieving an "A" on the exam, passing the entire course, receiving the degree at a graduation ceremony.

On the day of the test, there are many things to be done to ensure the best results, as well as the most calm outlook. The following stages are suggested in order to maximize test-taking potential:

Begin the examination day with a moderate breakfast, and avoid any coffee or beverages with caffeine if the test taker is prone to jitters. Even people who are used to managing caffeine can feel jittery or light-headed when it is taken on a test day.
Attempt to do something that is relaxing before the examination begins. As last minute cramming clouds the mastering of overall concepts, it is better to use this time to create a calming outlook.
Be certain to arrive at the test location well in advance, in order to provide time to select a location that is away from doors, windows and other distractions, as well as giving enough time to relax before the test begins.
Keep away from anxiety generating classmates who will upset the sensation of stability and relaxation that is being attempted before the exam.
Should the waiting period before the exam begins cause anxiety, create a self-distraction by reading a light magazine or something else that is relaxing and simple.

During the exam itself, read the entire exam from beginning to end, and find out how much time should be allotted to each individual problem. Once writing the exam, should more time be taken for a problem, it should be abandoned, in order to begin another problem. If there is time at the end, the unfinished problem can always be returned to and completed.

Read the instructions very carefully - twice - so that unpleasant surprises won't follow during or after the exam has ended.

When writing the exam, pretend that the situation is actually simply the completion of homework within a library, or at home. This will assist in forming a relaxed atmosphere, and will allow the brain extra focus for the complex thinking function.

Begin the exam with all of the questions with which the most confidence is felt. This will build the confidence level regarding the entire exam and will begin a quality momentum. This will also create encouragement for trying the problems where uncertainty resides.

Going with the "gut instinct" is always the way to go when solving a problem. Second guessing should be avoided at all costs. Have confidence in the ability to do well.

For essay questions, create an outline in advance that will keep the mind organized and make certain that all of the points are remembered. For multiple choice, read every answer, even if the correct one has been spotted - a better one may exist.

Continue at a pace that is reasonable and not rushed, in order to be able to work carefully. Provide enough time to go over the answers at the end, to check for small errors that can be corrected.

Should a feeling of panic begin, breathe deeply, and think of the feeling of the body releasing sand through its pores. Visualize a calm, peaceful place, and include all of the sights, sounds and sensations of this image. Continue the deep breathing, and take a few minutes to continue this with closed eyes. When all is well again, return to the test.

If a "blanking" occurs for a certain question, skip it and move on to the next question. There will be time to return to the other question later. Get everything done that can be done, first, to guarantee all the grades that can be compiled, and to build all of the confidence possible. Then return to the weaker questions to build the marks from there.

Remember, one's own reality can be created, so as long as the belief is there, success will follow. And remember: anxiety can happen later, right now, there's an exam to be written!

After the examination is complete, whether there is a feeling for a good grade or a bad grade, don't dwell on the exam, and be certain to follow through on the reward that was promised...and enjoy it! Don't dwell on any mistakes that have been made, as there is nothing that can be done at this point anyway.

Additionally, don't begin to study for the next test right away. Do something relaxing for a while, and let the mind relax and prepare itself to begin absorbing information again.

From the results of the exam - both the grade and the entire experience, be certain to learn from what has gone on. Perfect studying habits and work some more on confidence in order to make the next examination experience even better than the last one.

Learn to avoid places where openings occurred for laziness, procrastination and day dreaming.

Use the time between this exam and the next one to better learn to relax, even learning to relax on cue, so that any anxiety can be controlled during the next exam. Learn how to relax the body. Slouch in your chair if that helps. Tighten and then relax all of the different muscle groups, one group at a time, beginning with the feet and then working all the way up to the neck and face. This will ultimately relax the muscles more than they were to begin with. Learn how to breathe deeply and comfortably, and focus on this breathing going in and out as a relaxing thought. With every exhale, repeat the word "relax."

As common as test anxiety is, it is very possible to overcome it. Make yourself one of the test-takers who overcome this frustrating hindrance.

Special Report: Additional Bonus Material

Due to our efforts to try to keep this book to a manageable length, we've created a link that will give you access to all of your additional bonus material.

Please visit http://www.mometrix.com/bonus948/mttccogimpair to access the information.